Educating Teachers

Changing the Nature of Pedagogical Knowledge

CONTEMPORARY ANALYSIS IN EDUCATION SERIES
General Editor: Philip Taylor

Contemporary Analysis in Education Series

Educating Teachers

Changing the Nature of Pedagogical Knowledge

Edited by

John Smyth

 The Falmer Press

(A member of the Taylor & Francis Group)
London·New York·Philadelphia

UK   The Falmer Press, Falmer House, Barcombe, Lewes, East Sussex, BN8 5DL

USA   The Falmer Press, Taylor & Francis Inc., 242 Cherry Street, Philadelphia, PA 19106-1906

First published 1987

LB
1715
.E29
1987

Library of Congress Cataloging in Publication Data

Educating teachers.

   (Contemporary analysis in education series; 19)
   Includes index.
   1. Education—Study and teaching. 2. Teachers—
Training of. I. Smyth, W. John. II. Series.
LB1715.E29 1987 370′.7′1 87-20128
ISBN 1-85000-293-2
ISBN 1-85000-294-0 (pbk.)

Jacket design by Leonard Williams

Typeset in 11/13 Garamond by
Imago Publishing Ltd, Thame, Oxon

Printed in Great Britain by Taylor & Francis (Printers) Ltd, Basingstoke

Contents

General Editor's Preface

The education of teachers has always been problematic, a matter of contention and controversy, of competing and conflicting models and paradigms. Between the two World Wars the dominant approach was rooted in the notion of the mastery of methods derived from what came to be known as the *principles of education*. Sir Percy Nunne was perhaps the greatest, and best selling, of its exponents. But even as the principles of education school was holding sway in teacher education, a competing perspective based on the psychology of learning and teaching was growing in influence; an influence which since 1945 has held a foreground place in teacher education, together with the sociology, philosophy and history of education. It was J.W. Tibble who enshrined this *disciplines of education* paradigm in his classic work, *The Study of Education*.

Even as he did so the realities of teaching refused to be accounted for in terms of the disciplines. With noisy insistence the classroom claims its own explanatory system. The response is the work caught within the covers of this book; work which is potent for a better understanding of teaching and teacher education.

John Smyth is to be congratulated in ordering his talented contributors' work so that this book achieves the impact it does on our ideas of teaching and teacher education; an impact which represents a new paradigm for practice in the education of teachers; one for long waiting at the edge of our awareness. This book is a must, not only for teacher educators and intending teachers, but also for all involved with teaching; not least teachers themselves.

Philip Taylor
University of Birmingham
1987

vii

Introduction: Educating Teachers; Changing the Nature of Pedagogical Knowledge

John Smyth

This book takes as its backdrop the crisis of confidence in professional knowledge in general, and in teacher education in particular. Many of the papers, all of which have been specifically written for this volume, highlight the limitations, incompleteness and weaknesses of exclusive reliance on 'technical' or instrumental forms of knowledge about teaching. Those who argue that teaching should have a demonstrated scientific basis to it (Gage, 1978; Dunkin and Biddle, 1974; Hunter, 1984), and that teaching should adhere closely to prescriptions deriving from such research (US Department of Education, 1986), ignore the degree to which practitioner-derived knowledge is, in fact, trustworthy and relevant. By choosing to focus exclusively on the 'products' of other people's research, at the expense of the process by which understandings are reached, proponents of such views misconstrue the value of research. By seizing on the instrumental applicability of findings, they place a level of certainty on research that social scientists themselves would deny. Serious claims to a scientifically derived body of 'research on teaching' (sic) have now all but disappeared (Bolster, 1984). As Mishler (1979) notes, the positivist search for universal context-free laws has foundered largely on the grounds of their 'context-stripping methods' (Bernstein, 1976; Reason and Rowan, 1981). The scene is more likely to be characterized today by statements like: 'Meaning in context: is there any other kind?' (Mishler, 1979).

It is no accident either that the term 'pedagogy' appears in the title of this volume. It is true that the notion of pedagogy as expressed in some quarters has come to be misconstrued as the science of teaching or instruction, and to that extent it represents a narrowly scientist view that deserves to be severely discredited. Elsewhere in this volume I make the point that while pedagogy can refer to a systematic procedure for advancing learning, there is also a sense in which to act pedagogically means to act in ways that 'empower' learners. As I point out:

> Pedagogues ask questions, while articulating their theories about teaching and learning — they verbalize why they do what they do in their teaching, interrogating their knowing so as to uncover why it is they accept current practices, and questioning the veracity of the social conditions that support and sustain them.

Donald Schön (1983) has argued rather convincingly that professional knowledge based exclusively on the traditional disciplines is out of step with the changing situation across a range of professions, including teaching. He sees such knowledge as no longer being able to 'deliver' solutions on important social isues. In particular: 'The complexity, uncertainty, instability, uniqueness, and value conflicts which are increasingly perceived as central to the world of (current) practice ...' (p. 14) are no longer able to be handled simply by recourse to existing bodies of knowledge or accepted ways of acquiring such knowledge.

What Schön (1983) does is provide us with a way of fundamentally rethinking how we view professional practice, and the relationship between theory and practice. His thesis rests on the claim that where in the past professionals laid claim to 'extraordinary knowledge in matters of great social importance' (p. 4) and in return were granted unique rights and privileges, a number of factors have changed those circumstances. As well as media exposure of the extensive misuse and abuse of these privileges for personal gain, Schön (1983) points to a more important public loss of confidence in and questioning by society of professionals' claims to 'extraordinary knowledge'. By way of example:

> a series of announced national crises — the deteriorating cities, poverty, the pollution of the environment, the shortage of energy — seemed to have roots in the very practices of science, technology, and public policy that were being called upon to alleviate them.
> Government sponsored 'wars' against such crises seemed not to produce the expected results: indeed, they often seemed to exacerbate the crises. (p. 9)

It seems that, increasingly, professionals of all kinds are being confronted by situations in which the tasks they are required to perform no longer bear any relationship to the tasks for which they have been educated. As Schön (1983) so aptly put it, 'The situations of practice are not problems to be solved but problematic situations characterised by uncertainty, disorder and indeterminancy' (pp. 15–16). Practitioners are, therefore, becoming increasingly engulfed in wrangles over 'conflicting and competing values and purposes. Teachers, for example, are '. . . faced with pressures for increased efficiency in the context of contracting budgets, demands that they rigorously "teach the basics", exhortations to encourage creativity, build citizenship, (and to) help students examine their values' (p. 17). What is interesting about this dramatic shift, and its accompanying novel and complex array of responses, is that some practitioners have been able to find idiosyncratic ways of negotiating these realities, ways that amount to reaching. a modicum of manageability. While experientially acquired knowledge deriving from individual cases is not new to most professions, the rub comes in trying to codify it and accommodate to traditional discipline-based knowledge:

> Surely [we] are not unaware of the artful ways in which some practitioners deal competently with the indeterminacies and value conflicts of practice. It seems, rather that [we] are disturbed because [we] have no satisfactory way of describing or accounting for the artful competence which practitioners sometimes reveal in what they do. [We] find it unsettling to be unable to make sense of these processes in terms of the model of professional knowledge which [we] have largely taken for granted. (Schön, 1983, p. 19).

Clearly, what is required is much more than accommodation. Knowledge of the kind Schön (1983) speaks of is not of an instrumental kind to be 'applied' to practice — it is embedded in practice, and inseparable from it. Knowledge that comes about through knowing-in-action is of a fundamentally different kind: 'Often we cannot say what it is that we know. When we try to describe it we find ourselves at a loss, or we produce descriptions that are obviously inappropriate. Our knowledge is ordinarily tacit . . . our knowing is in our action' (p. 49). In other words, we often display skills for which we cannot describe the underlying rules and procedures. It is in thinking about what we do while we do it that we being to act reflexively and turn thought back on action — we engage in reflection-in-action. Generally, we do this in response to some puzzling, troubling or perplexing situation with which we are struggling. In Schön's (1983) words, the reflective practitioner acts as follows with regard to the circumstances of his puzzlement: 'As he tries to make sense of it, he also reflects on the understandings which have been implicit in his action, understandings which he surfaces, criticises, restructures, and embodies in further action' (p. 50). It is, therefore, through the examination, reformulation and testing of the intuitive understandings they hold that teachers can be said to be reflecting on their practice in Schön's sense. Erdman (1985) points out that in the world of teaching, it is the grind of daily practice that leads to it becoming increasingly more routinized and less reflective: 'This situation reflects both the non-discursive and artistic nature of teaching and its "busyness". Teachers seldom have time to talk about what they do. Nevertheless, they are profound knowers of the classroom scene; their perceptions and reasoning, motives and intentions can and should be studied' (p. 4). Schön's (1983) argument is, therefore, a neat counter to the simplistic criticism and outcries for a return to 'excellence in teaching' by merely tidying-up on the technicalities of teaching. By legitimating a more artistic and context-specific way of thinking about teaching, Schön (1983) provides teachers with a way of countering the claims to return to the widely voiced but non-existent universals of effective teaching.

It is not surprising to find a babble of voices within the teaching profession as people seek to unravel the tangled web of competing and conflicting values, goals, purposes and interests that comprise the professional practice of teaching. The rules of the game have indeed changed. Practitioner-generated knowledge that is embedded in and emerges out of action is coming to be seen increasingly as the basis for a new and emerging paradigm in the education of teachers. Taken-for-granted ways of applying specialized knowledge to resolve particular recurring problems no longer seem to work, if they ever did anyway. The foundations of the professional practice of teaching seem to have shifted dramatically from that of 'problem-solving' to one of 'problem-setting' (or problem-posing); that is to say, from a rational process of choosing from among possibilities that best suit agreed-upon ends, to a situation that opens up for contestation and debate the nature of those decisions, the ends to which they are to be directed, and the means by which they are achievable (Schön, 1983). Rather than relying upon tried-and-tested knowledge to be applied in all circumstances of a similar kind, the scene is becoming characterized by the application of knowledge acquired from previous particular cases.

All of this amounts to a shift: from a position where scientifically-derived knowledge was deemed superior, to a circumstance in which artistic and intuitive knowledge may be equally appropriate; from an a priori instrumental view of knowledge about teaching, to one that reflects knowledge as being tentative and problematic; and, from a view which presupposes answers to complex social questions relating to teaching, to one that endorses the importance of problem-posing and negotiated resolution.

When I first embraced the idea for this book, what I was searching for was a group of writers in teacher education whom I knew to be working actively with teachers at changing the *nature of pedagogical knowledge* in the way Schön (1983) had described in the professions generally. It was not hard to find those people, but as I explored further it became clear that it was not possible to talk about changes in pedagogy without also unravelling the way in which the *pedagogical context of teaching* itself contributed to and was enmeshed in the challenges and changes that were occurring. It became necessary, therefore, to add a second dimension to this volume, by including contributors whose primary preoccupation was with sketching out the changing contexts, structures and cultures of teachers' work lives.

On any issue as complex and controversial as this one it seemed insufficient merely to have challenged the nature of existing pedagogical practices — it was important also to have begun to grasp the 'nature of possibility'. Hence, the third section of this volume comprises contributions from a group of scholars and writers who have had a modicum of success in working with teachers to problematize their teaching through *pedagogical action*. What this group brings is a sense of 'what works' when teachers are invested with empowering ways of approaching their teaching.

Out of these initial speculations and the provocative thoughts of Donald Schön (1983) in this *Reflective Practitioner: How Professionals Think in Action* emerged the three loosely grouped sections of this volume:

pedagogical knowledge
pedagogical contexts
pedagogical action

John Smyth

References

BERNSTEN, R. (1976) *The Restructuring of Social and Political Theory*, London, Methuen.

BOLSTER, A. (1983) 'Toward a more effective model of research', *Harvard Educational Review*, 53, 3, pp. 294–308.

DUNKIN, M. and BIDDLE, B. (1974) *The Study of Teaching*, New York, Holt, Rinehart and Winston.

ERDMAN, J. (1985) 'Problematising field experiences for teaching', Unpublished manuscript, University of Wisconsin.

GAGE, N. (1978) *The Scientific Basis of the Art of Teaching*, New York, Teachers College Press.

HUNTER, M. (1984) 'Knowing, teaching and supervising', in HOSFORD, P. (Ed.), *Using What We Know about Teaching*, Association for Supervision and Curriculum Development, Alexandria, Va.

MISHLER, E. (1979) 'Meaning in context: Is there any other kind?' *Harvard Educational Review*, 49, 1, pp. 1–19.

REASON, P. and ROWAN, J. (1981) (Eds), *Human Inquiry: A Sourcebook of New Paradigm Research*, Chichester, Wiley.

SCHÖN, D. (1983) *The Reflective Practitioner: How Professionals Think in Action*, New York, Basic Books.

US DEPARTMENT OF EDUCATION (1986) *What Works: Research about Teaching and Learning*, Washington.

PART I

Pedagogical Knowledge

1   Replacing Pedagogical Knowledge with Pedagogical Questions

Alan R. Tom

Pedagogical knowledge is assumed to be useful to practising teachers. One recent teacher education reform report presumes that if only more research-derived knowledge were given to teachers, their performance would be dramatically improved (Holmes Group Executive Board, 1986). The term 'research-based knowledge' has become a revered goal. On the other hand, many scholars interested in pedagogical knowledge argue that a more useful source of such knowledge than discipline-based study is a teacher's own inquiry into his or her classroom activities and experiences (e.g., Elbaz, 1983). In any case there is considerable faith in the efficacy of pedagogical knowledge — personal or discipline-based — for improving teaching practice.

However, my own experience as a secondary school and university teacher suggests that pedagogical knowledge is only a minor element of improved teaching. Our hope that more knowledge about teaching practice — whatever its source — will significantly increase our potency as teachers fails to recognize the complex, interactive nature of teaching and fails to acknowledge the fundamental normative roots of teaching.

Such reservations, of coursee, have been frequently expressed in recent years. So what is new? Usually the next step in the argument of those who have lost faith in pedagogical knowledge is to relate teaching to the political and social context and to point out the sexist, racist, class-based nature of contemporary teaching practice. Awareness of these realities is important, but generally leads to a sense of resignation and helplessness on the part of the teacher. Criticizing current teaching practice is much easier than knowing how to construct a reasonable alternative to that practice.

I believe that what is needed is not so much more pedagogical knowledge as incisive pedagogical questions. In this chapter I explore what I mean by pedagogical questions. A major theme is that the focus of pedagogical questions differs according to one's understanding of the nature of teaching. I present a brief overview of four conceptions of the nature of teaching; then I outline some pedagogical questions which flow from adopting one of these conceptions: teaching as a moral endeavour. Lastly, I suggest how these questions might be used to design a pre-service professional curriculum or to guide staff development efforts.

Beneath the surface behaviours of teaching are rather contrasting conceptions of the essence of teaching. Four of these conceptions are: teaching as a craft, teaching as a fine art, teaching as an applied science, and teaching as a moral endeavour. As each of these four conceptions is discussed, I also offer critical comment on its adequacy.

To see teaching as a craft is to believe that the essence of teaching is found in the 'how-to' knowledge that teachers have accumulated over the years and have occasionally codified. Common sense and folklore are the sources of such knowledge. Often pedagogical knowledge is cast in such 'rules of thumb' as 'Don't smile until Christmas' or 'Be consistent in your treatment of students'. The fundamental criticism of such craft knowledge — even when it is more sophisticated than the above examples — is that such rules of thumb are conservative because past 'successful' practice is accepted without criticism, are simplistic because they emphasize the teacher's point of view, and are inattentive to the normative elements of teaching practice (Tom, 1984, pp. 140–3).

During the twentieth century, educational researchers — initially coming from psychology but later from other social scientific disciplines — soundly rejected the conception of teaching as a tradition-bound craft and gradually came to view teaching as an applied science. These discipline-based scholars thought they would discover scientific generalizations or laws about teaching-learning phenomena, and subsequently teachers would 'apply' these findings to the concrete problems of classroom practice. Sometimes the focus has been on finding dependable relationships between specific teacher behaviours and student learning outcomes (e.g., process-product research), but there has also been an emphasis on studying the impact of constellations of teacher behaviours (e.g., mastery learning or so-called active teaching). However, discipline-based findings on teaching-learning relationships have tended to be inconclusive, if not contradictory, narrowly focused on a variable or two, hard to relate to complex practical situations, and insensitive to the normative components of teaching (Tom, 1984, pp. 37–73, 135–40).

Perhaps in part as a reaction to the simplistic idea that teaching could be reduced to an applied science, a rival view emerged midway through the century, a view which stressed the similarity of teaching to such fine arts as music, painting, and acting. According to the fine arts conception of teaching, teaching can be viewed as an aesthetic activity, can be conceived of as an unfolding activity whose ends are often created in process, and can be seen as an activity influenced by events and contingencies more than by routines and prescriptions. But a fundamental difference between the fine arts and teaching practice involves the criteria by which the quality of each is judged. In the fine arts judgments of quality are grounded in aesthetic standards, while such criteria are of secondary importance in teaching. The stress in teaching is on the practical impact of the message to be communicated, not on the beauty of the communication effort. In addition, the fine arts conception of teaching ignores the normative component of teaching (Tom, 1984, pp. 129–33).

A fourth conception — I believe more adequate than the prior three — draws upon the practical arts more than the fine arts and gives central importance to the moral dimension of teaching. This conception I refer to as teaching as a moral endeavour. Teaching is a moral endeavour in at least two senses. First, there is an unequal power distribution between teacher and student, and this inequality makes their relationship inherently moral; the student, particularly the younger student, is subject to the good judgment of the teacher. The student, notes Hawkins (1973), in accepting a measure of control by the teacher is 'tacitly assured that control will not be exploitative but will be used to enhance the competence and extend the independence of the one controlled, and in due course will be seen to do so' (p. 9). Thus the teacher-student relationship entails giving the teacher control over the development of the student in desirable directions, while concurrently enhancing and extending the independence of the student. By accepting this obligation for fostering these desirable outcomes, the teacher assumes moral responsibility for the student (Tom, 1984, pp. 79–88).

A second sense in which teaching is a moral endeavour is that teaching presupposes that something worthwhile is to be taught through the curriculum. In part, the moral basis of the curriculum is grounded in the need to create a teaching plan by selecting some content instead of other content. Even when the teacher begins planning by selecting interesting content rather than first specifying objectives in a Tylerian planning model, the teacher still needs to choose among the universe of teaching content. This selection cannot be arbitrary, or we would fail to see the subsequent teaching as being educational. Peters (1965) is convincing on this point:

> [The concept] 'education' relates to some sorts of processes in which a desirable state of mind develops. It would be as much of a logical contradiction to say that a person had been educated and yet the change was in no way desirable as it would be to say that he had been reformed and yet had made no change for the better. . . . To call something 'educational' is to intimate that the processes and activities themselves contribute to or involve something that is worthwhile. (pp. 90–2)

Thus I am using the term 'moral' in a broader sense than referring to right conduct: 'moral' is defined as including valuational situations in which human relationships and desirable ends are at issue. But teaching, I believe, is more than attending to the moral basis of the student-teacher relationship and the teaching of worthwhile content through the curriculum. Teaching is also akin to such practical arts as coaching, gardening, and fishing in which certain ends, presumed to be valuable, are pursued with strategies which sometimes work and other times fail. Because the success of any particular strategy is problematic, we recognize that there is a craft involved in successful coaching, gardening, fishing, or teaching.

But this problematic basis of teaching craft can be considerably more sophisticated than the commonsense and folklore version of craft discussed early. Indeed the pursuit of particular teaching ends, with strategies whose efficacy is problematic, suggests that teaching craft involves much more than rules of thumb. Clearly rules of thumb or something similar are one element of teaching craft because successful teaching entails many routines or semi-mechanical sequences, processes which often befuddle the novice but which become second nature to the experienced teacher.

A second element of teaching craft involves the ability to analyze teaching situations, e.g., to reflect upon which of two sets of ideas ought to be taught first to a particular class, to decide whether an attempt should be made to extend and debrief a stimulating discussion or whether the class should be moved on to the next topic. Teaching craft thus entails the analysis of complex situations and, ultimately, the decision to pursue a particular strategy to deal with each teaching context. The results of an instructional strategy must be carefully monitored, and new strategies may well be necessary. Therefore, the analysis involved in teaching craft includes understanding a specific teaching context, selecting what appear to be appropriate strategies, and monitoring the results of provisional tries. Rules of thumb are part of the concept of craft in teaching, but craft involves keen analysis and measured decisions as well as rules of thumb, and skilled performance is an essential aspect of teaching craft (Tom, 1984, pp. 98–119).

In a fundamental way, viewing teaching as a moral endeavour brings together two divergent aspects of teaching. On the one hand, questions having to do with the moral nature of student-teacher relationships and of the selection of worthwhile content are placed side-by-side with questions concerning the daily interaction of teacher and student for the purpose of learning certain curricular content. Ironically, to see teaching as a moral endeavour entails looking at the same activities of teaching practice through two contrasting lenses — one lens empirically shaded and one normatively shaded.

To view teaching as equally, and concurrently, focused on craft and moral practical issues seems to be a more adequate view than to reduce teaching to an applied science, or to a fine art, or to a folklore-based craft. But the complexity of the moral endeavour conception of teaching is not easy to relate to the improvement of teaching practice. In the remainder of this chapter I suggest one avenue for bridging the gap between the moral endeavour conception and teaching practice. This approach involves generating pedagogical questions from the moral endeavour conception of teaching.

This question-posing approach to bridging between a conception of teaching and teaching practice is rather different from the norm. For both the teaching-as-craft and teaching-as-applied-science views of teaching, the bridge to practice tends to be through knowledge. This way of connecting a root conception of teaching and teaching practice is clearest in the case of applied science. In this instance, the potency of the conception of applied science is grounded in the idea that scientifically-derived knowledge is the major way by which teaching practice is to be improved. Over the years the belief that laws of teaching would ultimately be discovered has waned, but there is still faith that the discovery of pedagogical generalizations or of regularities among teaching and learning variables will significantly improve teaching practice. Similarly, there is hope among those who study how teachers come to learn craft knowledge that this personal knowledge can be codified in some

way and made available to all teachers. Codification of craft knowledge seems to be of most interest to those who hold a complex view
of the craft basis of teaching. When craft is seen as fairly simple
rules of practice, then modeling, often through apprenticeship, may
well be the primary mode for bridging between the craft conception
and classroom practice.

But using knowledge to bridge between a conception of
teaching and teaching practice suggests a much tighter link between
underlying metaphors for teaching and classroom realities. A more
reasonable approach is to derive pedagogical questions from the
moral endeavour conception. These questions can guide classroom
thought and action in particular directions without inferring or
proposing that somehow teaching practice can be deduced from the
moral endeavour conception. Thus pedagogical questions will not so
much tell us what to do as how we might proceed to address our
obligations and tasks as teachers; these questions, indeed, may at
times pull our thinking and acting in differing and perhaps conflicting directions.

What pedagogical questions ought we to ask if we think
teaching can profitably be viewed as a moral endeavour? While these
questions can be formulated in a variety of ways, it is important that
they begin with the reality of teaching and that they cause us to
address both the moral and craft elements of teaching. Thus I
propose that we initially examine the craft and moral basis of the
teacher-student relationship. Possible craft questions include: How
can I develop learning environments which entice youngsters to
want to learn a particular topic or skill? How can I both move the
classroom group along and respond to the interests of particular
individuals? Can a particular tangent which occurs in the course of a
discussion be integrated into the overall lesson? How can I make a
transition from topic 'A' to topic 'B'? Some of these craft questions
are generic (the first two), while others (the third and fourth) are
situation-specific. These questions tend to revolve around such classic problems of interactive teaching as motivation, balancing group
teaching and individual interests, guiding discussions, and making
transitions. The wording of the question is far less important than
that the content directs attention to enduring problems of the craft
of classroom teaching.

At the same time, the teacher needs continually to attend to the
moral dimension of the teacher-stuent relationship. Illustrative questions are: Is a particular topic significant enough for me to compel a
youngster to learn it? In an overall sense are my actions as a teacher

promoting and extending the independence of my students? When I do limit the freedom of my students or manipulate them, are there substantial educational reasons for these actions and not just an unconscious desire on my part to have power over other people? Again, these questions can either be generic or situational, and they may well lead to challenging the appropriateness of routine craft relationships between teacher and student.

A second level of pedagogical questions beyond the teacher-student relationship involves the third element in the teaching triad: subject matter. Subject matter has already been touched upon in many of the craft and moral-oriented questions focused on the teacher-student relationship. After all, teaching cannot occur without something being taught by the teacher to the student. Craft-based curriculum questions include: Where do I find the resources to develop a curriculum theme out of my initial interest in the study of social classes? In what way can I link the students' interests in peer relationships with a study of social class? Which aspect of English is most likely to start the year out with a bang? Which text has a reading level appropriate to my class? Craft questions on curriculum tend to concentrate on the skills of curriculum development and sequencing or on text selection.

Questions stressing the moral dimension of curriculum emphasize the value of studying certain topics, for example: Is it more important to teach everyday computational mathematics skills or to foster an understanding of mathematical concepts and processes? Do I devote time to the development in my youngsters of a healthy self-concept? Is it wise to spend another week on the term paper since some students are still confused about proper documentation and other skills I want to teach through this assignment? In contrast to the skill-oriented craft questions related to curriculum construction, the moral questions in this area are more speculative and are more directed to the wisdom of particular curriculum decisions.

A third level of pedagogical questions moves beyond the immediate realms of classroom relationships and curriculum content to examine the interconnection of teaching and schooling processes with the larger society. These questions tend to blur the craft and moral distinctions, but generally have a moral import, if not a moral focus. For example: Do schooling processes as now constituted tend to foster the reproduction of existing social and economic relationships? Does the career of teaching attract people who have both conservative leanings and a desire to control the lives of others? Is the proper role of the school to conserve the best of our heritage, yet also to challenge elements of that heritage? Ought the teacher to be held accountable for results (i.e., student learning) or for best professional practice? These wide-ranging questions are often of minimal concern to the practising teacher who must cope daily with complex teacher-student relationships and sophisticated problems of curriculum judgment and construction.

Strategically, therefore, I believe level one and level two questions — because of their immediacy to daily teaching activities — should be the first order of attention for the novice teacher. But level three questions ought not be inordinately delayed or be slighted, as the answers to these questions have the capacity to alter, even redefine, questions at the first two levels. Level three questions, however, often are of more concern to outsiders than to the practising teacher, especially when the teacher is a novice initially coping with craft concerns.

What might we do with these pedagogical questions? Such questions might be the stimulus for self-reflection on the part of experienced teachers. Or they might provide a framework to guide the staff development efforts of principals, department chairs, or supervisors. Or (most interesting of all to me) these three levels of questions — with a concurrent emphasis on the craft and moral dimensions of teaching — could serve as a superstructure on which to construct a pre-service professional curriculum. These questions — particularly the craft, but also some of the moral ones — have the capacity to organize the pre-service professional curriculum around the persisting problems of practice rather than around such traditional bodies of knowledge as social foundations, educational psychology, curriculum and instruction. As compared to topically organized knowledge, practice-based study tends to be a more potent form of learning for novice teachers.

Use of three levels of questions, moral as well as craft, for organizing a problem-based professional curriculum should lessen the conservatism craft-based professional curricula often embody. Yet having the entire professional curriculum deal at least in part with craft questions should help reduce the classic tension that novices usually feel between the theoretical demands of the professional curriculum and the practical requirements of schoolkeeping. On the other hand, novices and experienced teachers do not necessarily attend to moral-oriented questions, even when these pedagogical questions are grounded in the problems of practice. Great care is therefore required in designing the pre-service curriculum so that moral-derived questions are not pushed aside and lost.

One approach that should be avoided is the sequencing of pedagogical questions so that moral issues are raised only after the novice has mastered the craft of teaching. Important habits of thought and action are formulated during induction into teaching, and the teacher-in-training should be encouraged to consider the moral dimension of teaching from the very beginning of his or her preparation. The essence of good teaching is the ability to meld together the concerns embodied in both craft and moral pedagogical questions.

References

ELBAZ, F. (1983) *Teacher Thinking: A Study of Practical Knowledge*, London, Croom Helm.

HAWKINS, D. (1973) 'What it means to teach', *Teachers College Record*, 75, pp. 7–16.

HOLMES GROUP EXECUTIVE BOARD (1986) *Tomorrow's Teachers: A Report of the Holmes Group*, East Lansing, Mich., Holmes Group.

PETERS, R.S. (1965) 'Education as initiation', in ARCHAMBAULT, R.D. (Ed.), *Philosophical Analysis and Education*, New York, Humanities.

TOM, A.R. (1984) *Teaching as a Moral Craft*, New York, Longman.

2 What Knowledge Is of Most Worth in Teacher Education?

Landon Beyer

The 'crisis in knowledge' which this volume illuminates and analyzes is by now well-known. The critiques of positivism that have been offered, especially in the last twenty-five years, have made the older affiliation between education and science now seem both hasty and unproductive.[1] A reliance on psychometric analyses, isolated technical competence, linear thinking and instrumental reason, we must now candidly admit, is not the saviour of educational waywardness we once thought it was (or would become). Neither reliance on the epistemologically foundational knowledge from philosophy, nor the canons of empiricist sciene serve to legitimate educational theory or practice with any degree of certainly.[2]

Yet the ideas and ideologies underly teacher education in the United States still tend to embody such a perspective. In part because teacher education has been conceptualized in hierarchical, patriarchal, technocratic, and psychologized terms, the dominant culture in teacher education has embraced the tenets of positivism and technical rationality. Moreover, current proposals for teacher education reform in the US and elsewhere extend this reliance on technical rationality, as they search for 'the solution' to problems of teaching and schooling. The first part of this chapter documents this continuing reliance on technical knowledge in the domain of teacher education. The second portion argues for a reconstructed knowledge base for teachers and teacher education. Instead of a focus on technical rationality, linear thinking, and psychometric analysis, this alternative highlights two other interrelated ideas. First, since educational discourse and a great many teaching practices are political, moral, and ideological, the knowledge most appropriate for teacher education must be based in such social and moral traditions. This entails a rather fundamental restructuring in the way we educate teachers. Secondly, this alternative approach to teaching and teacher preparation must resist the temptation to prescribe in detail the routes toward improved teaching and programs designed to foster this with prospective teachers. Unlike most previous and contemporary reform efforts, we must offer alternatives that take seriously the notion of democratic participation and decision-making, as we alter the ideological biases within the knowledge that is thought to be of most worth in teacher education. To change these knowledge forms without also shifting our strategies for the reform of education is to be caught in the very dualisms (theory and practice, conception and execution, reason and emotion, fact and value, etc.) that have been generated out of the very hierarchical and patriarchal system of domination we seek to replace.[3]

I   The Culture of Teacher Education

We can understand the dominant culture of teacher education in the United States as embodying a largely technical, ameliorative, and vocational orientation. These values surround both the theory and research of teacher education as well as the practice of such programs. That teacher education in the United States today is dominated by what we might generalize as a 'technocratic rationality' can be demonstrated by the widespread acceptance of newer forms of competency-based teacher education, the testing of teachers, apprenticeship-based clinical teacher education, systems management approaches to curriculum development and program evaluation, behaviorist psychologies, and the nature of national accreditation and state licensing requirements.[4] For example, many approaches to competency-based teacher education (currently presented under the rubic of 'research-based teacher education') seek to foster the development of specific teaching skills (e.g., asking higher-order questions) or teaching strategies (e.g., direct instruction) apart from considerations of the curricular context within which the skills are to be employed or the ends towards which they are to be directed. The effect of these programs has been to trivialize the relationship between teacher and learner by assigning to the teacher the role of technical, value-free behaviour manager. Education is viewed as a problem in systems management and human engineering, while the solutions to the problems of teacher education are seen to lie within the grasp of 'science' and technology.[5] The moral and political issues embedded in the ongoing processes of teacher education are obscured as teacher educators focus their attention exclusively upon procedures to attain ends which are not openly examined.[6]

Furthermore, numerous studies demonstrate the consequences of the widespread and uncritical acceptance of apprenticeship-based clinical teacher education. For example, studies regarding the development of pedagogical perspectives during the student teaching experience consistently indicate that student teaching and other forms of field-based teacher education contribute to the development of 'utilitarian teaching perspectives' in which teaching is separated from its ethical, political, and social roots.[7] According to these studies, spending time in classrooms, getting students through the lesson on time and in a quiet and orderly manner, frequently become the primary basis for accepting or rejecting the use of a particular teaching activity. If a technique 'works', that is, solves the immediate problem at hand, it is often perceived as good or appropriate regardless of possible larger consequences or the existence of alternatives approaches. Within this perspective, techniques of teaching often become ends in themselves rather than a means toward some articulated, reasoned educational purpose. An ameliorative perspective is thus advanced that limits students' perceptions and actions.

Consequently, student teachers tend to accept the practices they observe in their field placements as the upper and outer limits of what is possible. Katz refers to this condition as one of 'excessive realism'.[8] The knowledge structures that students confront and the ways in which knowledge is communicated to children are largely accepted as natural and right. The school serves as a model for accepted practice; it is not itself an object for analysis or possible alteration. There seems to be little understanding, in such dominant technical approaches to teacher training, of either the socially constructed nature of knowledge or of the school itself, and almost no searching for alternatives to what is taken to be natural within those worlds.[9]

Closely related to the almost exclusive focus on techniques of teaching as ends in themselves in both competency-based and field-based programs are general conceptions of knowledge and pedagogy that permeate aspects of teacher education, including campus-based experiences. Bartholomew argues with regard to teacher education in Great Britain that in both the universities and schools the main form in which curriculum knowledge is presented to prospective teachers is as a predefined set of 'worthwhile' activities to be mastered.[10] Popkewitz makes the claim that this same externalized or objectivist conception of knowledge characterizes US teacher education as well,[11] and that as a result prospective teachers come to believe that knowledge is something that is detached from the human interactions through which it was constituted and by which it is maintained.[12]

Furthermore, as Bartholomew points out, a transmission relationship is the only possible conception of pedagogy that can exist between teacher and taught within such a conception of knowledge.[13] Accordingly, the message that is communicated to prospective teachers is that becoming a professional entails identifying knowledge that is certain, breaking it into manageable bits, and presenting it to students in an efficient fashion. Being a student means acquiring this knowledge and learning how to use it in a context which does not include criticism and has little patience with analysis. Freire has labelled this form of pedagogy the 'banking concept of education'.[14] Although the rhetoric of teacher education often encourages students to use liberal phrases and to affirm liberal slogans about the education of people in places other than the university, the facts of social interaction in the colleges (e.g., teacher-learner relationships) are similar to those found in the schools. The schools and universities work in consort to provide a powerful, conservative force for defending existing institutional arrangements from close scrutiny and modification.[15]

Another correlate of the technocratic rationality that has dominated the thinking and debate in teacher education is a problematic orientation that is usually individualistic. This orientation is often assumed in the debates over developing a curriculum for teacher education programs and is in turn imparted to education students through the curricular choices that result.[16] For example, one currently popular approach to the development of curriculum for pre-service teacher education is a 'personalized' approach.[17] The essence of this approach is that the content of a teacher education curriculum should be matched to the level of concerns that students are experiencing at a particular time. This approach further assumes that current concerns of students must be resolved (by a 'relevant' teacher education curriculum) *before* more mature concerns can emerge. Given the largely survival-oriented and instrumental perspectives described earlier and the results of empirical studies of teacher development,[18] this would mean that the curriculum for teacher education would be constructed primarily with a view toward helping student teachers survive more comfortably within a context that is largely taken for granted.

There is nothing inherently wrong with suggesting that the content of teacher education be constructed with regard for the motives and concerns of prospective teachers. In fact, a teacher education program that totally neglects student concerns is itself ethically suspect. However, the apparent lack of 'mature' development during pre-service training is often used by advocates of this approach as a justification for excluding any non-survival-oriented content from the pre-service teacher education curriculum.

> On the basis of the evidence now available, it seems reasonable at least to offer survival training to pre-service teachers. Such training might be particularly welcome immediately after first contact with teaching when survival concerns seem particularly intense.... The thought even occurs to us that *only* survival training should be offered during pre-service education and that all of the sophisticated substance of professional education ought to be offered during the in-service years.[19]

The significant aspect of this approach to curriculum development in teacher education is that teacher educators evaluate their roles solely in terms of their impact on education students (e.g., 'meeting individual needs') and not in terms of their impact on social systems. Along these lines it is important to remember that the 'survival concerns' of prospective teachers are not genetic endowments but concerns that are rooted at least in part in the current institutional contexts in which education students are expected to work. Just because teachers appear to develop in a particular way under present circumstances does not imply that this is the way we ought to help teachers grow.

The individualistic, technical, and ameliorative tendencies within the dominant culture of teacher education are being reinforced, and even extended, in some current proposals for the reform of teacher preparation. For example, the Carnegie Forum on Education and the Economy makes numerous recommendations for improving teaching and the quality of programs for preparing future teachers. It begins its summary in terms reminiscent of the earlier report by the National Commission on Excellence in Education, *A Nation at Risk*:[20]

> America's ability to compete in world markets is erod-
> ing. The productivity growth of our competitors outdis-
> tances our own. The capacity of our economy to provide a
> high standard of living for all our people is increasingly in
> doubt. . . .
>
> As in past economic and social crises, Americans turn to
> education. They rightly demand an improved supply of
> young people with the knowledge, the spirit, the stamina
> and the skills to make the nation once again fully
> competitive. . . . There is a new consensus on the urgency of
> making our schools once again the engines of progress,
> productivity and prosperity . . . success depends on achiev-
> ing far more demanding educational standards than we have
> ever attempted to reach before . . . [and] the key to success
> lies in creating a profession equal to the task. . . .[21]

Here the linkages among social prosperity, economic productivity,
educational 'excellence',[22] and reforms in teacher education are quite
openly stated. The use of economic language in this report — the
concern with productivity, high unemployment, supply and demand
considerations regarding teachers, performance and accountability
measures, and so on — is hardly an accident. Included on the
Carnegie Forum Advisory Council are the former head of Bell
Telephone, a Vice President of IBM, an Executive Vice President of
an investment firm, and the Chief Executive Officer of American
Can Company.[23]

The term 'competency' is often used in the Carnegie report as it
stresses the recommendation that a new Master of Teaching degree
become adopted as a prerequisite for certification. This program is
designed to 'prepare candidates to take maximum advantage of the
research on teaching and the accumulated knowledge of exceptional
teachers. It would develop their instructional and management
skills, cultivate the habit of reflecting on their own practice of
teaching, and lay a strong base for continuing professional
development.'[24]

The report stresses a technical approach to teaching through a
separation of theoretical from professional coursework, a focus on
activities enhancing classroom management and instructional technique, a commitment to the central importance of skill development,
and an emphasis on field-based experience guided by Lead Teachers.
Such emphases are extended in the report's discussion of incentives
and productivity in the teaching profession. In language that smacks

of the earlier emphasis on scientific management of schools and curricula,[25] the Carnegie report says,

> ... resources are never unlimited, so we turn out to be interested in the best possible performance at the lowest possible cost ... we believe improvements are not likely to be made until the structure of incentives for teachers and other school employees is redesigned to reward them for student accomplishment.
>
> But the issue is not just performance. The rate at which student performance must improve exceeds by far the rate at which school revenues can reasonably be expected to rise, even at the most optimistic levels.[26]

The relationship between student achievement and revenue expended on schools is taken for granted by the members of this group, constituting a part of the 'common sense' of education. The problem is that added expenditures will not keep pace with the increases necessary in student achievement. Again we see the utilization of technical, business-oriented language in the discussion of educational quality. The authors also say that for those of us facing pressure to improve schools, 'there is an important parallel here to the challenge faced by American business and industry.' This parallel lies in the concept of productivity:

> ... American business exposed to foreign competition [must] improve productivity. That pressure shows some promise of leading to a sweeping reassessment of long-standing production methods, the introduction of new technologies, innovative labor-management practices, improved forms of organization, and the introduction of new management methods — all in the search for quality and efficiency. American schools also need to produce a higher quality product with greater efficiency....[27]

The equivocation between business interests and educational excellence is here starkly and bluntly put. Like industrialists, educational managers and workers must emphasize increased productivity, the maintenance of a higher quality 'product', and gains in efficiency, through the adoption of new management systems, better incentives, and the use of new technologies. Utilizing the lenses provided by contemporary corporate America, the Carnegie Forum on Education and the Economy envisions an educational arena allied with the values, principles, procedures, and aims of our economic apparatus. What is good for General Motors, the authors seem to be reminding us, is not only good for the US generally, but for our system of schooling in particular. Hardly a new idea, this report surfaces at a time when economic problems beset large segments of American society, so that school improvement and business enhancement appear conjoined.[28]

Of the commissions and groups that have been working on teacher education reform during the last few years it is the Holmes Group that has attracted most attention from college and university faculty.[29] In attempting to increase its membership to well over 100 universities representing a substantial segment of our research community it is fair to conclude that this group is attempting to develop a cartel of like-minded institutions that will set policy for teacher education, and attempt to exert its influence in state legislatures, state departments of education, national and regional accreditation agencies, and indirectly, colleges and universities not themselves members of the Holmes Group. This group clearly forms a powerful political force in the contemporary call for reform in teacher education.

A central assumption of the Holmes Group report is that teaching, and teachers, are the central variables in improving the quality of public education:

> We cannot improve the quality of education in our schools without improving the quality of teachers in them. Curriculum plans, instructional materials, elegant classrooms, and even sensitive, intelligent administrators cannot overcome the negative effects of weak teaching, or match the positive effects of positive teaching. . . . The entire formal and informal curriculum of the school is filtered through the minds and hearts of classroom teachers, making the quality of school learning dependent on the quality of teachers.[30]

As the linchpin of educational improvements in our schools, the teacher plays a determining role. Thus teacher education is to be valued for the ways in which it can enhance the competence of the practitioner. Moreover, the quality of teaching is determined, the authors say, by the quality of student learning that takes place. As the primary aim of teaching, levels of learning can then be utilized in assessing not only practitioners, but programs for preparing them as well.

To justify their differentiation of the teaching profession into Career Professional, Professional, and Instructor classifications, and to provide teachers with the appropriate knowledge base they will need to be recognized as professionals, the Holmes Group acknowledges the importance of developing an approach to teacher education that will elevate its status. It is clear that for this group many of the potential candidates for the knowledge base that is required have been eliminated. For example, while supporting undergraduate study in the academic disciplines — on which they see professional education as relying — the study of education is not regarded as a co-equal partner or collaborator on a common project. This is shown in part by the Holmes Group's rejection of majors in education at the undergraduate level. Nor is professional education to be grounded in the social, historical, philosophical, or sociological foundations of education.

Further, curriculum as an aspect of educational studies, the Holmes Group claims, is 'one area about which we have little compelling information and theory',[31] thus disallowing another possible source of knowledge for teacher education. Yet there is a particular focus in the Holmes Group on an area of study that is presumed to be central for the requirements of teaching:

> Within the last twenty years ... the science of education promised by Dewey, Thorndike, and others at the turn of the century, has become more tangible. The behavioral sciences have been turned on the schools themselves, and not just in laboratory simulations. Studies of life in classrooms now make possible some convincing and counter-intuitive conclusions about schooling and pupil achievement.[32]

The behavioural sciences offer special advantages for teacher education: first, they are allied with a tradition of inquiry that lends credibility to education, as it can now be referred to as a 'science'. Second, this new 'science of education' can be implemented to achieve the primary aim of schooling: increased pupil achievement. Even though professional education is fundamentally unlike the academic disciplines that undergird it, to be differentiated from the foundations of education and curriculum studies, teacher education based in the behavioural sciences will aid in improving the overall quality of education. It will, thus, justify the stratification of the profession, and increase the respectability of teachers, teacher educators, and schools of education.

What these recommendations by the Carnegie Forum and the Holmes Group document is the continuance of ways of thinking that have dominated the culture of teacher education. In spite of the critiques that have proliferated regarding the epistemological assumptions of positivism and its influences in the social sciences and educational studies, as well as the reported dangers in programs of teacher preparation that take on a technical, vocational, and individualistic orientation, there is little evidence that such assumptions are being seriously reconsidered by those members of élite institutions now in a position to do so. It is especially important, in view of this, that we offer alternatives that take up the challenges presented by the contemporary 'crisis in knowledge', and go beyond the dominant technical rationality of teacher education.

II Teacher Education, Social Context, and Knowledge

Several things are required to change the current tendencies in the dominant culture of teacher education in the United States and elsewhere. In countering the tendencies of technical rationality, the insights of hermeneutics become especially relevant. Instead of an obsession with 'the' scientific method, systematic and linear thinking, and the various 'forms of reasoning' that presumably inhere in the disciplines, other perspectives and values become important. A central part of hermeneutic dialogue involves questioning received wisdom and notions of common sense. Those concerned with hermeneutic dialogue, Richard Rorty tells us:

> . . . are reactive and offer satires, pardoies, aphorisms. They know their work loses its point when the period they are reacting against is over. . . . They want to keep space open for the sense of wonder which poets can sometimes cause — wonder that there is something . . . which (at least for the moment) cannot be explained and can barely be described.[33]

It is this openness to wonder, mystery, and the unknown, the barely speakable, that may help revitalize a teacher education culture that has become stylized, often stagnant, and relies on overworked images and ideas.[34]

A rejection of technological rationality also carries important political and social consequences. One of the elements of technical, positivistic thinking is a reliance on the appropriate specialized, isolated expert. Since knowledge can be quantified and accumulated, the answer to a range of problems is the location of the expert who has acquired this knowledge. The alternative to this technological conscience:

> ... corrects the peculiar falsehood of modern consciousness: the idolatry of scientific method and of the autonomous authority of the sciences and it vindicates again the noblest task of the citizen — decision-making according to one's own responsibility — instead of conceding that task to the expert.[35]

A rejection of technological rationality thus carries with it both a humanizing and democratizing of knowledge and an individual and communal responsibility for action.

In addition, a new approach to understanding must recognize the ways in which political, social, and ideological contexts are enmeshed with knowledge and action. Instead of pursuing knowledge 'for its sake', or for the cultivation of sensitivity, task, or cognitive discrimination it can encourage, it becomes valued for the actions and involvements it makes possible. That is, knowledge is useful and valuable to the extent that it works toward personal and social realities that are empowering, that work toward socially just communities, and help achieve alternative worlds. The aim of teacher education, accordingly, ought not to be the achievement of prespecified outcomes that are rationalized, sequenced, and individualized, but the encouragement of practical reason that can help reconstruct a world dominated by inequality and alienation.

A key starting point for reorienting teacher education lies in the Aristotelian distinction between 'techne' and 'phronesis'. The latter concepts:

> ... appears in the fact of concern, not above myself, but about the other person ... the person with understanding does not know and judge as one who stands apart and unaffected; but rather, as one united by a specific bond with the other, he thinks with the other and undergoes the situation with him.[36]

To accomplish such a perspective, teacher educators must develop and assist their students in obtaining such 'ethical know-how', as well as accentuating the continuation of dialogue, democratic social relations, and a concern for non-linear wonder and uncertainty.

The sort of teacher preparation effort required to help achieve the aims outlined above would greatly differ from those programs reflecting the technical, ameliorative and individualistic orientation described in part I. It would necessitate placing teaching and schooling within that large array of social and cultural practices that dialectically interact with educational institutions.[37] This would help us move away from an individualistic, vocational preparation focus toward one founded on conceptions of social justice, dialogue, and democratic involvement. An important part of teacher preparation would focus on clarifying, for example, the connections among pedagogy, curriculum, and classroom social relations, on the one hand, and the larger patterns of social practices and cultural values that provide school practice with meaning, on the other. It would also include investigations into alternative values and practices, as we contemplate more responsive, socially just institutions and involvements.

Something else is clearly central in this alternative model for teacher education. It is clear that our past reliance on genuine knowledge sanctioned by the expertise of technological rationality has fostered the proliferation of reform movements that are hierarchical and patriarchal. The commitment to alternative political and moral visions enunciated here must be accompanied by a different view of reform and collaboration. While we can suggest the principles and ideas that should guide such a view, its detailed accomplishment can only happen in specific locations and in collaboration with those people — teachers, parents, students, administrators, etc. — involved in the day-to-day operation of schools and programs of teacher preparation. The commitment to ethical know-how, democratic social relations, and non-positivistic knowledge is not possible within the more typical context for reform that is hierarchical, divisive, and impositional.

A curriculum for teacher education committed to these ideas would include several orienting principles. First, a movement away from an excessively psychologized perspective would be replaced by one more responsive to philosophical, historical, social, and moral possibilities. As we broaden our perspectives on educational matters, the reductionistic tendencies of psychology have to be challenged so as to incorporate larger issues and ideas. Second, a vision of current practice as providing the parameters of education has to be replaced by one where these boundaries are seen as socially constructed and capable of being challenged and modified. Thus the end of teacher educaion need not be, as it now often is, the replication of current practices and activities. Third, extending the previous point, we must collaboratively work with students, teachers, and others, not only to reconsider current possibilities, but also to conceptualize alternative possibilities and how they may be morally and democratically accomplished.

All of these principles are practicable. While none is easy or without complex conceptual and strategic obstacles, programs based on them go some way to expose the limitations of current educational and epistemological presuppositions, and to offer the hope of enhanced human and social possibilities. Teacher education must alter its dominant cultural traits and work toward such possibilities.

Notes

1   See, for example, THOMAS S. KUHN (1970) *The Structure of Scientific Revolutions*, 2nd ed. enlarged, Chicago, Ill., University of Chicago Press; PAUL FEYERABEND (1978) *Against Method: Outline of an Anarchistic Theory of Knowledge*, London, Verso Edition; RAYMOND WILLIAMS (1961) *The Long Revolution*, New York, Columbia University Press; EVELYN FOX KELLER (1985) *Refections on Gender and Science*, New Haven, Conn., Yale University Press; RUTH BLEIER (1984) *Science and Gender*, New York, Pergamon Press and CAROL GILLIGAN (1982) *In a Different Voice*, Cambridge, Mass., Harvard University Press.
2   LANDON E. BEYER (1986) 'The reconstruction of knowledge and educational studies', *Journal of Education*, 168, 2.
3   LANDON E. BEYER and MICHAEL W. APPLE (Eds) (in press) *The Curriculum: Problems, Politics, and Possibilities*, Albany, N.Y., State University of New York Press, 'Introduction'.
4   See MICHAEL W. APPLE (1972) 'Behaviorism and conservatism: The educational views in four of the systems models of teacher education', in BRUCE JOYCE and MARSHA WEIL (Eds) *Perspectives for Reform in Teacher Education*, Englewood Cliffs, N.J., Prentice Hall, for a general discussion of the dominant instrumental rationality in teacher education. Also, as Herbert Kliebard points out, this form of rationality is not a new phenomenon within teacher education but has dominated the form of discussion and debate since the turn of the century. See HERBERT KLIEBARD (1973) 'The question in teacher education', in DONALD MCCARTY (Ed.) *New Perspectives on Teacher Education*, San Fransico, Calif., Jossey-Bass; and HERBERT KLIEBARD (1973) 'The rise of scientific curriculum making and its aftermath', *Curriculum Theory Network*, 5.
5   It is important to see this stress on 'science' as distinct from the practice of scientists. Rather than blaming the domain of science for the excesses noted here, it is more accurate to see these as influenced by an 'ideology of scientism' that is fostered by positivism but which is itself a reconstruction of the history of scientific practice.
6   See KAREN KEPLER ZUMWALT (1982) 'Research on teaching: Policy implications for teacher education', in ANN LIBERMAN and MILBURY MCLAUGHLIN (Eds), *Policy Making in Education*, Chicago, Ill., University of Chicago Press for a discussion of the problematic aspects of Competency-Based Teacher Education. Also see JOSEPH CRONIN

(1983) 'State regulation of teacher preparation', in LEE SHULMAN and GARY SYKES (Eds), *Handbook of Teaching and Policy*, New York, Longman for discussion of the technocratic influences of state policies regarding teacher education programs.

7   For example, see LAURENCE IANNACCONE (1963) 'Student teaching: A transitional state in the making of a teacher', *Theory into Practice*, 2, pp. 73–80; BOB TABACHNICK, TOM POPKEWITZ and KEN ZEICHNER (1979–80) 'Teacher education and the professional perspectives of student teachers', *Interchange*, 10, pp. 12–29; and TOM POPKEWITZ (1977) 'Teacher education as a problem of ideology', presentation at the Annual Meeting of the AERA, New York.

8   LILLIAN KATZ (1974) 'Issues and problems in teacher education', in BERNARD SPOKEK (Ed.) *Teacher Education: Of the Teacher, By the Teacher, For the Child*, Washington, D.C., National Association for the Education of Young Children.

9   For a more detailed analysis of the obstacles to teacher learning associated with current forms of field-based teacher education see KENNETH M. ZEICHNER (forthcoming) 'The practicum as an occasion for learning to teach', *South Pacific Journal of Teacher Education*; also see LANDON E. BEYER (1984) 'Field experience, ideology, and the development of critical reflectivity', *Journal of Teacher Education*, 35, 3, May-June.

10 JOHN BARTHOLOMEW (1976) 'Schooling teachers: The myth of the liberal college', in GEOFF WHITTY and MICHAEL F.D. YOUNG (Eds), *Explorations in the Politics of School Knowledge*, Driffield, Nafferton.

11 THOMAS POPKEWITZ (1979) 'Teacher education as socialization: Ideology or social mission', presentation at the annual meeting of the AERA, San Francisco, April.

12 See GEOFFREY ESLAND (1971) 'Teaching and learning as the organization of knowledge', in MICHAEL F.D. YOUNG (Ed.), *Knowledge and Control*, London, Collier-Macmillan for a detailed discussion of the assumptions embedded in an objectivist conception of knowledge.

13 BARTHOLOMEW, *op. cit.*, p. 120.

14 PAULO FREIRE (1970) *Pedagogy of the Oppressed*, New York, Seabury Press.

15 For a summary of the empirical evidence supporting this assertion see KENNETH M. ZEICHNER (1986) 'Individual and institutional influences on the development of teacher perspectives', in LILLIAN KATZ and JAMES RATHS (Eds), *Advances in Teacher Education*, Vol. 2, Norwood, N.J., Ablex.

16 This should not be surprising given the fact that, as Cagan points out, 'perhaps no other aspect of American social thought and culture is as widely acknowledged and deeply felt as that of individualism' (ELIZABETH CAGAN, 1978, 'Individualism, collectivism and radical education reform', *Harvard Educational Review*, 48.

17 FRANCES FULLER (1971) *Relevance for Teacher Education: A Teacher Concerns Model*, Austin, Tex., University of Texas R&D Center for Teacher Education.

18 For example, see FRANCES FULLER (1969) 'Concerns of teachers: A

developmental conceptualization', *American Educational Research Journal*, 6, pp. 207–26.

19 FRANCES FULLER, JANE PARSONS and JAMES WATKINS (1973) *Concerns of Teachers: Research and Reconceptualization*, Austin, Tex., University of Texas R&D Center for Teacher Education, pp. 46–7.

20 THE NATIONAL COMMISSION FOR EXCELLENCE IN EDUCATION (1983) *A Nation at Risk*, Washington, D.C., US Government Printing Office.

21 THE CARNEGIE FORUM ON EDUCATION AND THE ECONOMY (1986) *A Nation Prepared: Teachers for the 21st Century*, New York, Carnegie Corporation, p. 2.

22 'Excellence' has become the latest slogan in educational discourse and the rhetoric of reform in the US. For an analysis of slogan systems see B. PAUL KOMISAR and JAMES E. McCLELLAN (1961) 'The logic of slogans', in *Language and Concepts in Education*, edited by B. OTHANEL SMITH and ROBERT H. ENNIS, Chicago, Ill., Rand McNally and Company.

23 THE CARNEGIE FORUM ON EDUCATION AND THE ECONOMY, *op. cit.*, p.125.

24 *Ibid.*, p. 76.

25 See, for example, FREDERICK WINSLOW TAYLOR (1911) *The Principles of Scientific Management*, New York, Harper; SAMUEL HABER (1964) *Efficiency and Uplift: Scientific Management in the Progressive Era 1890–1920*, Chicago, Ill., University of Chicago Press; for the effect of scientific management ideas on schools see RAYMOND E. CALLAHAN (1962) *Education and the Cult of Efficiency: A Study of the Social Forces That Have Shaped the Administration of the Public Schools*, Chicago, Ill., University of Chicago Press; and HERBERT M. KLIEBARD (1975) 'Bureaucracy and curriculum today', in WILLIAM F. PINAR (Ed.), *Curriculum Theorizing: The Reconceptualists*, Berkeley, Calif., McCutcheon.

26 THE CARNEGIE FORUM ON EDUCATION AND THE ECONOMY, *op. cit,*. p. 89.

27 *Ibid.*

28 LANDON E. BEYER (1985) 'Educational reform: The political roots of national risk', *Curriculum Inquiry*, 15, 1, Spring.

29 THE HOLMES GROUP (1986) *Tomorrow's Teachers*, East Lansing, Mich., The Holmes Group.

30 *Ibid.*, p. 23.

31 *Ibid.*, p. 51.

32 *Ibid.*, p. 52.

33 RICHARD RORTY (1979) *Philosophy and the Mirror of Nature*, Princeton, N.J., Princeton University Press, pp. 369–70.

34 See DWAYNE HUEBNER (1975) 'Curricular language and classroom meanings', in WILLIAM F. PINAR (Ed.), *Curriculum Theorizing: The Reconceptualists*, Berkeley, Calif., McCutcheon for discussion of similar views of the field of curriculum.

35 HANS-GEORG GADAMER (1975) 'Hermeneutics and social science', *Cultural Hermeneutics*, 2, p. 316.

36 HANS-GEORG GADAMER (1975) *Truth and Method*, New York, Crossroad Publishing Company, p. 288.

37 For example, see Michael W. Apple (1979) *Ideology and Curriculum*, Boston, Mass., Routledge and Kegan Paul; MICHAEL F.D. YOUNG (1971) *Knowledge and Control*, London, Macmillan; KEVIN HARRIS (1982) *Teachers and Classes*, Boston, Mass., Routledge and Kegan Paul; and WALTER FEINBERG (1983) *Understanding Education*, New York, Cambridge University Press.

3   Being a Teacher: Towards an Epistemology of Practical Studies

John Pearce and Andy Pickard

To begin on a polemical note: in 1975 Sara Delamont, the prominent British educational researcher, wrote optimistically of the coming boom in classroom research.[1] She suggested that such research already possessed an established history of organized endeavour. It even had a pre-history — an heroic age when individuals ploughed their lonely intellectual furrows. The future, it seems, was assured. To an extent this prescience has been confirmed. Things have stirred in the educational woods: studies of 'real' classrooms with real teachers and children, if not a legion, are no longer so rare as to be a major publishing event, and while 'grand theory' retains a fearsome bite in teacher education, 'action research' has established a presence in in-service and some pre-service courses for teachers.[2]

And yet, and yet ... this kind of classroom research, practice to theory orientation still retains something of the feel of the ghetto: strong binding culturalities unite those on the inside but exclude outsiders. Practical studies are still talked about as the 'coming thing' — always the bridesmaid it seems. They have yet to achieve that organic relationship with teachers and others involved in education whereby the ideas and methods of 'action' research become the common sense of the profession. It is not our purpose here to examine why progress has been slow in this respect. It is likely that it is partly the product of intrinsic characteristics: the competing and contradictory philosophical and ideological bases of the research itself as well as a preoccupation with methodological purity (the 'loops' and 'hoops' syndrome); and it may be that too much energy has been absorbed in throwing up yet more mountains of data — a kind of happy empiricism. It is also clear that external limitations, such as research funding problems in recent years, have caused difficulties. All of this needs some unwrapping if the limitations as well as the possibilities of these new approaches to understanding educational processes are to be identified.[3]

We are concerned in this chapter with one particular but crucial element in practical studies — the underlying epistemology of such work. Given that in *context* terms teaching is such a complex and varied business, it is important that epistemological concepts cutting across the particularities of any one situation are identified. It is by this route that 'action research', to use that term generically, can make its contribution to the more qualitative judgment about teaching. It is by this means also that what teachers do can acquire an intellectual status in its own right.

In the most obvious sense, being practical means purposeful activity and we are concerned with understanding the phenomena of 'doing things' in conceptual terms. It is also clear that as an activity teaching is a highly selective business in the sense that not everything which happens in a classroom is regarded as practically relevant, even when it is part of the teacher's consciousness. It is understanding this selective and subjective quality of teaching which forms the heart of an epistemology of practical studies. We also argue that understanding teaching in this way involves understanding the contextual relationships of what is happening. A more theoretical approach is concerned with *all* children, *all* schools, even *all* societies, whereas teachers are involved with *this* child, etc. The problem of the relationship between general categories and specific cases has to be resolved and epistemologically incorporated.

The other major thrust of our argument is concerned with the relationship between the here and now (the present) and the not here and now (the not present). Dual claims of this kind are a characteristic of teaching. Sometimes they are very grand indeed ('I want all my children to grow up to be good citizens and good Catholics to ensure the salvation of their souls'); at other times they seem very mundane ('when you go across to the art room I want you to stand behind your desks and not touch anything'). However, we are concerned here with something more than teachers' ambitions. In phenomenological terms the present/not present relationship centres upon the conceptual accounts offered by teachers for the connections they see among events. Thus 'lining children up' is often related by teachers to 'starting the lesson': conceptually 'starting the lesson' covers both events. Or behaviour in one context (the classroom) is seen as being about behaviour in another (assembly, the bus queue at the end of the school day.) It is our argument that such claims, perceptions and explanations also require an epistemological status.

Our entry point into these issues is part of a transcript of a discussion between a teacher and an 'observer' recorded in January 1986. The transcript itself has no particular significance or merit beyond its status as a running illustration and sounding board for the following argument. We are, therefore, defying research conventions and providing no additional information about the school beyond the obvious fact that the discussion followed a maths lesson with a junior class.

THE TRANSCRIPT

Observer: Tell me what it was that you were aiming to achieve, what were the children doing, and what expectations did you have?

Teacher: Well, when I was thinking about what to do with them at this stage of their maths, I had a chat with their previous teacher and she suggested 'time' as a topic. I wasn't too keen — it seemed horribly obvious and rather too young for junior kids, but when I talked to them they didn't really have much idea of time at all. Just talking to the tables, I found that if I asked them what time it was, then with the exception of two or three children in the whole class, they really didn't have the vaguest idea of time at all. They couldn't tell me the time when I showed them the clock and they had no real idea of when they had their dinner.

Observer: I wonder why that is. As you said, 'time' is a pretty standard content. I bet these kids have done it every year since they came to school. And it surrounds them all the time — 'time for play', 'time for prayers', 'time to go home', bells ringing — all that.

Teacher: Perhaps it hasn't been done too well....

Observer: Possibly but maybe its a more complicated notion than we adults assume. It seems to me that many people operate quite happily without 'clock time'. Maybe kids are like that too. I noticed that you started with 'technical' time — your clock faces and related questions: it didn't seem very interesting.

Teacher:	But on Tuesday when I introduced it we talked as a class about dinner time.
Observer:	How did that go?
Teacher:	Not too bad but I struggled to get them all involved. I didn't have any real discipline problems as such but this table in particular were reluctant to talk. I tried most things — easier questions, direct questions, moving closer to them, smiling — the whole bit, without too much success.
Observer:	And what would success have been like?
Teacher:	[laughs] Oh nothing startling! If only Paul could have said a couple of things about what he did at home time — but I'm working on it.
Observer:	Yes, I was interested in Paul. He didn't seem to be doing too much about time except waste it in all sorts of interesting ways. In fact none of this table did much at all. It seems to me that you've got a problem there which is increased by your decision to go for group work rather than a class approach. You were so obviously preoccupied with the other tables that you didn't really make it to Paul and friends.
Teacher:	Well, yes, I realize that. What I am hoping is that once I get the rest of the kids on the topic, then I can concentrate on talking to Paul and the others. At a more general level I don't think a class approach is suitable here — the kids are so widely apart.
Observer:	Well that is something useful to monitor and think about. One last comment which you can rule out of order if you like as one of my obsessions. The children who were going over to the computer corner in pairs — all six were boys. Does that bother you? It bothered me rather.
Teacher:	I hadn't really thought about it. Wednesday is computer day for this class. It gets wheeled from each class in turn and today was our day. I didn't really organize it.

Our task, therefore, is to examine this conversation as a practical discourse, given the limitation that it is a discussion about activity rather than the activity itself. In the sense of 'doing things', the actionable elements are clearly the selection of a syllabus content (time) and the poor response of some of the children, especially Paul and friends. The gender abuse of the computer may possibly be a third element but its status seems rather problematic for the teacher.

To take Paul and friends first. The teacher appears anxious to establish what the problem is 'really' about; and she does this in terms of a relationship between the present and not present. The sentence, 'I didn't have any real discipline problems as such', is a description of past experience which is seen as sufficient to convey meaning to a fellow professional. It is also a claim about what has happened in their shared present ('you didn't see any manifestations of poor discipline did you?'); and crucially is an argument for the *appropriateness* of her actions now in effecting a desirable change. Thus the teacher has an image of acceptable not present which is influencing her perception of what counts as significant in the present. She provides a conceptual entity for the appraisal of both present and not present — 'involvement'. This is a powerful term which conjures up images of children talking to her and to other children about their work, volunteering information, possibly bringing material to school or reluctant to leave the work at the end of a lesson.

Unfortunately, the relationship between Paul and this not present is problematic; 'telling me a couple of things he did at home time' seems an altogether more lowly level of involvement. The teacher appears to be creating a conceptual gap between the class and Paul, who is in grave danger of becoming a special case — a danger dramatically reinforced by the observer's 'interest' in Paul (the smoke of special schools and psychologists appears above the horizon!). Almost in the same moment, however, the situation is redefined yet again: the issue becomes 'Paul and friends' and the status shifts. On the basis of this the teacher begins to identify her sequence for making present and not present cohere: she will concentrate on Paul's table while keeping the rest of the class busy.

In terms of content the teacher's strategies may be ambitious or relatively modest: from providing routine or undemanding tasks to encouraging the use of workcards or library searches. Concentrating on Paul's table will probably involve sitting with this group, identifying rather more appropriate tasks, etc. In phenomenological terms such practices are complex. Sitting with Paul and friends for the morning is explicable for the teacher only in terms of the sequence which involves these children in such a way that they understand 'time'. However, such practices also have their own intrinsic meanings: sitting with children is sitting with children. The means/ends relationships involved in approaching practical studies this way are complex because they raise the problem of the connection between the teacher's world and that of the children. Crudely, if Paul goes home and says, 'Miss sat with us today and it was really interesting. We talked about the time we did things and what we did' (assuming Paul is more forthcoming at home than he is at school), then the child's and teacher's experiences of the sequence are comparable. If, on the other hand, his account is, 'Miss wouldn't let us alone, we had to work all day. I hope she picks on someone else tomorrow', then quite clearly Paul has a different view of events and is unlikely to become involved.

The problem arises because the relationship between elements and aspects of elements and the overall sequence is frequently ambiguous. With reference to the transcript situation, it means that the way in which the teacher sits with the children, the way in which she holds back sometimes or comes forward on others, what she chooses to emphasize or ignore, are all going to matter in the way in which children begin to see things. Experienced teachers are aware of this dimension and go to work on ambiguous manifestations in such ways that meanings and understandings become transformed. Infant teachers, for example, are able to make scribble into writing or a blob on a page into a picture of mummy hanging out the washing (daddy in gender-conscious classrooms).

It is at this point that the epistemological significance of 'context' begins to come more clearly into focus. In the transcript the teacher makes several direct appeals to the relevance of context. Thus with other children her syllabus selection might well have been different, but with these children it has to be 'time'. Similarly, the gender abuse of the computer has nothing to do with her 'real' self but arises from school organization. Most revealing of all, perhaps, is the crucial statement, 'I tried most things — easier questions, moving closer to them, smiling — the whole bit.' Here we have the authentic feel of techniques which have been successfully employed in other contexts but are ineffective in this classroom. The conclusion is that context modifies not just the starting point of a sequence, as with the choice of time, but continually. It is unlikely, for example, that this teacher could literally abandon 'smiling' or 'easier questions', but the relationship between this and doing other things — the design of the work programme, etc. — is contextually influenced. It may be that for smiling to be effective, the children have to value both the work they are doing and the relationship they have with the teacher. Teachers who see themselves as being in a school where children hold antipathetic or hostile attitudes will have a different order of practices to produce a coherent relationship between present and not present.

It follows from this argument that, just as context influences the beginning and course of a sequence, it will also affect the point at which a teacher decides to bring things to a close. Theoretically it might be possible for the teacher in the transcript to extend the study of 'time' to the twenty-four-hour clock or the history of time-keeping from candles to the microchip. Once again, however, her response might be, 'not for *these* children'. Here we come up against the problem apparently inherent in such a subjective approach to practical studies and one which is epistemologically crucial: how to evaluate legitimately what we have described as a sequence.[4]

The complexity and something of a solution to this problem may be seen in the 'observer's' mini-lecture on 'time'. He suggests that the concept is 'richer' than the teacher's rather narrow view. In terms of our epistemology his argument is a massive extension of context to incorporate *all* schools where bells ring, etc. Unfortunately, this version of time is very ambiguous within the situation perceived by the teacher whose own version is totally unambiguous — time equals clocks. Consequently, there is no meeting of minds, as evidenced by the teacher's comment, 'perhaps it hasn't been done too well', which is a clear reference to formal time. Quite possibly the same critique would apply to observers raising the issue of the boys' monopoly of the computer. Here, however, he legitimates a rejection of practical relevance by suggesting that it is a 'personal' obsession.

We are suggesting here that, in terms of our phenomenological epistemology, a meaningful relationship has not been established between the possibilities available in teaching 'time' and the events of the classroom. This in turn indicates that a completed sequence is about the creation of just that kind of relationship whereby a teacher can meaningfully explain an event as an event and relate how such events cohere to form a whole. Thus in terms of our transcript example, if the teacher saw 'bells ringing' as a significant aspect of the children's ignorance and indifference (an alienating experience of time as something done to them?), then home-base sequencing would be a situation in which the teacher could point to children controlling their 'time' through choosing to spend it one way rather than another. For the teacher whose starting point had been a 'low level' view of time, children exercising such choices would be a completely different and unrelated event.

We can now begin to summarize our epistemology of practical studies. Practical studies means doing purposeful things, but doing things is not a matter of ad hoc occurrences. Successful teaching means holding elements together conceptually in such a way that present experience is related to experiences which are past and to those which are still to come. We can call this holding together sequencing, and the scale and complexity can vary enormously (involving Paul, keeping the class busy, interesting the children, making school regimes part of the children's perception of time, different contents for different abilities — and that was only on the basis of one small transcript). Part of the complexity arises from the contextual nature of teaching in which the definition of context shifts according to whatever action is being considered. Positivistic notions of context as the class, the school, the neighbourhood, or society, clearly will not do here.

One conclusion from the preceding argument is clear: the practicality of practical studies cannot be rooted in a particular predetermined content. No checklist of skills or body of theory can correlate with the complexity of what it is to be a teacher, because what teachers do is necessarily bound up with what teachers are. It is on this ground that the defence of a phenomenological epistemology as rational, even 'scientific' and 'objective', has to be made, although only a general indication of such a defence can be provided here.

When teachers engage in those activities which define teaching, they are engaging in something more than a role to be set aside as will: they are constructing themselves as *beings*. Thus, with reference to the transcript, Paul may have been socially constructed as a 'slow learner', but the teacher was also self-constructed as someone who cares about such children in particular ways. Moreover, because teaching is a cultural process and a public activity, being a teacher is both internal self (one's own values and experiences) and external self (a comprehensible engagement with other teachers, children, parents, etc. whose views either tally with or deny aspects of one's sense of being).

Given the complexities and contradictions of teaching, we would argue that when teachers struggle with their 'public' and 'private' selves, they are seeking to establish a sense of authentic being, a sense of self which can transcend moments of conflict, contradiction, or crisis. We are describing here the process through which the present may be transcended in the consciousness and experience of a teacher by a coherent awareness of the not present. Such a process involves standing back from events and the particularity of circumstances and allowing matters to develop with a reasonable degree of certainty about outcomes. For such teachers, teaching becomes a more flexible process and, we would argue, the world become a less threatening place. Their concept of the practical is such that, because what they do has a meaningful relationship with a series of events and situations, it follows that the effort expended in teaching is more economically utilized. In contrast, the teacher whose experience of present and not present is of an incoherent kind is always being forced to respond to the present in ways which make little sense in terms of past experience. The distinction is between, on the one hand, the teacher who is rational, coherent and consistent or at least can handle inconsistencies, and, on the other hand, the teacher who is inconsistent, incoherent and irrational.

It is important to say what the argument is not: it is not just a claim that all teachers are rational simply because they are teachers. Consistency qua consistency is not rational. The teacher who always beats children can claim consistency: rationality would grow out of the relationship between punishing children this way and the other claims made by such a teacher (discipline? authority? successful learning? order?). It would also grow from the relationship between this action and the meanings attached to it by others involved — the children, parents, other teachers. Nor is ours an argument for some consensual model of what it is to be a teacher. We recognize that even the most fundamental aspects of teaching, such as what it means to learn or to be in control of children, are disputed. Public rules are never objective and are there to be challenged by the teacher's own sense of authentic being.

Our argument is that consistency and coherence are part of the teacher's experiential world. The conclusion is that they should provide the basis of their epistemological world also. The epistemology we have identified and argued for here achieves this. It is related to the phenomenological world which teachers inhabit and, furthermore, it confronts and challenges those traditional public categories — lessons, subjects, classroom organization, types of children, etc. — whose currency has been so debased when trying to understand teaching.

Notes

1 G. CHANON and S. DELAMONT (Eds) (1975) *Frontiers of Classroom Research*, Windsor, NFER.

2 See, for example, the recently published J. SMYTH (Ed.) (1986) *Learning about Teaching through Clinical Supervision*, London, Croom Helm.

3 Some of the issues raised here are in the process of being unwrapped. See for example, W. CARR and S. KEMMIS (1986) *Becoming Critical: Education, Knowledge and Action Research*, Lewes, Falmer Press.

4 We label this particular problem *the getting out of Munich syndrome*. A student described thinking sequentially as going on a rather tiresome journey to somewhere pleasant — 'like Yugoslavia'. If the journey became too long, a teacher could always settle for somewhere relatively atmospheric — 'like Munich'.

4 Teachers' Knowledge of Teaching: Strategies for Reflection

Freema Elbaz

I have never been trained as a teacher. As a result, I don't know how to make lesson plans (at least, not 'properly'). Nor can I manage a classroom. Once a ruler was grabbed out of my hand; another time someone's name was scribbled on the front of my coat when I wasn't looking. On the other hand, I have had some successes: I once took a group of ninth graders through a double period of English, which they hated, and by the end of the second hour all of them were participating willingly and even learning. Being untrained gave me an advantage with respect to situations like these: not having been socialized into appropriate teacher behaviour, I didn't feel that my personal prestige was at stake when I acted inappropriately, and since I had no fixed categories for dealing with the situations (e.g., classroom management, motivation), I was able simply to approach them as interesting events, events which triggered long sequences of thought about what learning in classrooms in different places is like, and why. For example, the ruler-grabbing incident took place when I substituted in a very well-behaved grade 4 classroom in a Canadian suburb. On reflection, I later realized I had confused and incited the class by ignoring a series of minor misdemeanors which preceded the event. To understand why, one only needs to know that I had spent the previous year in an Israeli elementary school where very different rules of conduct obtained. So apart from being momentarily embarrassed, I gained an opportunity to reflect on the nature of the signals or cues (Ben-Peretz and Halkes, 1985) that are exchanged by pupils and teachers in different classrooms.

Such reflection, we know, is not a part of the occupational structure of teaching: there is no time for it, and teachers are seldom trained to reflect on their work. Yet teaching is both effective and worthwhile in large measure to the extent that the teacher is able to reflect critically on practice. Such reflection entails at least two things: first, that the teacher is able to test reflection through action designed to modify aspects of the learning/teaching situation; and second, that the teacher has some awareness of the knowledge used in such reflection. Recent work has significantly advanced our understanding of teachers' knowledge and of the teacher's perspective on educational events, but there is still ambivalence and uncertainty as to the implications of this research for the training of teachers and for the involvement of researchers and academics in the effort to improve schools. In this chapter I consider these implications by looking at the process by which teachers become aware of their knowledge.

For two years I have conducted seminars on teacher thinking for graduate students, almost all of whom were also teachers. The seminars were not directed solely at the elaboration of participants' knowledge, and began with the consideration of general issues arising out of recent research on teacher thinking; about half of the teachers involved, however, chose to focus on their own work. Their resulting oral and written presentations provided some indication of what the task of elaborating one's own knowledge of teaching can be for teachers (see also Yonemura, 1982; Lampert, 1985; and the work of Butt and Raymond, 1985).

Such experience shows that there is a large gap between what researchers produce as reconstructions of teachers' knowledge, even when this research is carried out explicitly 'from a teacher's perspective' (e.g., Elbaz, 1983; Clandinin, 1985) on the one hand, and teachers' accounts of their own knowledge on the other. I would like to assume that research on teachers' knowledge has some meaning for teachers themselves, that it can offer ways of working with teachers on the elaboration of their own knowledge, and that it can contribute to the empowerment teachers and the improvment of what is done in classrooms. In my encounters with teachers I have met with considerable interest and enthusiasm for the task of elucidating one's own knowledge, but the role of research knowledge in this activity is not obvious, and as teacher I am still searching for viable and effective modes of facilitating the process.

One initial obstacle is the perception of teachers that the investigation and elaboration of their own knowledge is not altogether legitimate as a research activity; some teachers may feel that the university is condescending to them, offering a watered-down version of research more suitable to their abilities. A second difficulty is that once teachers agree to focus on their own work, their concern with solving problems comes to the fore in a way that interferes with the deeper search for understanding. Hence teachers' analyses are often disappointing to the academic eye on first reading: they look for solutions to problems, and for easy accounts of the 'causes' of particular situations, and their analysis does not seem to attain the depth or comprehensiveness that they are capable of in regular academic work. Furthermore, there is a concern to lay the blame somewhere; in discussions teachers may be very critical of 'the system' in general, and equally aware of problems with the way that particular schools are run and organized, but when they begin to give account of their own work there is a discouraging tendency to accept all the blame for failure in a particular situation. Even worse, getting it all down on paper sometimes seems only to reinforce a defeatist attitude.

Nor do all the obstacles lie with the teachers. As instructor I am sure I convey, implicitly, my impatience and my feeling that the process ought to lead somewhere, and this undoubtedly curbs the urge to write autobiographically. Further, the place of a critical perspective in working with teachers is difficult to find: how does one avoid 'dumping' on the teacher by imposing one's more 'enlightened' view of the situation, yet at the same time assume some responsibility for engaging teachers in a process of critical reflection? Put the other way around, how does one work from and with the reality of the teachers without becoming bogged down in conventional views of schooling? And how can the views constructed by researchers, of teachers' knowledge drawn 'from a teacher's perspective', be of use in this process?

In thinking through these issues, the work of Paolo Freire has allowed me to gain a better understanding of the apparent conflicts between teachers' and researchers' knowledge, on the one hand, and between the need to accept the teacher's perspective and the desire to bring to bear a critical perspective, on the other hand. Freire speaks of problem-posing education as a collective process in which participants reflect on their situation, coming to perceive it as an 'objective-problematic situation' and acquiring the ability to intervene in reality as they become more aware of it; this process is seen as analogous to the decoding of 'an enormous, unique, living "code" to be deciphered' (Freire, 1970, p. 103). We can identify three phases in the decoding process. The first stage is one of sympathetic observation and recording of everything in the situation, as it is seen by the observer. In the following stage, the reports of all participants are presented, and each exposition 'challenges all the other decoders by re-presenting to them the same reality'; this confrontation necessitates a reconsideration of the situation and new analyses, which are again played off against one another. This is a process of dividing and reintegrating the total situation, and involves bringing forth the contradictions or 'limit-situations' which characterize the reality of participants. The final phase is one of structuring a program of educational action based on the nucleus of 'limit-situations' which has been identified.

While my work with a high-school teacher, aimed at elucidating her practical knowledge for purposes of research and conceptualization, is far indeed from the context and purposes of Freire's work, it seems to me in retrospect that the different phases of analysis in that study are analogous to the first two phases of investigation described by Freire. Thus, the first phase of the study involved focusing on the experiential world of the teacher — looking at it as she experiences it, sympathetically, and as far as possible in her own terms. The period which followed involved analysis of the teacher's knowledge using different sets of terms: first the content of her knowledge was elaborated in terms of everyday categories (subject matter, instruction, etc.); then the various orientations of knowledge were examined (social orientation, personal orientation, etc.), and finally the analysis touched on the rules, principles and images which make up its structure. These different modes of analysis were played off against one another to verify and integrate the various understandings. The concept of 'image' served as a device for expressing the integration of the teacher's knowledge; and finally the concept of cognitive style was developed to give an account of the totality of the teacher's knowledge. This account expressed some at least of the contradictions inherent in the teacher's work, although the study did not extend to the stage of action and thus cannot be considered a dialogical study in Freire's terms.

In a similar way, I would suggest that working with teachers on the elaboration of their knowledge involves a movement through the three stages, and primarily a back-and-forth movement between the descriptive and the analytic, then between the analytic and the synthetic phases, and ultimately moving to action. Looking at the process in terms of these three stages gives me a better understanding of some of the difficulties I have encountered in working with teachers, and also helps me to make more appropriate choices of means to further the process at each stage.

As suggested, an initial problem encountered is the reluctance of some teachers to accept the elaboration of their own knowledge as serious scholarly work. One student in a seminar approached me, a few weeks after the group had decided that each member would choose a personal issue or problem in teaching to focus on, and asked to write a seminar paper on the approach to teacher thinking of a particular Jewish religious philosopher. The request discouraged me, suggesting as it did that the purpose of the seminar had been missed altogether. But in line with Freire's stipulation that 'the point of departure must always be with men in the "here and now", which constitutes the situation within which they are submerged, from which they emerge, and in which they intervene', I agreed to the topic; if the academic reality and its canons were of such importance to this student, the concern must be honoured. The justification for this decision came with the discussion that was engaged when the paper was presented orally to the class: it provoked one of the most intense sessions of the seminar, in which preconceptions and prejudices concerning religion were brought forward and confronted.

Another instance of the need to produce work that resembles the standard academic paper is L.'s project. She was troubled by her eleventh grade language class — it was difficult to interest students in the material, their very poor reading skills did not seem to be improving, and classroom climate was tense. Rather than confront this situation directly, L. decided to carry out a carefully controlled comparison of her work in this class with her teaching in another class at the same level and doing the same work; significantly, the second class, which L. enjoyed teaching, was composed of adults studying towards a diploma in a post-secondary technical college. L. placed considerable emphasis on standard observation procedures, found someone who didn't know her well to carry out the observations for her, arranged to teach the same material both times, and generally took pains to control as many aspects of the situation as possible. Again these measures were justified by the resulting presentation in which L. was able to convey vividly the situation in both classes; the controls had obviously helped her to distance herself sufficiently from the painful aspects of her teaching to make this confrontation possible.

Once teachers are embarked on the process of examining their teaching and their knowledge, there seems to be a tendency to shortcut the first, descriptive phase. Indeed introspective, descriptive writing can seem to be static and divorced from action, something one does quickly in order to get on with the task at hand. For the instructor it sometimes seems a very individualistic process which does not bring together the members of a group.

J., who had decided to develop a project to eliminate streamed math groups in grade six, commented that she began this project 'from a clear ideological position'. At one point in our group discussions she described how, as a teenager in a large South American city, she believed that all youth her age attended high school as she did. The moment at which she discovered that she and her friends were members of a very small, privileged minority was obviously a critical point in the development of that ideological position, yet she never wrote about it, probably because it simply did not seem important enough to her. Maher and Rathbone (1986), in developing the notion of educational autobiography from a feminist perspective, asked students to write on topics such as schooling and IQ ('When I learned how smart I am'), schooling and family finance, and memorable rewards and punishments. The idea of directly imposed topics seems, at first glance, to run counter to the spontaneous, personal quality we associate with autobiography, but in fact such topics may serve to bring a group together as members share experiences brought to paper in response to the task.

Later in the process there may be difficulties getting into the phase of analysis. Researchers are familiar with this difficulty: on the one hand, it is hard to get started without predetermined analytic terms; on the other hand, terms found in the literature do not necessarily suit the unique situation with which one is dealing. In my experience teachers do not seem to take readily to the terms used by researchers; my students rarely adopted terms of analysis from my own or other researchers' work, and the categories they developed often seemed to me to be muddled or simplistic. This is a rather threatening situation for researchers — we want to feel that our work is of some use to practice, and it is tempting to conclude that teachers are simply less talented than we are at probing and analyzing knowledge of practice. It is important to remember that for teachers, categories of analysis serve the organizational function of ordering their material in a personally meaningful way; the discreteness of categories and their theoretical sophistication are properly of no particular interest to teachers.

Another problem is the tendency to jump to conclusions or solutions without really taking apart the situation. Sometimes this is a sign of fatalism — the teacher has already concluded that change is not possible. M. described two contrasting experiences which had led her to such a conclusion. In the first instance she had spent three years with a vocational class; the students had many difficulties in learning, for which none of M.'s training had prepared her and initially she was at a complete loss. Gradually she acquired understanding of the students' problems by consulting with the school counsellor and attending courses in remedial teaching. She also participated in a research project on school change in which, guided by the researcher, M. led group meetings in which the several teachers who taught her class analyzed problems in depth, generated and tried out solutions. After this experience M. viewed herself, and no doubt was seen by the school administration, as someone who could deal effectively with problem students. She was given a new class, a grade 11 vocational class. M. sailed in full of confidence, and found that nothing worked. The students' basic skills were weak and they were behind in every subject; their other teachers refused to invest the time needed to cooperate in a problem-solving group; parents felt it was too late to turn the situation around. The students were uncooperative at first, but once they saw that M. meant business they did the assigned work, and eventually learned enough to pass the school leaving exams. But their attitude to the school, the class and M. herself remained one of sullen indifference. M. was totally dispirited by her inability to reach the students and alter the classroom climate. The other teachers in the seminar pointed out that M. had come to this new class after they had experienced two years of failure and inattention to their problems; she had nevertheless been able to bring them up to the level of the external examination. M. acknowledged this, and saw that in her previous class many additional factors worked in her favour. Yet her failure to create a warm and trusting relationship with these students plagued her, and M. felt that eventually she would leave teaching.

M.'s account of her experience puzzled me: she was aware of all the factors working against her with the grade 11 class, and had had an impressive success with the earlier class. Similarly L. had taught effectively in the setting of the technical college and could understand why the same strategies did not work with the high school class. But both teachers focused only on the negative aspects of the situation.

This dilemma is addressed by Freire's analysis of the dialectical relationship between reflection and action. To the extent that the teacher is able to analyze the situation in depth and perceive its inherent contradictions, her ability to act to change that situation is enhanced; but insofar as she sees no options for action that will bring about change, her ability to perceive the situation will in turn be limited. This point brings us to the importance of a dimension of intervention in the elaboration of teachers' knowledge. Teachers necessarily think in terms of projects and intentions; the impetus to problem-solving is a legitimate one for the teacher. As researchers with a history of 'no significant differences' we are justifiably reluctant to adopt premature solutions, but we ought not to impose our hesitation on the teacher. It does not follow that we should encourage teachers to rush into projects for change. Rather, it is only by envisioning alternative ways of doing things that we can become fully aware of the 'limit-situations' which make up our reality, and conversely this enlarged awareness makes possible the discovery of new solutions to problems. In the seminar it was typical for participants to give rational advice of the form, 'What would happen if you tried X?' This strategy was ineffective precisely because the teacher could not see the point of trying *anything*. A better approach to such fatalism might be by first confronting this 'lack of a task', as Freire puts it, and then attacking the blocked situation by a form of brainstorming in which alternative actions are generated without a rational monitoring procedure; even absurd or impossible solutions help to bring awareness of both limits and possibilities in the situation.

In conclusion, a consideration of my experience with teachers examining their own knowledge, seen in terms of both my own earlier work and Friere's frame of reference, brings to the fore a number of possibilities for further work with teachers. In the early phase of such work we see the value of autobiographical writing, but we should not dismiss other types of writing as tools for enhancing teachers' awareness of their situations. Later on it becomes important to generate and exchange different views, using whatever theoretical and practical devices seem appropriate; group reflection is invaluable in bringing about this exchange. Finally, it is essential to envisage and entertain concrete alternative courses of action which follow from the reflective process; only then can the process become self-sustaining, enabling the teacher to proceed independently.

References

BEN-PERETZ, M. and HALKES, R. (1985) 'Cues and culture: Personal knowledge of teachers in the interpretation of classroom situations in intercultural settings', presented at the OISE Symposium on Classroom Studies of Teachers' Personal Knowledge, Toronto.

BUTT, R. and RAYMOND, D. (1985) Presentation of work in progress at the OISE Symposium on Classroom Studies of Teachers' Personal Knowledge, Toronto.

CLANDININ, D.J. (1985) *Classroom Practice: Teacher Images in Action*, Lewes, Falmer Press.

ELBAZ, F. (1983) *Teacher Thinking: A Study of Practical Knowledge*, London, Croom Helm; New York, Nichols.

FREIRE, P. (1970) *Pedagogy of the Oppressed*, New York, Seabury Press.

LAMPERT, M. (1985) 'How do teachers manage to teach? Perspectives on problems in practice', *Harvard Educational Review*, pp. 179–94.

MAHER, F. and RATHBONE, C.H. (1986) 'Teacher education and feminist theory: Some implications for practice', *American Journal of Education*, 94, 2, pp. 214–35.

YONEMURA, MARGARET (1982) 'Teacher conversations: A potential source of their own professional growth', *Curriculum Inquiry*, 12, 3.

5 Student Knowledge and the Formation of Academic Discourse: A Case Study[1]

Glenn Hudak

For radical educators like Paulo Freire[2] and Ira Shor[3] learning is a transformative experience. This process not only entails that the student reflect on self and society, but also the realization that as a human being he/she can actively participate in history as an agent of social and political change. A central component to these 'critical' pedagogies is the integration of student knowledge into the academic curriculum. Here student knowledge serves as the primary content of the curriculum, where 'features of everyday life are isolated as themes of study.'[4] The authentic learning experience begins with that with which the student is most familiar: his/her own knowledge of the world.

In this chapter I present the findings of a recently completed investigation of a high school mass media class.[5] The objective of this study had been to reinvestigate the role student knowledge plays in the formation of an academic discipline. The genesis of this project was the sense of 'panic' I felt after reviewing several well-written case studies which document how the process of schooling literally excludes student knowledge from the academic curriculum. Studies at the elementary,[6] junior high,[7] and secondary levels[8] indicate that student knowledge has no legitimate status in the classroom.

To make matters worse, these conclusions regarding the role of student knowledge in the classroom often undermine proposals for radical reform at the classroom level. Consider the conceptual problem embedded in Robert Everhart's study of a junior high school.[9] For Everhart, student attempts to include their knowledge into the classroom agenda (via resistances) ultimately serve to create and maintain a sharp separation between student and school knowledge. At the level of day-to-day activities within the classroom practices associated with student knowledge (i.e., resistances) exacerbate the rift between student and school knowledge at two fronts. First, by their own admission, students did attmept to 'bug the teacher', i.e., to disrupt the normal flow of classroom events. Under these circumstances it seems quite natural for the teacher to attempt to curtail such disruptions, and to refocus student attention toward the planned agenda. As a consèquence, student knowledge was routinely dismissed from any serious consideration by the teacher. Second, while bugging the teacher, the activities associated with resistances simultaneously reinforce group solidarity, i.e., they strengthen ties among students. This, of course, led to the maintenance of student culture. Taken together, teacher dismissal and the strengthening of group solidarity work to insure that student knowledge remains outside the parameters of legitimate classroom knowledge.

It is from this perspective that Everhart concludes that resistances reinforce existing conditions within the school, rather than actually challenging or structurally altering school knowledge. The power embedded in resistances is shown to operate in such a manner as to intensify peer relations, while minimizing concern for classroom knowledge. In essence resistances reinforce the common-sense meanings associated with work and play.[10] Work is something that is teacher-directed and, like a dull headache, it is something that the student must put up with in order to at least pass the course. Play represents student interests, student ways of knowing and acting; it is their knowledge. For the student, the primary goal of going to school becomes that of maximizing play and minimizing work whenever and wherever possible. As such, the agenda for the course remains unaltered; to challenge the agenda structurally is tantamount to students taking work seriously. That is, there would have to be a fundamental shift in student priorities. This, in turn, does not seem possible in Everhart's framework: for student priorities to shift, the very organization of the school must change; and this cannot happen as long as students continue to disrupt classroom activities. In essence the process of schooling represents a vicious cycle of tight control over student actions and student attempts to break control, which in turn reinforce the necessity for continued control over student actions. On the basis of Everhart's findings there is no official, legitimate place for student knowledge in the curriculum.

While Everhart's study illuminates the relationship between social practices and knowledge production, there exists a fundamental conceptual problem related to the study as a whole.

Everhart suggests that the way to break out of this vicious cycle is for teachers to resist the imperative of the bureaucratic structure. That is, teachers ought to strive to aid students to develop emancipatory interests; i.e., a critical perspective toward schooling and society. This sounds good, however at the level of day-to-day activities within the classroom Everhart provides no concrete linkages to suggest how this should occur. Instead, Everhart makes a conceptual leap by integrating a Habermasian framework into the study. That is, school knowledge is represented by technical interests, student knowledge is represented by practical interests, and emancipatory interests can be obtained essentially by synthesizing both. The problem with this is: how does one accomplish this synthesis, given that students and teachers essentially view the world from 'separate realities'?[11] What evidence do we have to suggest that there is a connection between student knowledge and school knowledge? For teachers to actualize a program of emancipatory interests, there must already exist at some level a 'field' which would allow student and teacher knowledge to interact — hence the synthesis of technical and practical interests.

The problem is that while Everhart makes connections between knowledge and social practices, his framework is not sufficiently broad to investigate the communicative environment of the classroom. Indeed, a possible solution for Everhart would be to show that the inclusion of student knowledge does at one level maintain a separation between school and student knowledge, and that at another level, say the communicative dimension, student knowledge does interact with school knowledge in such a manner as to play a significant role in the formation of classroom knowledge. Hence, there may be some basis for suggesting that emancipatory interest — a critical pedagogy[12] — is possible.

To this end, I began to look at the formation of the curriculum from the perspective of discourse production. My goal was to explore the possibility of expanding the domain of investigation to include not only concrete linkages between social practice and knowledge (as Everhart does), but also the communicative interactions involved. Such an investigation would show how both social and communicative interactions between student and teacher produce 'a specific way of talking (and thinking)'[13] about a subject, i.e., a discourse where 'the discourse is not about objects; rather the discourse constitutes them.'[14] I wished to explore how an academic discipline is constituted and if student knowledge contributes to the constitution of the discipline. The focus of this study would not be the formation of classroom knowledge per se, but rather the constitution of an academic discourse.

The Inquiry

To understand the role of student knowledge in the classroom, I chose to study a high school mass media course. I wished to investigate a situation where students had prior familiarity with the subject matter of the course, in this case TV, radio, film — i.e., mass media. In such a situation, I reasoned, students would have something to 'say' about the media. Next I would ascertain if student information was integrated into the classroom agenda. Here my focus was on the development of the curriculum-in-use[15] in this media course. Finally, if student knowledge were found to be part of the curriculum-in-use, then it would be possible to claim that for at least one subject — media studies — the foundations for emancipatory pedagogy are possible.

The setting for this study was a single high school mass media course. Twenty-four students were enrolled, thirteen of them male, and eleven female. The instructor was male. Throughout the study he was identified as Mr Albert, a pseudonym. The course was offered as an elective within the English department. Only high school juniors and seniors (eleventh and twelfth grades) were allowed to register. There were no formal prerequisites for the course. No texts were used; the instructor used films as a means of presenting information.

Data for the study were collected for the entire length of the course, i.e., for a full semester. The course met five days a week for fifty minutes each day. The total contact time with members of the class was approximately 105 hours.

The research design consisted of three stages: (1) observation — interviews; (2) organization of material; and (3) analysis of data. Classroom observation served as primary data for the study. The intent was to gather accurate descriptions of social and communicative interaction between students and teacher. These data later served as the basis for analysis. Informal interviews were also included throughout the semester as a means of clarifying student/ teacher actions.

Material was organized by establishing a broad taxonomy of teacher approaches to the study of the media. During the semester, data revealed that the teacher tacitly approached the media from three distinct knowledge orientations: commonsense, cultural and technical.

> *Commonsense orientation*: Lessons identified under this heading were found during the first two weeks of class. These lessons were perceived by the teacher as an introduction to the course as a whole. During these lessons the teacher encouraged students to state their opinions about topics presented in class. The term 'commonsense' was derived from the observation that student comments were frequently 'off-the-cuff' statements that did not require much effort or reflection, i.e., they appeared to be 'commonsensical', spontaneous remarks.
>
> *Cultural orientation*: Chronologically, lessons identified under this heading followed the commonsense orientation, and preceded the technical orientation. The primary aim of these lessons was to introduce to the student the social, cultural, and historical foundations of contemporary media practices.
>
> *Technical orientation*: These lessons were devoted to the expliation of the technical aspects of video and film production.

These three orientations formed the general framework for the organization of material and analysis of data.

The conceptual framework for this study has been to view the production and constitution of 'legitimate' classroom knowledge in terms of the formation of discourse within the institutional setting provides an overall framework.[16] Here the production of discourse entails an actual 'struggle' between two opposing forces. Generally speaking, this struggle is played out in terms of the institution versus the individual or group. The power of the institution resides in its ability to control, select or organize knowledge. In essence institutions tend to 'contract' the parameters of legitimate knowledge by controlling access to and flow of information. On the other hand, there exist social forces which seek to be infinitely open, to 'expand' the parameters of legitimate knowledge, where members tacitly attempt to legitimate knowledge forms which are not officially sanctioned by established institutions.

To ascertain the 'direction' in the parameters of classroom knowledge, i.e., expansion or contraction, I made one methodological move: the 'movement' was translated into the boundary strength between internal (school) and external (student) knowledge. A 'weak' boundary between internal and external knowledge meant that students were able to draw upon and 'use' their knowledge during classroom discussions; that is, the parameters of legitimate knowledge had expanded to include student knowledge. At the other extreme, a strong boundary between internal and external knowledge meant that student responses to teacher inquiries were restricted to information presented in class, and that students had limited access to their own knowledge; that is, the parameter of legitimate knowledge had tended to 'contract', to exclude student knowledge from classroom discussions regarding the media.

The Nature of Academic Discourse

This section will explicate those practices and procedures which came to constitute an academic discourse in the media. I will show how the parameters of legitimate knowledge continued to contract from the commonsense orientation through the technical orientation. Regular classroom sessions were divided into the three knowledge orientations. To ascertain the parameters for each orientation, the primary methodological strategy was to focus on the boundary strength between internal (classroom) knowledge and external (student) knowledge.

Commonsense Orientation

The analysis of commonsense orientation revealed that the boundary strength between internal and external knowledge was weak. This meant that in general discussions characteristic of this orientation students were encouraged to draw from their own knowledge of the media. Mr Albert, the teacher, asked students to state their opinions and to be 'open-minded' when listening to the views of others. He stated that in general discussions there were no explicitly right or wrong answers and that each student was entitled to his or her opinion. Relatively speaking, students appeared to have enjoyed this format for discussion. Reasons for students liking this format included the following: (1) given student familiarity with the media, they found it easy to give 'off-the-cuff' answers; (2) the classroom discourse included student opinions, that is, student knowledge was granted legitimate status; (3) the legitimacy of student knowledge meant that they could control some aspect of the classroom discourse by interjecting comments. The discussion was not totally defined by Mr Albert.

However, in the second lesson an incident occurred which came to constitute the first prohibition on the classroom discourse. After the film 'Why Man Creates' was shown, Mr Albert initiated a discussion. In the midst of this discussion a student called out, 'the film was dumb!' This comment was followed by a moment of silence in the classroom. Then other students voiced their dissatisfaction with the film. The agenda that Mr Albert had planned for the lesson came to a sudden halt. Students began to have their own discussion of the film. Mr Albert's response was surprising, given the understanding that student opinion was to be honoured. Mr Albert silenced the class by publicly reprimanding the student. This action tacitly led to the establishment of the first rule for classroom discussion: students were not to challenge or question Mr Albert's agenda. The reprimand of the student graphically conveyed to others that not all student comments were legitimate. Students could draw from their own experiences; they could state their opinions; however, they could not question or critique the material presented by Mr Albert. The establishment of rule one essentially contracted the parameters of legitimate knowledge by prohibiting certain aspects of student knowledge.

This contraction of parameters meant that the boundary strength between internal and external knowledge increased. Increased boundary strength served to control access of information entering the discussion and as such reduced student control over the terrain of the discourse. The fact was that students could *not* say anything they wished. Their comments were valid only to the degree that they remained within the limits defined by Mr Albert. The range of possible discussion topics was reduced and student autonomy over the discussion process was therefore reduced.

Cultural Orientation

The contraction of parameters shrank the domain of the classroom informational environment by increasing the boundary strength between internal and external knowledge. As the informational environment decreased, so did student control over the discourse.

This was accomplished through a radical transformation of the knowledge orientation itself.

Briefly, the cultural orientation was characterized in the analysis as being a 'relational' mode of knowing. Its 'logic' is 'synthetic' in that this orientation attempts to bring together the various dimensions of media practices through the integraton of several academic disciplines. As the analysis revealed, however, the promise of the cultural orientation was never realized in the media course. For example, during one lesson on the history of photography, the film 'This Is Edward Steichen' was shown. The film revealed, among other aspects of Steichen's life, that his wife was a great deal younger than he was. After the film was shown, Mr Albert attempted to discuss Steichen's perspective on photography. Students, however, had a different agenda in mind. They asked, 'How could she kiss him?' As Mr Albert attempted to refocus the discussion on Steichen's philosophy, students continued to talk among themselves about Steichen, the 'dirty old man'. This difference in interests led to a disruption of Mr Albert's agenda, a disruption which students appeared to have really enjoyed.

The disruption led to two further prohibitions on classroom practices and discourse. Tacit rule number two was that students were to direct their comments to Mr Albert and not talk among themselves, for it appeared that intra-student communication led to class 'disruption'. As student collaboration increased the students' ability to include their comments in the discussion, it also increased student control over the discourse and reduced Mr Albert's ability to control the agenda for the discussion session. Rule two, then, sought to fragment student communication/collaboration. If students could *not* talk among themselves, then it was possible to avoid further disruptions. Tacit rule number three was that students were to keep their comments 'clean'. Sexuality appeared to be one topic which brought students together and led to student disruptions of the agenda. By prohibiting the discussion of issues involving sexuality some of the impetus for collaboration could be reduced. Taken together, rules two and three continued to contract the parameters of legitimate knowledge by further limiting student behaviour and increasing the boundary strength between internal and external knowledge.

To operationalize rules two and three, the teacher appeared to increase the tempo of discussions. This transformed the character of the discussion sessions from relatively informal format to question and answer sessions. In prior lessons student responses to Mr Albert were characterized as rambling, off-the-cuff statements. Increased tempo limited the time available for response. Hence, student responses were compressed and usually limited to one word or a short phrase. (For example, 'When was the first photography developed?' The response was '1848'.) The increased tempo truncated the relational aspect of the cultural orientation. Students were not asked to reflect on the cultural or social foundations of the media. Instead, the discourse was reduced to the identification of discrete facts. Rules two and three not only limited student actions and knowledge, but transformed the essential character of the cultural orientation by removing 'reflection' and 'synthesis' from the pedagogical process.

By the last lessons of the cultural orientation, parameters had contracted to such an extent that student knowledge had been virtually defined out of the discourse: the students had no legitimate means whereby they could introduce their opinions into the discussion. The student's voice in the classroom had been 'silenced'. Students responded to this exclusion by withdrawing from legitimate discussions; only after much coaxing from the teacher did students respond to his questions. In essence students covertly resisted exclusions from the discourse by withdrawing from the discussion. As a result the social relations between teacher and students deteriorated to the point where each responded to the other, at times as adversaries. This 'gap' between the teacher and students was not bridged during the remaining lessons found in the cultural orientation.

Technical Knowledge

The pattern of contraction continued throughout technical knowledge. The boundary strength for initial technical knowledge lessons was strong, and discussions focused almost exclusively on information presented within the classroom. There was little evidence of students drawing from their own experiences. However, these lessons were met with moderate student enthusiasm for the material, for various reasons. First, students did not have to discuss the 'boring' social or cultural foundations of the media any longer. Second, the instrumentality of the technical orientation appeared to match student expectation of what a media course should cover, i.e., how to make video tapes and films. Third, the 'analytic' procedure used to disseminate technical information about production processes appeared to be compatible with student expectations. Students had little difficulty 'taking apart' production procedures and indentifying specific technical terms. Since this method was familiar to students, they were able to anticipate questions that Mr Albert would normally have asked. The result was greater student control over the terrain of the discussion. There appeared to be a compatibility of students' expectations, teacher agenda, and the primary method for study of the technical aspects of production. In essence students and teacher were moving in the same direction. As a result there was no evidence of student resistance during initial lessons. Both students and teacher appeared to have fun in these lessons. The 'gap' between student and teacher appeared to have been momentarily bridged. The key to these 'successful' lessons appears to have been new control, a new approach to the media, the most importantly an increase in student access to and control over parts of the discussion.

The breakdown of student enthusiam corresponded with a continual contraction in the parameters of legitimate knowledge. As lessons progressed there was a marked increase in the amount of class time used for the showing of films and a decrease in time for discussion. This meant that the discussion itself had to be compressed for Mr Albert to remain on his schedule. Hence, the tempo of the discussion increased. As in the case of cultural knowledge lessons, increased tempo meant that discussions had to become very focused. There was no longer time for students to collaborate among themselves. Student responses had to be compressed to a single word or phrase: they could not ask questions; they could not reflect on material presented. Reflection was truncated from the pedagogical process. The students' role during discussion was reduced to identifying technical terms as presented in the films. With reflection and collaboration removed from classroom discussion, the promise of the technical orientation was never achieved. That is, the instrumentality of the technical orientation was deleted from the discourse. Students did not learn 'how to' construct a video or film. Instead, they identified discrete terms which were stripped of their essential relationships with each other.

The contraction of parameters literally squeezed the fundamental instrumentality of this orientation out of the picture. With it went student incentive for studying the technical aspects of production. Students no longer had any legitimate avenue for introducing their opinions into the discussion. Students had lost control over the terrain of the discourse. They were once again backed into a corner where the only mode of including their opinions was to resist Mr Albert. Both overt and covert resistances emerged; social relations had once again deteriorated to the point of mutual antagonism, and a 'gap' had again been created between teacher and students. However, unlike the conclusion found in the cultural orientation, there was evidence to suggest that both teacher and students actively sought to bridge this gap (though the motivation for doing so was quite different for each).

The Culture of Discourse

The pattern of contraction indicates that the parameters of legitimate knowledge were radically reduced for each knowledge orientation and that the discourse was essentially constituted through a process of 'rarefaction'. This concept, which is adopted from Foucault, is defined as 'those internal procedures which deplete meaning from the discourse. They constitute a growing scarcity, a dwindling of meaning in that ... the discourse reveals not plentitude of meaning, but scarcity. Thus, the internal procedures of rarefaction consist in discourses which exercise their own control, which limits themselves....'[17] The important point is that the struggle over control of the discourse led to a depletion of meaning, a growing scarcity of interpretation. For each knowledge orientation there is evidence that the struggle between student and teacher led to a strengthening in the boundary between internal and external knowledge. For the commonsense and cultural orientations this process of contraction was initiated by student attempts to include their knowledge in the classroom agenda. In the technical orientation the process of contraction was initiated by the over-use of films. That is, the conflict between student and teacher was teacher-generated. The result was that for the cultural and technical orientations the domain of legitimate classroom knowledge came to consist solely of discrete bits of ('teacher-owned') information.

Furthermore, as an internal classroom process, rarefaction came to socialize both student and teacher. By 'socialize' I mean 'process of making people "safe". This process acts selectively on the possibilities of a man's actions by creating through time a sense of inevitability of a given social arrangement, and through limiting the means of permitted change.'[18] Indeed, rarefaction operated as (1) a mechanism of self-censorship where the struggle between Mr Albert and students defined points of 'controversy', i.e., differing interpretations of media practices, and (2) over time came to develop a 'sense of inevitability' not only over what one discussed with regard to the media, but also how one was to interact with this information.

To illustrate this point I will focus on the last lesson in the technical orientation — the events which occurred after the film 'Solo' was shown in class. The film documents a mountain climber, Mike Hover's journey to the top of the Grand Tetons. What was striking about this lesson was that the discussion of the film was so congenial. Mr Albert had asked students to identify various technical terms found in the film 'Solo'. Student response was somewhat enthusiastic. For instance, at one point students debated, on their own, whether one shot in the film was 'moving-camera' or not. Given the prior gaps and struggles between Mr Albert and students, it was difficult to imagine that these same students were really as interested as they appeared to be in these particular topics. Why the sudden interest in identifying technical terms?

The answer appeared to be that 'Solo' was to a certain extent the 'inevitable conclusion' to the long hard struggle between Mr Albert and the students. Lessons had come to the point where the discourse had been so depleted that to avoid further confrontation both students and teacher tacitly 'normalized' relations. As in a chess game, both Mr Albert and students had come to a stalemate. Mr Albert wished to regain his audience, since teaching to a group of bored, restless students was no pleasant experience. To this end Mr Albert allowed students more time to discuss information presented in class. Interviews with students made it clear that they wished to pass the course. To this end students avoided issues or opinions that led to conflict in the past, e.g., calling the film 'dumb'. With all other avenues of discussion defined out of the agenda, the only 'safe' move was to accept, though not necessarily believe in, the current state of affairs which they had created.

To this extent the discussion and interpretation of the movie had to remain at a surface level. While students may have found the content of the film enjoyable, which added to the congenial atmosphere, the discussion was construed within narrowly defined parameters. It was not surprising that students did not pursue any issues beyond what was asked by Mr Albert. For example, Mr Albert: 'An instance of the long-shot.' Student: 'The side of the mountain, to show how small he was next to it.' This type of interrogation was all that was possible under these circumstances. Normalization, then, is indicative of the neutralization of conflict between student and teacher. It is essentially a pragmatic move on the part of the actors.

Here the constitution of a 'safe' discussion was the result of real human concerns: concern on the part of the teacher to have a pleasant lesson and concern on the part of the students to pass the course. Rarefaction of the discourse, however, greatly reduced the options available for student and teacher action. Interestingly it was the ability of student and teacher to act upon the actions of each other which generated the rarefaction process; and through rarefaction the discourse was rendered 'safe'. No parent or administrator ever entered the media class. The very social dynamic of the media class came to constitute its own form of censorship, its own form of containment. The members of the media class limited their own possibilities for action.[19]

Concluding Comments

This study identified points of struggle which occurred between students and teacher. In the commonsense and cultural orientations the initial conflict was initiated by student attempts to include their opinions in the discussion, e.g., calling a film 'dumb', and the discussion of Steichen as a 'dirty old man'. In the technical orientation the initial conflict was generated as students began voicing their dissatisfaction with the number of films shown in class. The result of this struggle was that the content of classroom discussions was rarefacted. Here the tension created through the expansion-contraction of knowledge parameters essentially removed student (and teacher) knowledge from the domain of classroom discussions.[20] Thus the content of classroom discussions was stripped of its former richness; what remained was characterized as discrete bits of factual information.[21]

Of importance was the discovery that even though the struggle between student and teacher did rarefact the content of the course, a 'particular way of talking' about the media was nonetheless constituted, i.e., a 'safe' discourse. The safe discourse meant that by the end of the course both students and teacher avoided the discussion of issues that would fuel further conflict. Furthermore, 'safe' describes not only *what* was said between students and teacher, but also *how* it was said to avoid conflict. By the end of the study students and teacher 'normalized' relations so as to attain their respective goals (e.g., pleasant lesson for the teacher, passing the course for students).

Throughout this study we found that student knowledge played an integral part in defining the curriculum-in-use in this media course. This conclusion was made possible by expanding the domain of current ethnographic investigations to include the formation of the discourse. At the level of the discourse there exists a 'field' where student and teacher knowledge interacts, thus making it possible to initiate critical pedagogies at the classroom level.

Notes

1 I wish to acknowledge and thank Kathleen Gershman and Harriet Powers of the Center for Teaching and Learning for their assistance in the preparation of this chapter.
2 PAULO FRIERE (1973) *Pedagogy of the Oppressed*, New York, Seabury Press.
3 IRA SHOR (1980) *Critical Teaching and Everyday Life*, Boston, Mass., South End Press.
4 *Ibid.*, p. 99.
5 GLENN M. HUDAK (1985) 'Communicating, learning and discourse production in the classroom: A case study of a mass media curriculum', PhD dissertation, University of Wisconsin.
6 MICHAEL W. APPLE (1979) *Ideology and Curriculum*, Boston, Mass., Routledge and Kegan Paul, particularly chapter 3. In this chapter Apple, with Nancy King, discuss how kindergarten children learn the distinction between 'work' and 'play', i.e., the distinction between school knowledge and 'merely my knowledge'.
7 ROBERT B. EVERHART (1983) *Reading, Writing and Resistance*, Boston, Mass., Routledge and Kegan Paul.
8 LINDA M. MCNEIL (1983) 'Defensive teaching and classroom control', in MICHAEL W. APPLE and LOIS WEIS (Eds), *Ideology and Practice in Schooling*, Philadelphia, Penn., Temple University Press. McNeil concludes her study by pointing out that 'defensive' teaching strategies employed by secondary teachers 'seems to make the students withdraw into their own personal information (their "real" knowledge)' p. 139. Again we find evidence of a split created between personal and school knowledge; and how personal knowledge is removed from the classroom agenda.
9 EVERHART (1983), *op. cit.*
10 See APPLE (1979), *op. cit.*, chapter 3.
11 EVERHART (1983) writes, 'resistance to school-based knowledge through regenerative knowledge does not oppose as much as it forms a separate reality' p. 229.
12 See in EVERHART (1983) Appendix A, 'Lesson Plans'.

13 CATHERINE BELSEY (1980) *Critical Practice*, New York, Methuen, p. 5.
14 MICHEL FOUCAULT, quoted in MANUEL ALVERADO and BOB FERGUSON (1983) 'The curriculum, media studies and discursivity', in *Screen*, 29, 3, May/June, p. 31.
15 APPLE (1979), *op. cit.*, p. 51.
16 MICHEL FOUCAULT (1981) 'The order of the discourse', in ROBERT YOUNG (Ed.), *Untying the Text*, Boston, Mass., Routledge and Kegan Paul.
17 *Ibid.*, p. 49.
18 BASIL BERNSTEIN (1977) 'Social class, language and socialization', in JEROME KANABEL and A.H. HALSEY (Eds), *Power and Ideology in Education*, New York, Oxford University Prss, p. 476.
19 The analysis presented in this study is limited; to provide a complete picture of this process of containment we need to explore and make linkages between internal classroom processes and influences external to the classroom.
20 In HUDAK (1985) I present data to show how the teacher's personal knowledge of the media was also removed from the classroom agenda.
21 Here my findings are similar to Everhart's, namely his discovery of 'reified' knowledge. See Everhart (1985) chapter 3.

PART II

Pedagogical Contexts

6 Teachers' Knowledge from a Feminist Perspective

Sara Freedman

In the workshops I conduct with teachers, I always begin by asking them why they entered teaching. The two most frequent responses are: (1) because I love working with children and (2) because it fits in well with raising a family. Most of these teachers are women, especially in the 'lower' grades. They take for granted their dual roles of teacher and mother. They are acutely aware of the difficult nature of balancing both roles, while pointing out that, at least as far as working conditions are concerned, being a mother and being a teacher are often compatible.

When we discuss the major areas of conflict they face as teachers, they report that they are most upset by their encounters with parents. 'As a teacher I hate parents and as a parent I hate teachers.' They see both students they feel are neglected by their parents, and students pushed too hard by their parents. In the first case, teachers often report stories of deep personal involvment with children, of working with children on emotional or moral issues that the students are facing, many of which involve family conflicts. In the second case, they tell of children who grow tense from pressures to succeed, and parents who demand extra work, numerous conferences outside normal school hours, and two years of reading progress in a matter of months. These two descriptions of parents' relationship to their children often mirror descriptions the teachers give of their own teaching. They too neglect children. They too pressure children beyond the students' capacities. Sometimes this happens because they are simply too spent or too disinterested, sometimes because of pressures from above, scheduling crunches, or overcrowded classrooms. They talk about being torn between the desire to help certain students and anger at their mothers, in particular, for making such help necessary.

I too have faced these tensions as a teacher, feeling extremely attached to many of my students while facing enormous anger or distance from a number of parents. It particularly concerned me that the tension was between two women, the woman teacher and the mother, and both saw each other as the enemy. This chapter addresses this issue by raising a number of questions: What are the responsibilities of a teacher to her students? What are the boundaries between the role of the teacher and the role of the parent? Who sets these boundaries, both intellectual and emotional, and what purpose do they serve? How do these boundaries reflect and affect other divisions within schools and families, as well as society at large?

In seeking answers to these questions, one finds little attention to the issues they raise in research about teachers or in courses that train prospective teachers. In the literature that does address the problem, the origin of these tensions, particularly the way they are shaped by the larger framework of the school system or the family, is not discussed. Instead, the literature talks about the harmful effects on the students when parents and teachers find themselves in conflict; the teacher is warned that she must be careful not to become emotionally attached to her students, or a particular student. The warning is generally couched in terms of a taboo. (Although the pronoun 'she' is never used in these writings, one can assume that it is to a 'she' that such advice is directed, for how many men are presumed to need such a warning?)

Not surprisingly, several of the widely quoted authors on this subject are women (Lightfoot, 1978; Katz, 1980; Scarr, 1984). They bring to our attention the important emotional labour that women are expected to perform in our society, both in the workplace and in the home. However, their work runs the risk of accepting the continued ghettoization of emotional labour to the world of women, in the very fact that they encourage us to value this kind of 'woman's work' without raising the parallel questions of who is *not* doing this work, and how this division of labour fits in with other divisions of labour, both in the education system and in the family. There is little in this body of work that describes or critiques the role of men in avoiding an affective role, or how society has attempted to divorce emotion from intellect, and assign each of these two attributes to a different sex. We learn little about the role of principals in schools, for example, in creating this division of labour, or how fathers' work lives and emotional makeup reinforce these role separations in the home.

Instead, the emphasis is on delineating clear boundaries between mothers and teachers, in order to decrease role confusion and tensions. Writers emphasize the need to separate the work of women in the family from the work of women in the school, so that women do not perform emotional double duty. This they believe is important not only for women, but more so for their children and students. They write about the potential for competition between teacher and mother, and the importance of having one person serve as impartial, semi-detached judge, while the other performs the functions of a passionately attached advocate.

Lilian Katz, for example, in an article entitled 'Mothers and Teachers: Some Significant Distinctions' (Katz, 1980) argues for something she awkwardly calls 'optimum detachment'. She believes teachers need to be reminded to exercise this form of emotional tightrope walking precisely because the role of women, and specifically mothers, in our society is changing. The new pressures under which many women find themselves are affecting not only the institution of the family but other social institutions as well, especially schools. Katz (1980) argues that there is increasing pressure being placed on teachers by parents of children in day-care centers, preschools, and primary classes to meet the needs of their children, which go unsatisfied because of the busy working lives of their mothers (in many cases, single mothers). In other words, *mothers* are negligent in their emotional duty to their children. She believes this blurs the boundaries between the home and the school, something she disapproves of because it violates the responsibility 'society enjoins on parents to their young children [which] is quite different from that which it expects from teachers, nurses and other professionals' (Katz, 1980, p. 49). While the job of the teacher is 'optimum detachment' which requires 'selfconscious and deliberate efforts to distance themselves', the job of the mother is to exercise optimum irrationality [where] the emphasis is upon the depth and strength of what we sometimes call 'ego involvement' (Katz, 1980, pp. 54–5).

Once she defines the family as the place in which all of a child's emotional needs should be met, the solution is obviously not to question whether the family alone, and the mother in particular, should meet that need but somehow to force mothers to continue responding to their children in ways that have been traditionally assigned to mothers in our society for the last several hundred years. The teacher should in no way rush to fill the vacuum of children's presumed emotional needs, because this would upset what Katz accepts as the natural order.

Arguments for the separation of powers between teachers and parents are grounded on the way authors (Dreeben, 1968; Newson and Newson, 1976; Lightfoot, 1978; Katz, 1980; Scarr, 1984) with this viewpoint look at the two touchstones of modern-day society — love and work. Grounded in the tradition of Parsonian sociology, they believe not only that love and work are two distinct ways of being, but also that they are exercised in two separate places — the family and the workplace. 'The traditional Parsonian view of work-family separation held that universalistic, specific, emotionally neutral, and performance-oriented norms dominate the work world, whereas particularistic, diffuse, emotional and quality — (or ascriptive) oriented norms dominate the family' (Kanter, 1977).

These authors (Newson and Newson, 1976; Lightfoot, 1978; Katz, 1980; Scarr, 1984) seem to accept the differences as part of the natural and therefore acceptable functioning of these institutions, and of the people within them. All families are seen as loving and stable, as havens in a ruthless and uncaring world. Conflicts and power differences within families are not acknowledged. Much of the description of families is a nostalgic recollection of the ideal industrialized white middle-class family, created in the nineteenth century, rather than modern-day or even latter-day reality. We are told that parents have lifelong attachments to their children, that those attachments are boundless, and the responsibilities of parents are inescapable and all-encompassing. 'Society enjoins on parents [responsibilities] quite different from that which it experts from teachers. . . . For one thing [they] have no fixed hours. . . . Parents of preschool children never go off duty' (Newson and Newson, 1976, p. 400). The reality of divorce, of children from several marriages living with step-parents, of the unwillingness of many fathers to pay child support are simply not acknowledged.

Sarah Lightfoot, in *Worlds Apart*, offers a similar description of family ties:

> Parents have emotionally charged relationships with their children that rarely reflect interpersonal status or functional considerations. Children in the family are treated as special persons, but pupils in schools are necessarily treated as members of categories. From these different perspectives develop the *particularistic* expectations that parents have for their children, and the *universalistic* expectations of teachers. (Lightfoot, 1978, p. 22)

Lightfoot, in thus defining mothers' work, seems to legitimize mothers' concerns when they are explicitly asking for special attention for their children. The ritual of much of what is called 'parent participation' — the mainstay of which in many American public schools is deciding which teacher will teach your child next year — offers a fine example of this viewpoint. Pressure on schools has been building to let parents in, and the goals of equal opportunity, democratization and accountability have been blended into one overriding mechanism in many schools, that of convincing parents that the way to ensure their child's success in school is to place the child in the 'best' teacher's class. The legitimate concerns of parents for quality education, and the need by educational authorities to give lipservice to an often-expressed belief in democracy has been translated into a minimalist view of the democratic process, one that encourages parents to believe that one's own interests are separate from, and in competition with, the interests of others.

Class placement, as the ritual is called, starts in the spring of each year when each classroom teacher divides the children she is currently teaching into reading 'ability groups'. She next allocates an equal part of each group among the number of classes that will be taught in the next highest grade. At the same time, the principal typically sends a letter to all parents in the school asking for their suggestions and comments as to where their child should be placed in the coming year. Middle-class mothers stalk classrooms, interview and assess teachers, and on the basis of this brief courtship, decide whether they have found a suitable match for their child. Middle-class mothers thus act as lobbyists for their children, their own special interest group. The principal then readjusts the class lists on the basis of the parent request. The system precludes all parents from participating, for working-class mothers and single mothers simply do not have the time to make such forays. The changes are always conducted in secret, with the power of the principal over both parents and teachers bolstered.

Parents are not given information about, nor asked to consider the issue in terms of race, class, or sexual composition, nor does the system encourage parents to ask what kind of class composition they would like their child to experience. The broad appeal for personal, individualized information about a parent's child specifically legitimizes drawing the principal's attention to one's own child, divorced from the needs of others or considering how those needs might be reconciled or mutually supported.

Because the ideological cover for this process is the desire for increased democratization in the schools, requests must be couched in terms that stress the emotional well-being of the child rather than a raw straining of ambition. Thus the system depends upon mothers being psychologically and emotionally attuned to their children so that they can act as articulate and convincing advocates. Private information, the kind the mothers know through the intimate involvement with their children, is thus transmuted into public policy. For a mother to state concerns about the overall racial, class, or sexual differences in or outside of school would seem to be overstepping her boundaries. Indeed, a mother who ignores or chooses not to submit a request to the principal feels, and is often made to feel, she is either negligent, naive, or sacrificing her child's needs to a kind of unmaternal, harsh, and abstract principle of equal opportunity.

The mother's realm, the family, is directly juxtaposed to the classroom, the realm of the teacher. The teacher is expected to consider the students in her classroom on the basis of 'universalistic' standards. She is discouraged from maintaining any long-term relationship with the child, and is encouraged to remove herself from the historical record of the child. She is told she will be judged by how closely she adheres to those standards. Again, the need to remind teachers of these criteria suggests that they either try to use other standards, or administrators believe they do. 'Even those teachers who speak of "loving" their children do not really mean the boundless, all-encompassing love of mothers and fathers but rather a very measured and time-limited love that allows for withdrawal' (Lightfoot, 1978, p. 23). Thus women outside the home are confined to the realm of the 'universal', and frequently admonished not to allow an understanding of the emotional makeup of their students to interfere with the division of their classes along more objective standards. It is assumed that if they do follow such standards — generally established not by themselves but by standardized testing, administrative fiat, and university-based research teams — they will be protected from the emotional turmoil of children.

Mothers are expected to operate in the opposite fashion. While inside the family they are expected to be self-sacrificing; in facing society they are pushed to be selfish where other family members' needs are concerned, in that they are asked to put the perceived needs of their families above those of society's. A measure of how devoted a mother is to her family is how tenaciously she works for its particular needs above and often against the needs of other families or any other social institutions.

A dispassionate model of behaviour — which in our society is generally identified with men — is held up as the ideal for teachers, and explicitly juxtaposed to what is defined as its opposite — the passionate, idiosyncratic, and empathetic model of behaviour generally identified with women in our society.

Critics of mothers and teachers who attempt to step out of their gender-defined roles set by society could perhaps be counted as proponents of encouraging teachers, if not mothers, to move away from the narrowly confining role of women as affective, nurturing proto-mothers in school. It could well be argued, however, that schools would be unable to function if teachers took categories such as Lilian Katz's seriously. Perhaps if children's emotions could be easily defined, diagnosed, and treated, with the proper 'treatment' given to each child — a treatment agreed upon by experts on the basis of sample behaviours of children — then teachers could simply choose the right treatment, and the child would fall into line. Alas, or fortunately, that is not the case, as any one who has spent time working with children can tell you. Instead, teachers must, and good ones do, depend upon their empathy, their observation, their acceptance of each child as particular, when they teach them, talk to them, prepare them for the next grade.

Creating a bureaucracy in schools allows some people to distance themselves from students, teachers, and others — formalizing relationships and setting up specific times and timetables for when they will sit down and work with someone. That does not mean, however, that everyone in a school has the luxury of such clear boundaries of time and emotions. Just as a father can leave home and expect the wife to clear up any emotional loose ends that come up during the day, so too are schools set up so that some people can set the rules while others are left to, and expected to, continue the daily, intimate involvement that is required to put those rules, or a reasonable facsimile of those rules, into practice. It is easy for a principal to believe that it is the rules, and the clear expectations and boundaries, that create adherence to them, because he does not see all the negotiating, all the recourse to individual ties that appear at a distance like standardized results.

Even though principals rely upon the intuition and emotional involvement of women teachers, they continue to speak in formal terms when explaining the workings and accomplishments of schools. Thus teachers are enjoined to be distant, impartial, and somehow therefore fair. To do this correctly, they also must follow the dicta from above — a not insignificant reason for trying to convince teachers to equate empathy with discrimination. Talk of 'teacher proof' materials, for example, carries with it the assumption that if teachers are allowed to teach idiosyncratically and with a degree of emotional involvement, they will inevitably be led to make distinctions amongst their pupils that would inhibit rather than enhance the equal opportunity, or simply the just rewards, of all.

It is crucial to recognize that the dicta about the proper involvement for parents and teachers come out of a socially constructed situation in which parents are given sole responsibility for children, with no rights to help in that care and responsibility, and others are excluded from sharing that care, whether they wish to give it or not. If one recognizes the way the roles of mothers and teachers have been constructed, and the ends they serve, then one can begin to break down these categories and the need to see society as held together by the maintenance of a series of dichotomies — the home and the school, the husband and the wife, the schoolmarm and the mother, the principal and the teacher.

The separation of teacher, student and family is only maladaptive in a society such as ours which isolates families from each other, punishes them for seeking help or community, and encourages them to compete with other families for scarce resources. In that context, anyone from outside trying to penetrate the very closed circle of the family threatens the entire social structure of individual, competitive families. One is penalized and seen as unnatural if one cares about others outside the circle of one's own family, and conversely a mother in particular is seen as selfless if she cares exclusively for the members of her own family. The fact is that children today could not be brought up in our society without the care and attention, and frequently devotion, of many people other than their biological parents.

The panacea of transforming 'woman's true profession' into a male model of detached professionalism will not work. Admittedly, teachers today are not always happy with the way they combine their interest in working with children and their need to keep them on grade level. They frequently feel that although they are expected to perform both tasks, their intellectual work is frequently devalued by administrators and others who make most of the decisions about curriculum, and their emotional work is unrecognized or considered harmful by many parents. Being a 'professional', a term often used when a principal feels a teacher has overstepped her boundaries, frequently means accepting the curriculr dictates from above, while being detached yet emotionally attuned to her students. 'Professionals trying to walk this tightrope end up being *generally* motherly: an absurd contradiction in terms' (New and David, 1985).

Rather than encouraging teachers to block their moral and nurturing sensibilities in regard to children and their families, the schools should seek to *extend* this way of thinking beyond the confines of the presently prescribed circle of care, the nuclear family, or its mirror image in the school, the individual classroom. They should be able to exercise these qualities, while at the same time being encouraged to develop the intellectual capacities of themselves, as well as their students. This would require a small revolution in the structure of the school, and in the relationship between principals and other administrators and teachers. Conversely, mothers should not have the entire emotional burden of raising children. Neither should this responsibility and joy be shared only with the women teachers. In the end, the raising of children is a societal issue, one in which we all have responsibilities, and one from which we all draw sustenance.

References

DREEBEN, ROBERT (1968) *On What Is Learned in Schools*, Reading, Mass., Addison-Wesley.

KANTER, ROSABETH MOSS (1977) *Work and Family in the United States: A Critical Review and Agenda for Research and Policy*, New York, Russell Sage Foundation.

KATZ, L.G. (1980) 'Mothering and teaching: Some significant distinctions', in KATZ, L.G. (Ed.), *Current Topics in Early Childhood Education*, Vol. 3, pp. 47–63.

LIGHTFOOT, SARA LAWRENCE (1978) *Worlds Apart: Relationships between Families and Schools*, New York, Basic Books.

NEW, CAROLINE AND DAVID, MIRIAM (1985) *For the Children's Sake*, London, Penguin Books.

NEWSON, J. and NEWSON, E. (1976) *Seven Years Old in the Home Environment*, New York, Halsted Press, 1976.

SCARR, S. (1984) *Mother Care/Other Care*, New York, Basic Books.

7 Accommodation and Tension: Teachers, Teacher Role, and the Culture of Teaching*

Robert V. Bullough Jr

When a beginning teacher enters a school for the first time, she enters more than a building; she enters a culture of teaching that has evolved in response to school structure and wider cultural values that establishes what is the appropriate teacher role. To function successfully within the school, the beginning teacher must come to terms with this role and the values that sustain it. She has a great deal of help in doing so. School structure — the way work is organized and evaluated — presses for conformity. Students, other teachers, administrators, and parents all indirectly, and occasionally directly, encourage compliance. But accommodation does not always come easily. Life within schools is complex, confusing and oftentimes contradictory, with the result that teachers do not always behave in ways consistent with institutional priorities.

In this chapter we explore the culture of teaching, the tensions and contradictions that accompany the teacher role, and how teachers' accommodation to the role not only reproduces the culture but offers possibilities for its transformation.

Teacher Role Characteristics

In the broadest of strokes the culture of teaching, reflecting the influence of school structure, can be characterized in a few unpleasant terms: it is presentist, conservative and individualistic.[1] However, this is not the whole story. As Sara Lightfoot has rightly

---

* I wish to acknowledge the important part played by my colleague Andrew Gitlin in the conceptualization and drafting of this chapter.

noted, when teachers are listened to carefully their 'voices deny easy categorization'.[2] What is heard reveals tension and conflict. The culture of teaching is clearly not all of a piece. Think, for example, of the shocking differences that exist among schools where differing economic, political and religious values and commitments are played out, even while the structure itself appears identical. Class, which has profound impact on the culture of teaching, is a case in point. Teachers in working-class schools often have lower expectations of students and place a greater emphasis on factual knowledge than do teachers in élite schools.[3] In these settings, and even between departments within the same school, teachers see their roles and the purposes of education differently. Nevertheless, there are certain common threads.

Public Service and Instrumental Rationality

Successful accommodation to school life requires negotiating a position between one's own personal interests and values and the interests and values that are embedded in the institutional and community context. At some points these converge, at others they diverge sharply. Analysis of the two major sets of values and interests that have formed the boundaries of the teacher role reveals the depth and complexity of the negotiating problem teachers face. The first is the value of public service which, while weakening as a motivation for entering and staying in teaching,[4] persists as a strong interest. The second, instrumental rationality, and its handmaiden, what we call technocratic mindedness,[5] reflects a powerful institutional interest that rationalizes school structure while subtly altering the focus of public service and lowering its intrinsic value.

Public service has long been a high value of the Western world. Plato, for example, commended the virtues of public service through describing the role and responsibilities of the guardian class. At its extreme, the highest good is to suppress individuality in every aspect of life to serve the state.[6] The ideal of service profoundly shaped the culture of teaching; teachers sought to serve and were expected to be self-sacrificing, morally upstanding servants to a higher good. Early, this higher good was connected closely with religious values,[7] later, community values in a more general sense came to the fore along with the value of helping young people.

In the United States the values of public service were solidified, strengthened and reshaped through the feminization of teaching which was justified on economic grounds — women were willing to work for a third to half of what male teachers demanded — and on moral grounds. Women were the perfect servants: they embodied the higher virtues of patience, high moral character, gentleness and a capacity to love while being, in the words of Cyrus Peirce, principal of the first American normal school, 'free from [the] eccentricities and infirmities off genius'.[8] As public servants women were expected and willing to sacrifice all for the good of others, particularly children, and not inclined, or seen as able for that matter, to establish their own aims. Rather, they would do as they were told.

Instrumental rationality also has a long history in the Western world, reflecting the rise of science and technoloy. For teachers its importance lies in how it has shaped institutional life and redefined the aims of public service, where institutional interests are taken to be synonymous with the public good. The good servant, therefore, puts the interests of the institution ahead of other interests. Throughout this century American educators have been consumed with the quest to establish ever greater levels of institutional efficiency: how to get more for less. To achieve this aim schools were organized around the model of American business, which was understood to enjoy its success because of the influence of presumably scientific rationalization. Like other forms of labour, teaching was reshaped. Specialization, systematization and firmly established hierarchical roles and responsibilities became the rule of the day.[9]

The organization of schooling along the lines of the factory did not exhaust the influence of pseudo-science on the culture of teaching. It also has had a powerful effect on how education and education-related problems have been understood. A mindedness emerged that complemented, justified and furthered institutional imperatives. An essential part of instrumental reason, at its extreme, is an uncritical acceptance of the method of science, narrowly construed and when in the hands of appropriately trained experts, as the only reliable means for problem solution. To achieve the accepted end of efficiency — an objective necessity to which the public servant teacher gives obeisance — experts created ever more sophisticated means which were then supposed to be carried out by teachers who occupied the middle rung on the hierarchy.[10]

Making certain teachers do as they were told required careful supervision. At its core instrumental reason betrays a fundamental interest in prediction and control under the assumption that only in this way is it possible to obtain efficiency. So experts who know the educational good, and who understand and control the means of knowledge production, establish rules and regulations to govern the behaviour of those charged with attaining the good. Others, supervisors, administrators and sometimes curriculum coordinators, seek means for making certain the rules and regulations are obeyed. The proper role of the teacher, therefore, centres on providing efficient instruction.

It is into this mix that the neophyte teacher brings his or her own values and interests. For most, internalization of several of the elements of the culture may have already taken place. As students, teachers learned some of the values of the culture of teaching, particularly those stemming from instrumental reason. They may, for example, believe that the proper role of the teacher is instruction and accept as reasonable limited involvement in goal setting. They also bring to teaching the desire to serve which in large part comes to be defined instrumentally. But tensions do arise. There is tension between public service and instrumental values, as well as between these values and one's own personal interests. For example, to serve is to obey, to follow institutionally established rules and regulations. Yet there are often instances where doing what is supposed to be done runs counter to the interests of individual students. At such moments the second sense of service re-emerges, the one that likely led the teacher to enter teaching in the first place, where the aim of service is to help young people however and wherever possible, and to this end rules are broken.

In numerous ways personal values modify the institutionally established teacher role and influence the culture of teaching which maintains it. To be sure, the influence is soft and subtle, because school structure, the power of ideology of public service, and the demands of instrumental rationality press the teacher to set aside conflicting personal values, but nevertheless it is there. If we but listen to the voices of teachers, what we hear are the words of uneasy compromise and of unfulfilled but lingering dreams, dreams of the kind of teacher they want to be.

Teacher Role and Reproduction

Accommodation is seldom complete. Their voices communicate ambiguity, frustration, and sometimes confusion. This is especially clear when they speak of what it is to be a teacher and the ideals that drive them to teach, and when they speak of their relations with other teachers and students. The teacher voices that follow come from observation notes and a set of twelve interviews conducted with a group of junior high school teachers with whom we worked over a two-year period.

Teaching and Teaching Ideals

The task the teachers assigned themselves was to produce a professional statement by exploring what it means to be a teacher. After working independently for two weeks, items were collated and a single document was put together for discussion. At the meeting the first item was read: the professional teacher 'has acquired a high degree of knowledge and skill in his field and keeps it current.' Almost immediately emotions began running high. One teacher excitedly remarked, 'Our field has more to do with survival than professionalism', and then, in a more calm voice and with some embarrassment, admitted she really 'didn't have ideas [about teacher professionalism] of her own, as usual.' She simply did not think of teaching as a profession but she thought she ought to. Another teacher wanted to discuss the second item: 'appears self-confident; handles pressure well.' This teacher thought to be professional was to 'appear expert', to put on a show for administrators and parents in order to, as another teacher quipped, 'maintain an image'. What followed was a discussion of why teachers are not professionals: 'We're so far removed from being professional ... [we] don't have any of the stuff [of professionals].' Another thought teachers were not professional because they were not 'trustworthy' — they have not proven themselves worthy of being considered professional. In the spirit of public service, to be considered worthy means putting students 'at the forefront' of everything done, but often this does not happen and institutional interests dominate.

These teachers did not believe anyone actually considered them professionals, nor did all of them believe they were worthy of such a designation, whatever it meant. They were public servants, as one teacher explicitly noted, and therefore talk about professionalism made little sense: servants are not professionals. Specifically, they did not have the degree of control over their work necessary to function professionally, which they lamented, even while expecting others to alter their situations for them. As one teacher remarked, teachers 'are too highly educated to be in the situation [they are] in' but it is 'too much work' to change things. They were dependent on experts, while simultaneously feeling guilty and resentful for not doing something about the situation themselves. As public servants, however, they were not supposed to seek power, and they did not. Instead, they were to be contented with their lot in the classroom, but they were not.

School structure and the culture that has evolved within it justify the view that teaching is synonymous with instructing: managing materials and persons, organizing and presenting information, duplicating and passing out worksheets, and so on. But here too tension emerges. To improve teaching means becoming better skilled technically, and finding activities that 'work'. Instrumentally, ideas that work are time and cost efficient and contribute to the smooth running of the institution which is always in danger of disruption. These commitments show up when teachers meet together to talk; they rarely talk about the aims of education; what they want to know is how to do something better. They show very little patience with anything that is not 'practical' and make quite a show of how silly 'theory' is. Indeed, in one meeting where one of the authors pressed a theoretical point, he was attacked as 'arrogant'. Thus the charge that the culture of teaching is presentist, only concerned with the here and now. Yet when a group of experts is organized to produce a curriculum teachers feel resentful at being excluded; teaching is apparently more than instructing, it includes having a say in goal setting: (from the same set of interviews) 'They are changing the science curriculum.... It was done at the board level, strictly at the board level. They have someone who did a couple of little studies — and I'm sure [they] were paid very well for their little studies — and presented it to the board.... There was no input. There was no committee. There was nothing.... We're down on the rock bottom with the kids where we see it and they're [those who designed the program] up sitting on their thrones making these decisions.' This teacher badly wanted to be involved in the process of writing programs and yet she was torn: to do so was not part of her role as teacher and besides she could not be involved even if invited because, given the pace of work, 'There's just no time. They don't give us enough time.'

For the most part teachers, particularly elementary school teachers, claim to have entered teaching because of liking to see young people grow and develop. They take joy from serving them and become excited when they see a light come on in a child's eyes. A science teacher put it this way: 'I love that feeling when you feel like you don't need any other tool. They don't have any papers or books. You're just standing there talking to them and communicating with them and they're taking [in] your ideas. . . . I love that . . . they're really learning and they're responding, and asking questions. . . .' Another teacher remarked: 'I love just being in the classroom. . . . When the kids catch on, or when they kind of get motivated and you see it, or when I'm trying something and I see this is going to work so I can keep moving that way.' It is this kind of service that keeps teachers teaching. But it is also this ideal that is most threatened by instrumental rationality.

When faced with a disillusioned public eager to have proof of getting the most value out of the money they spend on education, teachers, following the lead of various experts, have responded by trying to become increasingly time and cost efficient. Although often unhappy about it, they accept as proof of efficiency increases in standardized competency test scores. To accomplish this aim, teachers have altered their curricula and instruction to assure higher degrees of content and instructional validity. In the process of seeking increased efficiency, they have helped further rationalize schooling and thereby been party to decreasing the area over which they have control and further weakened their claims to professional status. The harder they work to become more efficient managers, the more many of the values they most cherish, ones that perhaps initially encouraged interest in teaching, are weakened.

Teacher Relationships

Public service values and instrumental reason justify and help maintain the kind and quality of relationships encouraged by school structure. We will only consider here teacher-student and teacher-teacher relations, again noting sources of tension. School structure and the culture of teaching generally encourage teachers to view students as clients in need of various treatments made necessary by the labels they carry. The student is an accumulation of these labels: 'gifted', 'talented', 'emotionally disturbed', 'intellectually handicapped', and the like.[11] Each schooling category has a preferred treatment, a 'how', attached to it. The skilled teacher knows what these are and appropriately applies them, making certain to maintain his or her objectivity. The task of the teacher, in short, is to identify student 'needs', which are institutionally defined lacks of various kinds, as precisely as possible and to fit a treatment to them. This is done presumably for the good of the student, who in the process is sorted and further labelled in the name of educational efficiency.

Teachers go along with this even while often being unhappy about it: 'Last year they made two advanced classes ... so we pulled out all of the kids ... but left in all of those that still had reading disabilities and learning problems. I had no one in my classes to help the kids be motivated, [no] stronger and better learners [for the others to model].' This teacher failed a fifth of her class and felt terrible about it — 'It was really bad' — even while seeing no alternative.

Situations like this are distasteful to teachers. They do not like what is being done to the students or to their relationship with them. In response some try even harder to establish warm, caring relationships with young people. But they do it in part because personal values and the values of public service are at times at odds with those of instrumental reason. While instrumental rationality, and the technocratically minded researchers, teachers, and administrators who push these values, foster fitting young people into ever-finer categories for ever-more-powerful treatments, public service as feminized, and the personal values of teachers, give a prominent place to seeing the child behind the label.

Public service values and instrumental rationality have also influenced teachers' views of other teachers and their understanding of them. Again, structural constraints are for the most part confirmed by teacher beliefs. The public servant in the teacher insists that 'a collective image of good and moral teachers is necessary for the maintenance of their individual status. A lowering of collective standards, they fear, might lead to chaos and disruption among students and might present a less than united front to intrusive parents.'[12] To achieve these ends, teachers suppress their emotions,[13] and engage in a subtle policing of one another, with the result that many teachers withdraw and become increasingly isolated while others become increasingly competitive. They also frequently, but privately, criticize one another, blaming other teachers for educational failure.[14] This is one source of teacher conservatism; teachers discourage one another from taking risks. It also may be a factor contributing to the development and maintenance of teacher individualism, the desire to go it alone.

As noted in Gitlin's chapter in this volume, the ever-present influence of evaluation — parent, student, fellow teacher as well as formal systems for evaluation — profoundly affects teachers; they feel vulnerable, insecure. Like their students, teachers are scrutinized at every turn. In response, the public servant frequently develops a hypersensitivity to being evaluated and recoils from it. They see it as, in the words of an English teacher, a 'snooper thing'. This sensitivity comes in part from the public servant's willingness to continue to take upon him or herself ever greater responsibilities, along with the realization that there is no way fully to satisfy a fickle and demanding public. Failure and guilt come with the job;[15] compromise is necessary. As a seventh grade math teacher put it: 'You're trying to do all these things to sort of meet everybody's needs and then you sort of have the dominant feeling of society that you're a piece of shit.' They fear rejection and resent not being appreciated for making so many sacrifices. But instrumental reason demands that evaluation take place; and current reform efforts aim at making certain that it does. For example, career ladders — which are predominantly based upon instrumental values — emphasize evaluation as essential to success, with the result that teachers *will* be sorted and rewarded differentially.[16] They *will* compete, as individuals, for increased rewards and they will adjust even while realizing that ultimately school success is dependent upon cooperation — something longed for but discouraged by school structure and the culture of teaching.

At its very centre the role of teacher and how teachers understand it is fraught with ambiguity. Each teacher who assumes this role must necessarily work out his or her own compromises in order to function adequately within the institution while simultaneously preserving cherished values. The necessity of compromise is reflected in the culture of teaching, which provides means by which teachers are able to find or create reasonably meaningful institutional lives.

Cultural Responses

The arena within which teachers adapt, and in the process make and remake the culture of teaching, is the classroom. While instrumental rationality drives administrators and would-be school reformers to push open the classroom door ever further, the student side of the values of public service and teacher's personal values press to keep it closed. The classroom is the teacher's sanctuary. It is by withdrawing into the privacy of the classroom, the teacher's realm, where, in order to preserve the value of modeling, teachers have been 'given the leeway and responsibility of vitalizing any classroom lesson', that partial resolutions are found.[17]

The sanctity of the classroom is a central element of the culture of teaching, which is preserved and protected through teacher isolation and a hesitancy of parents, administrators, and other teachers to violate it. Isolation is often identified as a horrible aspect of the role of teacher. Few researchers, however, have carefully considered its utility (or that of conservatism, presentism and individualism); isolation is linked to autonomy in the minds of teachers. And autonomy is a high cultural value.[18] There is considerable truth in the statement that once a teacher closes her door she is in control. Admittedly, control is limited by the intrusion of standardized testing and increasingly by efforts at teacher evaluation, nevertheless, teachers' *experience* of the classroom is that they are for the most part in charge. They cherish their autonomy even while expressing distaste for their isolation. How they use this autonomy, even if constrained, has a bearing on how well or how poorly they function within the institution. It is behind closed classroom doors that they work out tentative solutions to the problems that confront them without fear of being questioned.

Scholars have recently become interested in how teachers creatively adapt to school structure. They have become especially interested in teacher resistance to institutional expectations. Clearly, teachers do engage in contrary action, or more often figure out ways of minimally complying with distasteful requirements in order to preserve higher values, usually arising from personal commitments but also from the desire to serve students well and effectively.[19] For example, teachers have been observed smuggling 'elements of unstructured practices into an administratively-imposed program reflecting a structured [view of teaching].'[20] They also 'domesticate' curriculum innovations so that they better reflect contrary teacher values.[21]

While the security of the classroom allows teachers creatively to accommodate to institutional life, to forge a role that is more or less satisfying, such a response is not without problems. It makes certain that the more distasteful elements of school life, those aspects that are miseducative for teachers and students, are likely to go unchallenged: a dependency on expert opinion, insecurity, an unwillingness to take public risks, a denigration of personal interests coupled with a growing alienation from work, an ambiguous celebration of isolation masquerading as autonomy, a suppression of emotion, distrust of other teachers, and a narrow concern with the means of education to the neglect of educational aims. Not seeing solutions, or believing that the strength of institutionalized role boundaries makes solutions unlikely, many of the best and brightest simply choose to leave teaching. But there is hope.

On the surface the culture of teaching appears monolithic — it is frequently and easily caricatured as such — but in reality it is, as we have been arguing, fragmented. Even the sources of its most fundamental values, public service ideology and instrumental rationality, are fraught with contradiction. These points of tension within teachers' understanding of their work make it susceptible to change. Given the culture of teaching and current trends in school reform, which aim at shoving open the classroom door even wider, we can expect an increase in conflict. This appears inevitable. Also the persistence of the student side of public service values and teachers' deep frustration with institutional barriers that inhibit their attempts to respond in personally satisfying ways to students (and to other teachers) suggest change is possible. Teachers want schools to be different from the way they are. They want a different role. The potential is there, the question is how to go about realizing it.

Notes

1 ANDY HARGREAVES (1984) 'Education policy and the culture of teaching: Some prospects for the future', Paper presented at the American Educational Research Association Meeting, New Orleans, April, p. 4.
2 SARA LAWRENCE LIGHTFOOT (1983) 'The lives of teachers', in LEE S. SHULMAN and GARY SYKES (Eds), *Handbook of Teaching and Policy*, New York, Longman, p. 255.
3 See, for example, JEAN ANYON (1980) 'Social class and the hidden curriculum of work', *Journal of Education*, Winter.
4 GARY SYKES (1983) 'Public policy and the problem of teacher quality', in SHULMAN and SYKES, *op. cit.*, pp. 111–13.
5 See ROBERT V. BULLOUGH JR, STANLEY L. GOLDSTEIN and LADD HOLT (1984) *Human Interests in the Curriculum: Teaching and Learning in a Technological Society*, New York, Teachers College Press.
6 For a more extensive discussion see ROBERT V. BULLOUGH JR, ANDREW D. GITLIN and STANLEY L. GOLDSTEIN (1984) 'Ideology, teacher role, and resistance', *Teachers College Record*, Winter.
7 See PAUL MATTINGLY (1975) *The Classless Profession*, New York, New York University Press.
8 Quoted in PATTI LATHER (1984) 'Do good girls make good teachers? Gender and the shaping of public school teaching', Revision of a paper presented at the National Women's Studies Association Conference, June, p. 3.

Robert V. Bullough Jr

9   See Raymond Callahan (1962) *Education and the Cult of Efficiency*, Chicago, University of Chicago Press.
10   On the power of experts in American society see Robert Bellah *et al.* (1985) *Habits of the Heart: Individualism and Commitment in American Life*, Berkeley, Calif., University of California Press.
11   For an excellent discussion of labelling see Michael Apple (1979) *Ideology and Curriculum*, Boston, Routledge and Kegan Paul, chapter 7.
12   Lightfoot, *op. cit.*, p. 247.
13   Christopher M. Clark and Penelope L. Peterson (1986) 'Teachers' thought processes', in Merlin C. Wittrock (Ed.), *Handbook of Research on Teaching*, New York, Macmillan, p. 289.
14   See Sara Freedman, Jane Jackson and Katherrine Boles (1983) 'Teaching: An imperilled profession', in Shulman and Sykes, *op. cit.*
15   For a discussion of teacher guilt see Seymour B. Sarason (1982) *The Culture of the School and the Problem of Change*, Boston, Mass., Allyn and Bacon, p. 200.
16   For a good critique of career ladders see Samuel B. Bacharach, Sharon Conley and Joseph Shedd (1986) 'Beyond career ladders: Structuring teacher career development systems', *Teachers College Record*, Summer.
17   Mattingly, *op. cit.*, p. 180.
18   See Robert V. Bullough Jr and Andrew D. Gitlin (1986) 'Limited autonomy: Teacher decision making, ideology and the reproduction of role', *New Education*, Fall.
19   For a discussion of teacher resistance see Robert V. Bullough Jr and Andrew D. Gitlin (1985) 'Beyond control: Rethinking teacher resistance', *Education and Society*, Winter.
20   Clark and Peterson, *op. cit.*, p. 289.
21   *Ibid.*, p. 291.

8 Knowledge, Culture and the Curriculum: Implications of a Five-Year Ethnographic Study of Transition from School

James C. Walker

Teachers are trained and credentialed through specific institutional procedures to enable them, among other things, to develop knowledge in students. Many teachers come from a personal and social-class background where the kind of knowledge generally endorsed in schools, and the manner of its organization and transmission, is familiar. In short, educational knowledge, generally, is congruent with the professional and personal culture of teachers. This is not always so with their students, particularly when they come from divergent personal, social-class and ethnic backgrounds.

This chapter presents some reflections on relations between teacher and student cultures on issues concerning knowledge, culture and power, developed during the course of a study of the articulations between student and teacher cultures in an inner city school. It urges that we look closely at the interaction between cultures in the school context, to identify and build upon the knowledge contained in the cultures of both teachers and students. I commence with a brief description of the study, whose main findings are published elsewhere.[1]

The 'Stokeham' Study

Using ethnographic methods, the study investigated the relation between specific youth cultures, formal schooling, and the transition from school to employment, unemployment, or further study. Contact was maintained for five years with selected students of an Australian single-sex school from when the subjects were aged around 16 years until they were 21. Nearly all staff teaching the subjects were also interviewed.

'Stokeham Boys' High'[2] occupied restricted space in a heavily built up and congested mixed residential, commercial, and industrial environment. The population was ethnically extremely diverse. A traditional Anglo-Celtic working class had had to adjust to waves of immigrant newcomers. The majority of pupils remained working-class or went into family shops and other small businesses. A few became professionals.

The study concentrated on four friendship groups, each displaying a distinctive culture. It examined the relations between a culturally ascendant group, the 'macho' (mainly 'Aussie') footballers, a group of upwardly mobile Greek boys challenging the footballer ascendancy, and ethnically diverse group of 'nice guys', and three boys who were stigmatized as 'poofs' and reacted in an alienated way to their peers and to much formal school activity.

Despite the cultural diversity among the students, they all had difficulty handling the form and content of the official curriculum. Similarly, their teachers, most of whom came from middle-class backgrounds and lived in much more comfortable areas, had difficulty adjusting to, or even understanding, the cultural backgrounds and perspectives of the students. To use a technical term, the *intercultural articulation* between students and teachers — the communication and other cultural practices — tended to be divergent rather than convergent. The major exceptions to this were in school sport and in the desire of most students included in the study to gain credentials for employment purposes.

At Stokeham there were various and sometimes competing views of what counted as knowledge, and more particularly of what counted as valuable or useful knowledge. These views were rooted in the different cultural perspectives, implicit in the practices and social relations of students and teachers, on education, work, gender, sexuality and family life. But the articulation of these views occurred on two levels, formal and informal, in somewhat contradictory ways.

Educational Knowledge

On the formal level the teachers' culture assumed *authority* in matters of knowledge and, through the structure and content of both explicit and implicit curricula, put into practice a view of what counted as *educational knowledge*. This was taught in class, implicit in teacher-student exchanges, tested, and mastery of it was necessary for gaining credentials. Students acknowledged the social power of this knowledge insofar as it led to credentials. They were also aware of its claims to authority and of the teachers' socially sanctioned status as experts in it. On the whole they did not challenge this authority and expertise. When they responded negatively to official educational knowledge, it was because they could not see its relevance to their own lives and problems. Many teachers had similar misgivings about the curriculum and their own ability to address students' problems.

On a more informal level, however, both students and teachers recognized that all Stokeham cultures contained knowledge. It came in numerous sorts and had various spheres of practical applicability. It was produced in the practical contexts of everyday life. Teachers' views of students' employment prospects, for instance, often turned on assessments of how 'cluey' and 'street wise' they were about human relationships generally and the world of work in particular. It was to this informal knowledge that teachers and students referred in their appraisals of the relevance and practical usefulness of the formal curriculum.

In an important respect these two levels were contradictory. To see how, we need to note two fundamental asymmetries in attitudes to formal and informal knowledge. First, because teachers did not see themselves as authoritative on the informal knowledge in students' cultures, they were generally unable or unwilling to view the mastery of such knowledge as an integral part of their role *as educators*. With a few exceptions, their view of students' informal cultural knowledge was that it was external to teachers' own experience and problems and, if it had to be mastered, this was because it would be helpful in establishing rapport and good communication with students, which could then be exploited in teaching the formal curriculum in the classroom. Here it is important to note that the majority of students took exactly the same externally intrumentalist attitude toward the formal knowledge of teachers' culture. You had to deal with it in order to handle the constraints placed upon you by the inevitability of coexistence with another culture. But it remained external to the main goals of your own cultural practice.

Second, teachers could see the cultural and even the class location and applicability of students' informal knowledge, rooted in the practical circumstances of life in Stokeham, and many of them recognized the difficulties which their own *personal* middle-class backgrounds placed in the way of their work with the Stokeham boys. Nevertheless, there was little evidence that they recognized the cultural location of the knowledge constituting the official curriculum, rooted in the practices of middle-class professionals. This, along with the abilities needed to master it, tended to be seen as universally validated and authoritative, even if not universally useful to all students. It is important to note that students took the same universalist view of officially legitimated educational knowledge.

Thus teachers tended to display both a reluctance to take students' informal knowledge and cultural perspectives seriously in determining what should comprise the official curriculum, and a recognition that students' perspectives worked for students in certain contexts and that an understanding of them could improve educational practice. Intercultural understanding could have pedagogical value but little impact on curriculum and evaluation. The outcome was at best a strengthening of students' externally instrumentalist attitude to the curriculum. Formal educational knowledge, even when judged irrelevant to students' problems, remained privileged, and teachers' authority on what was to be learned remained unchallenged, despite the recognition of various cultural perspectives on knowledge. The dominance of privileged educational knowledge undercut the curricular potential of other perspectives; and the recognition of value in other perspectives undercut teachers' confidence in formal educational knowledge, mostly without providing a clear curricular alternative.

Similarly, students tended to display both a reluctance to take teachers' formal knowledge and cultural perspectives seriously in determining what should inform their own understanding of the world and their goals in life, and a recognition that teachers' perspectives worked for teachers in certain contexts and that an understanding of them would improve credentialist prospects. This attitude persisted into post-schooldays, with formal institutions, including colleges of Technical and Further Education, the Commonwealth Employment Service and the place of employment, viewed primarily as sources of either credentials or money. For solutions to one's personal problems one continued to rely on informal cultural resources and networks of friends and family. At school intercultural understanding between students and teachers could have socioeconomic value, but little impact on the substance of students' cultures or their evaluation of formal knowledge. This had the same outcome as teachers' attitudes: at best a strengthening of students' externally instrumentalist attitude to the curriculum.

While teachers' authority within their professional sphere was acknowledged, students' evaluation of knowledge as 'interesting' or 'really useful' remained framed within their own cultures. Cultural divergence remained entrenched, and much valuable knowledge, especially in natural and social science, history and the arts, which could have been learned and shared through more penetrating intercultural articulation, remained culturally confined.

In pointing out the contradictory and limited aspects of this outcome I do not wish to suggest that it was entirely negative. As mentioned, virtually all the boys included in the study and their parents wanted the credentials they thought necessary for a good job, and teachers mostly recognized this entirely legitimate desire. Given the present structure of our economy it is as much the democratic right of Stokeham students to aspire to qualifications and economic prosperity as it is the right of students at any other school, and it is not the province of teachers, policy-makers or educational researchers to deny this right or make it difficult to exercise, whatever they think of particular students' prospects. On the contrary, it is their job to assist all students in pursuit of this legitimate aspiration.

Rather, the point is that teacher-student cultural divergence tends both to make credentialist aspirations more difficult for students to pursue and to prevent the development of students' understanding of options (not necessarily in conflict with credentialism) other than those deriving from either credentialism or those framed in their own existing cultural perspectives. More effective intercultural articulation is what is called for, not an attack on the credentialism of students in lower socioeconomic groups. If it is thought that present credentialing practices are too narrow in form and too dominant over other educational values, this problem emphatically should not be addressed by steering lower socioeconomic groups away from credentialism. This would be presumptuous and undemocratic; it would also mislocate the source of the problem, which is the general structure of credentialing itself and its relation to opportunities in the labour market.

So far as Stokeham is concerned, it is clear that the articulation between teacher and pupil cultures made it difficult on both sides to maximize the students' chances of gaining good qualifications. The contradiction we have noted made it difficult for students to gain from their formal education an understanding of other options. Given the credentialist orientation of both teachers and students, it is a clear example of a problem *shared* by students and teachers, and therefore a point of interaction between teachers and students where they could find common interest in negotiating solutions in their mutual interest. Here we are making a pragmatic assumption: unless we start with the perceived problems of people in their current social context, and points of contact between people with different roles, perspectives and cultural backgrounds, we will not come up with effective ways of expanding options.

The Politics of Knowledge

These differentials in status of knowledge tend to undermine the success of both teachers and students in pursuing goals and solving problems, and are thus the cause of a shared problem: limited educational effectiveness. Any solution acceptable to both teachers and students will need to be compatible with each party's being able to pursue their legitimate objectives without compromising their capacity to do so. Resolution of the contradiction will involve mutual acceptance of a broader and more open definition of what constitutes genuine educational knowledge. In principle there would need to be a recognition that on both sides there is genuine knowledge and expertise. At Stokeham this was recognized *informally* to a considerable extent: many teachers tried to build upon the informal knowledge of students. The next step is to avoid prejudging the intrinsic curricular relevance or irrelevance of knowledge from whatever source, to work on the assumption that this is to be tested in practice, and that both teachers and students be prepared to adapt and revise their cultural programs. There was some preparedness to adapt, for instance in teachers' pedagogy and in students' preparedness to do the work teachers asked of them, which in some cases was extended into the curriculum, but only in some subjects and in a limited fashion.

To extend it further would mean teachers abandoning, not their claims to professional expertise in their specialized teaching subjects or their role as adults and educators responsible for the learning and welfare of their students, but *their institutionalized professional privilege on knowledge in general*. In practice those teachers who were worried about 'relevance' and student alienation from much of the formal curriculum were implicitly conceding this, many of them working as well as they could within the institutionalized constraints of the formal curriculum and the credentialing structure to adopt a more open and critical attitude to what could count as valuable educational knowledge.

Thus there was already a basis in practice for an effective resolution of the contradiction, and some weakening of its hold on the curriculum. To extend it further would require a more fundamental reorientation of attitudes to the curriculum via a rethinking of teacher's roles as knowledge professionals. For the abandonment of claims to professional privilege on knowledge in general means *recognizing the contingent cultural relativity not only of students' knowledge but also of those areas of knowledge in which teachers have special expertise.* It does not mean taking the view that all knowledge is *necessarily* relative to particular social-class, ethnic, gender or age locations or that it is only 'genuine' knowledge from within the perspectives of cultures formed in those locations.

For example, in analyzing the data in the Stokeham study I adopted the view that teacher culture, which includes the usual range of curriculum subjects, is a social-class culture, broadly identifiable with the 'new middle class'.[3] Many writers who have recognized this point have gone on to make the mistaken inference that knowledge is therefore 'culturally relative' in the sense that it is *essentially* tied to such perspectives and that its genuineness as knowledge depends on whether it serves the interests of the social groups whose knowledge it is. This inference has then been used as the basis for two further, quite different and incompatible conclusions.

First, some have mounted the élitist argument that because knowledge is socially relative, for example to social class, it is the job of educators to correct the perspectives of working-class students by initiating them into the culture of the demonstrably superior social class. Since working-class culture is inferior, and to remain within its parameters is to be disqualified on the whole (unless you become a pop star, etc.) from upward social mobility, working-class students should be given the opportunity to succeed in an uncompromisingly traditional curriculum, and to remove this possibility is to sell them short. Second, others have argued from a perspective supposedly acknowledging 'working-class interests' that to impose middle-class culture on students is an oppressive intrusion which depowers working-class students and indeed the working class as a whole. There should therefore be a 'working-class curriculum' which maintains intact the essential perspectives of the class. Since the school curriculum reflects a form of middle-class culture, so the argument runs, it is oppressive to impose middle-class culture on working-class students. What we need is a curriculum which not only reflects and respects the integrity of working-class culture, but also does not seek fundamentally to change that culture or to draw students away from it. We would in this case have a starkly distinct working-class curriculum.

In between there are those who would solve the problem by distinguishing between 'academic' and 'non-academic' rather than middle-class and working-class students, however much the two distinctions might tend to be coextensive in their application. Either way, and even in the middle, the assumption is that schooling can either assist students to join the middle-class professional strata or else leave them where they are.

The real trouble is that although there is an element of truth in each of these positions they are put forward statically and fail to recognize the real *processes* of schooling, including cultural variety and individual initiative, concentrating rather on prespecified outcomes. They do not attend to the *problem contexts* of working-class schools and, because one way or another they tend to structure the curricula of those schools, they prevent teachers from attending to the problems too.

As against the essentialism of these non sequiturs, which serve to polarize class perspectives in education, it can be argued that middle-class teachers and non-middle-class students have much to learn from each other and that it is largely up to them in practice to test what is educationally valuable through discussion and experiment. For teachers to drop the universalism implicit in professional middle-class culture does not mean dropping objective standards for evaluation of knowledge; it simply means that such evaluation can occur in the classroom just as it can in university laboratories and academic journals. It may be quite unlikely that a hypothesis well-established in nuclear physics will be falsified in a Stokeham classroom; although it may be quite likely that a sociological hypothesis subscribed to by educational researchers will be. But that is not the point. Rather, the abandonment of generalized claims as knowledge professionals means that educators teach their students that all knowledge is hypothetical, open to correction and revision, and that there is no necessary prejudgment as to where interesting hypotheses might emerge. In particular, no class or culture has a monopoly of educationally valuable knowledge.

This point needs stressing, and is relevant to the question of the relation between formal, codified and institutionalized knowledge, especially that knowledge for which the term 'science' is usually reserved, and informal knowledge such as that embedded in the cultural perspectives of the Stokeham boys. There is no necessary reason why scientific knowledge, or scientific methods, must be confined to the general culture of the professional middle class. There are no sound grounds for assuming that it is *essentially* incompatible with either the interests or perspectives of other social groups, however much, as a matter of historically contingent fact, students like those at Stokeham found such knowledge alien or difficult to incorporate within their perspectives.

For example, the careers teacher drew upon general economic knowledge about the structure of Australian industry and the labour market, endeavouring to present it in a way which addressed the employment opportunities and problems he believed would confront his students. He also kept up to date with specific local trends in the demand for labour and bore them in mind when advising individual students. This knowledge was conceptualized and codified in the standard frameworks of social science which he, as a trained teacher with a science and social science background, as well as some experience in industry, understood well, within which he was culturally 'at home'. Most of his students were not at home with it. Moreover, they had their own sources of knowledge about the economy and the local labour market which were in some but not all respects in advance of his so far as local conditions were concerned, but in comparison lacked the general explanatory and predictive power inherent in the teacher's explicitly scientific perspective. Furthermore, he was somewhat diffident about the role of what he described as his 'middle-class values' in his deployment of his expert knowledge in teaching and advising. Finding the professional intellectual framework difficult if not alien, students would often trust their own informally acquired beliefs when they conflicted with the careers adviser's message, and were in some cases sceptical or indifferent to the whole business of careers lessons anyway.

The problem here was not that the professional's explicitly scientific approach was essentially incompatible with the students' informal approach. Nor was it that the students' approach was essentially unscientific: indeed students used procedures of observation and personal experiment, of generalization, explanation and prediction in their own everyday pragmatism. Nor was it that the professional's beliefs were true or false only within his culture and the students' only within theirs. When we acknowledge that knowledge is culturally relative in the sense that it is always learned and expressed within the frameworks and in the material location and practices of particular cultures, we are far from adopting the view that what is true for one person can be false for another, that what is true on Monday can be false on Wednesday if we have undergone a cultural shift on Tuesday. To say that knowledge is open to correction and revision presumes some objective standards of truth and falsity; it does not preclude them.[4]

The point is that to persuade someone thinking and acting within a cultural perspective divergent from your own requires discovering the *touchstone*,[5] or common ground, between the respective cultures. Touchstone is discovered or constructed by identification of shared problems and extracting, from our understanding of those problems, shared standards we can use to assess the merits of our various points of view and the respective practical options available to us.[6] In the case of careers lessons, there was no doubt about where this touchstone was to be located: it started with the common belief in a real world of jobs and unemployment outside the school. To deepen it and build on it the teacher needed to explore students' cultural discourse and understand its roots in their practical experience. For teacher and student, this could be a thoroughly scientific project, whether conducted in the formal or informal mode. Formalization expands the overall power of knowledge and it is in the interest of all students to appreciate this and be able to draw upon it where this helps with their goals and problems. But abstract learning in the formalized mode is better done and more effective when it grows out of the informal learning of everyday life, when there is *cultural continuity* in the learning process.

Many educationists have commented on the need to teach the scientific attitude of critical thinking and open inquiry rather than to present knowledge as a set of final facts established by experts whose activities are beyond the ken of school students. What I am arguing for here is an extension of this point into the context of interaction between cultures. It is one thing to present professionally predefined educational knowledge of the major curriculum subjects in an open and critical way; it is a further step to open the curriculum to sources of knowledge and wider cultural perspectives from beyond the professional culture of teachers.

By the same token, within a framework of critical openness and preparedness to experiment, it should not be assumed that students' cultures are sacrosanct either, that they should automatically override teachers' perspectives; and it is obvious that teachers, not students, must maintain overall professional responsibility for what occurs in their classrooms, just as they have a certain legal responsibility for the welfare of their students. In the last analysis they can do no other than rely on their own judgment within the context of their official responsibilities. Their judgment will embrace, as did the Stokeham teachers', matters which transcend the interests of particular cultural groups, whether formed on class, gender, age, ethnic, or professional lines. Acknowledgment of common problems does not mean failure to recognize that there are unshared problems and conflicts of interest, and that when these arise within the ranks of students, teachers will need to establish priorities, considerations of equity and individual differences. One striking features of the Stokeham context was the complexity of these problems facing teachers. In the overall process of intercultural give and take I am advocating, some students may end up giving more than others. Whether or not this results in their taking less, benefitting less in the long run, is another question.

Conclusion

The view of teachers' professional knowledge I have presented suggests that it needs to be constantly reconstructed, *in practice*, in contexts of intercultural articulation with students, especially when students' cultures diverge from those of teachers. This is desirable not simply because it would make communication, and therefore teaching, easier; more than that, it enables a coherent and practically powerful process of learning for both teachers and students, enhancing their capacity to pursue their goals and solve their problems, and contributing to the ongoing improvement and reconstruction of educational theory and practice. The view I have presented acknowledges the *contingent* social and cultural relativity of knowledge, but denies that this impugns its objectivity or reference to social and natural reality. On the contrary, the power of knowledge depends on its objective reference. In education the trick is to be clear about the practical contexts in which that reference is developed and applicable.

Notes

1 WALKER (1987a, 1987b, 1987c).
2 The names of the school, all persons (except the researchers) and many

institutions and places in the study have been changed. The research was funded by grants from the Education Research and Development Committee and Sydney University's Research Grants Scheme, which are gratefully acknowledged. My thanks also go to the NSW Department of Education and the Principal of 'Stokeham Boys' High' for their kind permission to conduct the study in the school. There is no way I can adequately acknowledge the support of the principal, staff, and especially students of 'Stokeham' throughout the course of the research.

3 Following BERNSTEIN (1977).

4 The relevant philosophical distinction is between our theory of truth and our theory of evidence. See WALKER and EVERS (1984).

5 See WALKER and EVERS (1982); WALKER (1985).

6 Some suggestions on how touchstone might be used in curriculum development are outlined in WALKER (1987c, 1987e).

References

APPLE, M.W. (1982) 'Curricular form and the logic of control: Building the possessive individual', in APPLE, M.W. (Ed.), *Cultural and Economic Reproduction in Education: Essays on Class, Ideology and the State*, London, Routledge and Kegan Paul.

BERNSTEIN, B. (1977) *Class, Codes and Control*, 2nd ed., London, Routledge and Kegan Paul.

WALKER, J.C. (1986a) 'Romanticising resistance, romanticising culture: A critique of Willis's theory of cultural production', *British Journal of Sociology of Education*, 7, 1, pp. 59–80.

WALKER, J.C. (1986b) *Towards a Materialist Pragmatist Theory of Culture and Intercultural Articulation*, mimeo, Sydney, Department of Social and Policy Studies in Education, University of Sydney.

WALKER, J.C. (1987a) *Louts and Legends: Male Youth Culture in an Inner City School*, Sydney, George Allen and Unwin.

WALKER, J.C. (1987b) *Learning Cultures: Teachers and Students in an Inner City School*, Sydney, George Allen and Unwin.

WALKER, J.C. (1987c) *School, Work and the Problems of Young People: A Cultural Approach to Curriculum Development*, Canberra, Australian Schools Commission.

WALKER, J.C. (1987d) 'Greeks versus Aussies: Male youth culture, school and work in the inner city', *Youth Studies Bulletin*, 7, 1.

WALKER, J.C. (1987e) *Educative Leadership for Curriculum Development*, Armidale, University of New England in Association with ACT Schools Authority and NSW and Victorian Departments of Education.

WALKER, J.C. and EVERS, C.W. (1982) 'Epistemology and justifying the curriculum of educational studies', *British Journal of Educational Studies*, 30, 2, pp. 312–29.

WALKER, J.C. and EVERS, C.W. (1984) 'Towards a materialist pragmatist philosophy of education', *Education Research and Perspectives*, 11, 1, pp. 23–33.

9 Common School Structures and Teacher Behaviour*

Andrew D. Gitlin

Critics are quick to point an accusing finger at teachers for educational failure.[1] These rebukes, however, rarely consider the influence of school structure on teacher behaviour. As a result, reform efforts often leave intact the structures which at least partially account for what teachers do in schools. In an attempt to refocus the problem of educational failure, this chapter describes some of the powerful elements of school structure and how they influence what teachers do. But first, two caveats are in order: (1) while we will be speaking of common school structures, individual schools do differ in ways of consequence to school reform; (2) school structure does not *determine* how teachers behave. Rather, teacher behaviour reflects a compromise between teacher values, ideology, and the press of school structure. Understanding why teachers do what they do, therefore, requires that structure and ideology be scrutinized. This chapter focuses primarily on structure; elsewhere in this volume culture and ideology are dealth with (see Bullough, chapter 7).

Common School Structures

Core Curriculum, Approved Textbooks and Rationalized Programs

Almost all schools in the United States have a district mandated core curriculum. The core curriculum identifies the objectives for a

---

* I wish to acknowledge the important part played by my colleague Robert Bullough Jr in the conceptualization and drafting of this chapter.

particular subject area and lays out the sequence in which they should be taught. The general nature of the core curriculum allows teachers some leeway in what they do, however, it sets the number of objectives to be accomplished in an academic year and is used to redirect those who stray too far from the approved pathway.

District approved textbooks also help identify the scope and sequence of objectives to be accomplished. Even though in principle most teachers could alter the text in any manner they desire, 90 per cent of the time teacher instruction follows the text.[2] One reason teachers stick to texts is that it saves planning time and protects them from possible criticism about the selection of curricular objectives. Approved textbooks, therefore, encourage teachers to cover certain objectives in a particular order by providing significant fringe benefits to those who do so.

More than either core curricula or district approved textbooks, programs using a rationalized curriculum form directly shape what teachers do. The rationalized curricular form consists of predetermined behavioural objectives that are put in a sequence along with pre- and post-mastery tests for each objective. This form, which was thought to make curriculum 'teacher proof', first gained popularity in the 1960s.[3] With the current push to 'take account of and provide for student individuality in learning rates and style',[4] most elementary schools have in place one or more programs which use this curricular form.[5] Some school programs are entirely rationalized. A prominent example found in many parts of the United States is the Individually Guided Education [IGE] school.[6]

When implemented on a school-wide basis, rationalized programs more or less obligate teachers to cover specified objectives; to do otherwise may impede students' movement through the entire sequence. Moreover, because mastery of post-tests determines how fast students progress through the sequence, the teacher must carefully consider the priorities reflected in the test questions when making curricular decisions.

Compartmental Organization

Following the model of most large bureaucracies, schools divide their clients into a number of categories for treatment. Students are divided by grade level and then within a grade by academic ability. This type of tracking can be informal as in the establishment of reading groups in a classroom, or formal as in the identification of students for placement in honours and advanced placement English courses. Interest and anticipated destinations also divide students. Those wishing to go to college are placed in a preparatory track, while others who have no intention to go to college are placed in a vocational track.

Compartmentalization makes it necessary that schools find ways efficiently to divide up the day and to move students from classroom to classroom. On the secondary level most schools use forty-five-minute periods and bells to signal the beginning and end of the class. One result is that teachers often see as many as 200 students a day. On the elementary level teachers see fewer students but are required to be expert in as many as six or seven subject areas.

School Hierarchy

Hierarchy characterizes the relationships of administrators, teachers and students. Administrators are at the top because they set a variety of school policies, determine where supplementary funds are spent, control to a large extent teacher evaluation, and distribute responsibilities such as being department chair or coach. Teachers find themselves in a responsive mode, reacting to the particular context established by administrators, while at the same time they are competing with one another for the small rewards the principal offers. Students, of course, are on the bottom rung, without control.

In the last few years another layer has been added to the school hierarchy with the introduction of career ladders.[7] These create a middle management position in which a few teachers will act as liaison between administrators and the vast majority of teachers.

Other distinctions among teachers are based on the status attached to particular groups. Usually, science and mathematics teachers, for example, are more respected in the school than are shop, physical education or art teachers. High school teachers have more status than do elementary school teachers.

Teacher Evaluation

Most teachers are formally evaluated by their principal. Unfortunately, principals have little time to be involved in such a complex task and usually are able to visit a teacher's classroom only once or twice a year at most.[8] The brief visits limit feedback to easily observable aspects of teaching such as how quiet the students are, the organization of the lesson, and teacher enthusiasm.

More goes into the evaluation, however, than the actual visit. Principals also use a number of informal criteria to judge teacher quality. For example, principals and vice principals typically review teachers' grades to make certain not too many high or low grades are given. They also consider how well a teacher's students do on standardized tests. When this criterion is applied, the best teacher is assumed to be the one who gets the most students to score well. Finally, the number of students who are sent down to the office is also used to judge a teacher's ability to manage the classroom. The fewer problems for the office, the better the management.

Teacher evaluation as commonly experienced in schools makes it likely that rewards and punishments are doled out with little indepth understanding of what teachers hope to accomplish or what they do in their classrooms.

School Structure and Teacher Behaviour

Evidence from our own work and others, who have investigated the impact of structure on teachers, indicates that common school structures encourage a teacher role that emphasizes management and technical skills, isolates teachers from one another, and 'disconnects' them from their students.[9] To elucidate the nature of this influence, we will focus on four aspects of the teacher role: curriculum making, teacher skills, teacher relations, and teacher/ student relations.

Curriculum Making

It is commonly assumed that a major responsibility of teachers is the making of curriculum. But in practice school structure makes likely that teachers have very little say in determining curricular objectives. The activities designed to meet those objectives are also constrained by the extensive use of standardized tests.

Observations of a secondary school English class provide an example of this type of constraint on curriculum making.[10] During the two weeks the teacher was observed, the class was reading *Pygmalion*. For the most part the students read the play out loud and the teacher asked questions about the plot and the parts of the play. The question arises: what role did the teacher play in curriculum making?

The teacher had almost no leeway in choosing the play because the selection had to come from the recommended list for the junior year. Although the teacher had some say in designing the lesson, the content was shaped by the forthcoming advanced placement test. The teacher felt that students would have enjoyed and benefitted from a discussion of the relationship between the working class and the aristocracy, and the chauvinism of men. But lessons of this kind would have penalized her students on the test. As a consequence it seemed prudent to teach to the test, focusing on the plot sequence and the parts of the play. The teacher hoped to do more than facilitate good test scores in the next unit, but even this is doubtful given limited time and the number of objectives left to be covered before the students finished their junior year.

The press of structure on curriculum making is also felt at the elementary and middle school level. This influence is most directly related to the popularity of rationalized programs. The experience of a sixth grade social studies teacher working in an Individually Guided Education (IGE) school provides an example.[11] One of the objectives in the prepackaged social studies unit on the Industrial Age was 'to discover that the period of industrializaton was a time of rapid and great change in the production of goods.' To meet this predetermined end the teacher decided to have half the students make desserts individually, while the other half divided tasks in an assembly line manner. The point was to show that the assembly line is more efficient than having one person do an entire job. What does this activity tell us about curriculum making? Clearly, the teacher had no say in determining the objective for the lesson. Furthermore, means were to a large degree determined by the post-test. This influence became apparent in conversation with the teacher after the lesson. She noted that the activity seemed to emphasize the benefits of the assembly line while ignoring the drawbacks. The reason given for this slant was that the activity had to bring home the efficiency point because that was a question on the mastery test at the end of the unit.

For these teachers, and many others, curriculum making has become limited to a process of finding ways to facilitate ends predetermined by others. In a sense teachers have been forced to manage the curriculum while others make it.

Teacher Skills

School structures make it necessary for teachers to spend a great deal of their time using technical skills; skills which give teachers the control and precision necessary efficiently to deliver bits of information to students and increase test scores. These skills include efficiently moving students from one objective to another, correcting and grading tests and papers, keeping students in line, and providing documentation on what a student has learned. When used often enough, these skills assume a greater place within the teaching role.

At Flowing Brook, an elementary school based on the IGE philosophy, the dominance of technical skills has turned teachers into dispatch officers whose duty it is to monitor children and send along those who are ready for additional work while holding others back for more instruction:[12]

> pupils and teachers are divided into three teams according to the age of the children ... the children's day is spent doing paper and pencil tasks from a worksheet or workbook. The teacher explains the assignments, and the students complete them at their desks.... When students finish, they either hand their papers in and quietly line up at the teacher's desk for correction, or meet with the teacher as a group for correction. The general pattern is one of teachers explaining how to do assignments and correcting completed work while students do the assignments and have them checked off.... Almost every teacher sits, head bent over the desk, correcting papers. (p. 44)

Much the same result was found at a middle school that had a GEMS [Goal-Based Educational Management System] curriculum.[13] Teachers who used the GEMS curriculum were observed to follow this pattern:

> At the beginning of the class period the teacher would lecture for about five to ten minutes introducing new topics, correcting misconceptions, or perhaps supplementing required work. After answering questions, the teacher passed out the recommended GEMS ditto and students worked at their seats for forty to fifty minutes. Whiles students were busy with the dittos, teachers would record posttests and answer questions. (p. 227)

Within GEMS, the challenge of the work day was to correct miscues, pass students on post-tests, record grades and in general keep all the students moving forward to the next mastery skill. As was true of the IGE teacher, the importance of technical duties helped form a teacher role which centred on moving students from one predetermined objective to another.

Secondary school structures also give priority to technical aspects of the job. The sheer number of students makes paperwork an essential aspect of survival in a complex bureaucracy. Because grades are a sort of social currency, the documentation of student evaluations must be precise, again increasing the amount of paperwork required to do the job of teaching. Finally, there is a growing number of secondary students who refuse to play the school game, which exchanges credentials for compliance, and who often disrupt the classroom. While some school critics have praised this behaviour as a challenge to the sorting function of schools,[14] it leaves the teachers with little choice but to find ways to assert control. To do otherwise assures negative teacher ratings and slows the pace of learning for the other students. As a result, teachers devote a great deal of their energy to maintaining classroom control, another technical aspect of teaching.

Besides these common structures, evaluation also plays a role in encouraging a technical teaching emphasis. This emphasis is clearly illustrated in Donald Thomas' description of his secondary English literature class.[15] Wanting to bring some 'wonder and perplexity' to the classroom, Donald decided to do something different with the recommended unit on Jonathan Edwards. Donald drew the blinds, asked the students to raise their desktops in simulation of Puritan pews, and setting a lectern atop his desk, delivered in muted Edwardian tones the fire and brimstone of *Sinners in the Hands of the Angry God*.

By the teacher's account the lesson was a success given that 'the students set gaping and transfixed in their pews' (p. 221). The supervisors had a different assessment. Seemingly unaware of the students' engagement with the lesson, they focused on a different set of concerns. They asked, 'What had been the objectives? What had the children learned? How did [the teacher] propose to measure this learning objectively? What skills had the students employed and what had been my strategy for reinforcing them? [and] Was [the teacher] aware that he used slang?' (p. 221). In a sense, the supervisors were reflecting the common view of schooling as a place where bits of information are transferred from the knower to the novice and counted. But what effect does this type of evaluation have on teachers?

For Donald, the evaluation process encouraged him to develop activities which had precise measurable objectives. Creativity was something attempted by the young and restless.

> I see now that in many ways it was the kind of lesson that only a young teacher might try, valor seeming the better part of discretion, and theatrics the lessor part of precision. Today it would not occur to me to leap upon a desk, and more's the pity, for in that impulse lay a certain logic that I have since come to appreciate. (p. 221)

In sum, survival in the present school structure requires that teachers spend much of their time using the developing technical skills. As teaching becomes more of a technical enterprise, the creative and conceptual aspects of teaching become progressively less important and the teacher role less human and humane.

Teacher Relations

The increasingly hierarchical nature of teacher relations, the need for teachers to compete for scarce resources, the large number of students housed in a single school, and the emphasis of formal and informal evaluation schemes makes it likely that teachers will interact on a limited basis and, when they do, only focus on technical issues.

Teacher interaction is limited primarily because of the tight scheduling required to transfer large numbers of students in and out of classrooms. Elementary teachers, for example, often do not have planning periods. They are literally with students from the moment they enter the classroom. But even when they have planning periods, they rarely have more than forty-five minutes a day to discuss classroom practice and educational aims. Secondary teachers are in much the same situation. If they are to interact with other teachers it must occur during the planning period or in their own time.

Competition also constrains teacher interaction. At one elementary school, for example, teams were in competition for who gets the recess time that does not interfere with reading, which team has access to the skills room and what objectives will be taught by whom.[16] In competition, teachers often lose sight of the common condition they face and instead become increasingly critical of one another. '[Team] three was unable to come to a compromise in meeting with [team] two regarding recess time, so [team] two will have to go with early recess which cuts into reading.... We did check our books and we have had to send our kids to early recess since 1974' (p. 207). This type of competition is likely to worsen with the implementation of career ladder reforms which raise the salary of a few teachers at the expense of general increases.

School structures also constrain teachers in what they talk about. Observations of team planning meetings that occurred over a two-year period at a middle school indicated that conversations focused exclusively on 'discipline, scheduling, field trips, and special events such as parent teacher conferences'.[17] Never was there any discussion of what should be taught in the classroom or what teaching methods would best achieve certain results. Why was this so? First, the IGE structure found at the school laid out all the required objectives, making discussion of teaching aims redundant. Second, because teacher evaluations were based primarily on efficiency concerns such as 'excellent timing — half an hour was perfect for the lesson' and 'timing — very good',[18] there was a pay-off in making sure the team looked good in these areas.

At the secondary level the press of structure is much the same. When teachers have a planning period, their most immediate task is to mark papers, record grades, and keep track of student latenesses and absences. When there are over 200 students to sort and discipline, teachers at best only have a few minutes to discuss other types of educational issues with colleagues.

The structure of schools limits teacher colleagueship. If teachers are to behave as professionals and help each other critically consider their teaching practice in ways that go beyond the technical, they must do so in their own time. Further, they must do so with the knowledge that this effort is unlikely to have a pay-off in terms of teacher evaluation.

Teacher-Student Relations

Most teachers, as Goodlad suggests, enter the field because of a commitment to 'understand children's learning problems and to provide constructive guidance'.[19] To fulfil this intention teachers must develop close relations with students and have an opportunity to use their knowledge of these young people to shape educational experiences. Unfortunately, common school structures make this difficult.

At the elementary level a number of structural factors combine to disconnect teachers from students and constrain their ability to adjust curriculum to student needs. The vast number of students that teachers must see in itself limits the amount of time a teacher can spend getting to know individual students. When student numbers are combined with a fast work pace, the potential to do any sort of reflection on student needs is limited. Further, grading systems that view students as empty vessels to be filled with the knowledge found on standardized tests make it unnecessary for teachers to analyze student needs and wants. Instead, needs are determined by student performance on post-tests. This orientation to teaching is reflected in the following statement by a middle school teacher: 'I had a great year, 42 of my students got to the final predetermined objective in math.'[20]

Nowhere is this type of constraint more dramatic than in observations of Jacob [fictitious name], a second grade student in an IGE school.[21]

> Jacob has a worksheet in front of him that he should be working on. He seems to be doodling.... Jacob stands up and wanders over to the teacher [and] saunters back.... He stands up and moves his chair around. The teacher has left her desk and is working with a small reading group. He sits down, then stands up and wanders over to the teacher. He speaks to her briefly, picks up a worksheet, and walks back to the desk. He checks to see if the teacher is watching and then ... begins to use his desk as a drum, a muffled, almost silent drum. He sneaks over to a neighbor for a quick visit ... the teacher is busy and doesn't notice.... Jacob hasn't made a single mark on his worksheets. (pp. 48, 49)

During this observation period the teacher let Jacob slip into the empty spaces of classroom life. Why was this so? First, there was little point in finding out what objectives might interest Jacob, considering that the needs of the students were determined by the rationalized curriculum. Second, the teacher was kept so busy trying to shuffle students from one predetermined objective to another that she had little time to consider differences in learning styles or needs. Finally, because most teachers are rewarded or praised for a quiet classroom, there was no pressing reason to confront Jacob on his lack of involvement. The irony is that Jacob could be totally disconnected from his teacher, while the teacher was fulfilling her obligations, as shaped by the school structure.

At the secondary level the impact of school structure is much the same. The large number of students, the pace of work and the rewards of a quiet classroom where students do well on standardized tests both limit and shape teacher-student relations. In addition secondary teachers have a special problem that most elementary teachers do not face: large numbers of students who are turned off from school because they have consistently lost out in the contest for rewards. Because the presence of even a few of these students can influence the tone of the entire classroom, teachers often adopt an authoritarian stance deemed necessary to keep the classroom moving smoothly ahead. By doing so they sacrifice close personal relations to push students along a predetermined course as fast as possible.

Conclusion

Common school structures have helped create and maintain an alienated work experience for teachers. Teachers are alienated from their work process because the primary tool they use to shape educational experiences for students, the curriculum, is no longer theirs. Instead, they manage a curriculum whose goals and aims are determined for the most part by others. Teaching as curriculum management deskills teachers, while putting a premium on clerking skills needed to make certain each student moves efficiently along a predetermined path. It is not surprising, therefore, that most teachers withdraw into their classrooms and try to find minimal ways to comply with structural priorities. But withdrawal is no solution. Isolation limits feedback and professional growth while concealing common problems and constraints.

The structure of schooling presses teachers to become cogs in a machine that is less interested in educating students than in filling them up with what is considered to be legitimate knowledge. Teachers often recognize this, and are troubled by it:[22]

If the pace was such where there were breaks anywhere in the day, where I could focus on more curriculum things or just more individual things with kids it would make a lot of difference.... But it's one thing after another — there's no break at all.... That's the machine that we have going —

simply plug the kids in where they pass on the placement tests and then move them forward according to what they are able to handle. (pp. 229, 230)

If we are to struggle against the unwarranted constraints on the teaching role and the resulting mechanistic view of education, then reform efforts must alter the common school structures which shape teacher behaviour.

Notes

1 Criticisms have ranged from mindlessness (see ROBERT SILBERMAN (1970) *Crisis in the Classroom*, New York, Random House) to reproducing social inequalities (see JEAN ANYON (1981) 'Social class and school knowledge', *Curriculum Inquiry*, 11 January, pp. 3–42.

2 See KENNETH KOMOSKI (1985) 'Instructional materials will not improve until we change the system', *Educational Leadership*, 42, April, pp. 31–7.

3 Popular programs include Science Research Associates (SRA) 'Individualized Learning Through the Reading Laboratory' series by D.H. Parker and G. Suannell and DISTAR Language by Engelmann.

4 JOHN GOODLAD (1984) *A Place Called School: Prospects for the Future*, New York, McGraw-Hill, p. 105.

5 Example of such programs include: Art Is Education (AIE), Utah System Approach to Individualized Learning (USAIL), Continuous Progress in Spelling (CPS), Language Experiences in Reading (LEIR), Science Curriculum Improvement Study (SCIS), Science — A Process Approach (SAPA).

6 HERBERT J. KLAUSMEIER (1976) 'Individually Guided Education: 1966–1980', *Journal of Teacher Education*, 27, Fall.

7 For a discussion of career ladders, see *Education Leadership*, 42, 4, December 1984/January 1985.

8 GOODLAD, *op. cit.*, pp. 302–3.

9 For a discussion of school structure and teachers' work see ANDREW GITLIN (1983) 'School structure, teachers' work and reproduction', in M.W. APPLE and L. WEISS (Eds), *Ideology and Practice in Education*, Philadelphia, Penn., Temple University Press; ROBERT BULLOUGH and ANDREW GITLIN (1985) 'Schooling and change: A view from the lower rungs', *Teachers College Record*, 87, Winter, pp. 219–37; MICHAEL APPLE (1983) 'Curriculum form and the logic of technical control', in APPLE and WEISS, *op. cit.*, and R.W. CONNELL (1985) *Teachers' Work*, Sydney, George Allen and Unwin.

10 These observations of a cooperating teacher were initiated better to understand the context student teachers would enter.

11   For a more detailed description of this activity see GITLIN, *op. cit.*, p. 200.
12   See ROBERT BULLOUGH, STANLEY GOLDSTEIN and LADD HOLT (1984) *Human Interests in the Curriculum: Teaching and Learning in a Technological Society*, New York, Teachers College Press.
13   For a more complete discussion of how the GEMS structure affects teachers see BULLOUGH and GITLIN, *op, cit*.
14   Paul Willis argues that this type of behaviour challenges the taken-for-granted role of schooling which exchanges credentials for compliance. For a complete discussion of student resistance see PAUL WILLIS (1977) *Learning to Labor: How Working Class Kids Get Working Class Jobs*, Westmead, Saxon House.
15   DONALD THOMAS (1985) 'The torpedo's touch', *Harvard Educational Review*, 55, May, pp. 220–1.
16   For a detailed discussion of team competition see GITLIN, *op. cit.*
17   BULLOUGH and GITLIN, *op. cit*, p. 230.
18   GITLIN, *op. cit.*, p. 206.
19   GOODLAD, *op. cit.*, p. 171.
20   ANDREW GITLIN (1980) 'Understanding the work of teachers', PhD dissertation, University of Wisconsin, p. 132.
21   BULLOUGH, GOLDSTEIN and HOLT, *op. cit.*
22   BULLOUGH and GITLIN *op. cit*, pp. 229–30.

10 Life Histories and Teacher Knowledge

Peter Woods

The educational literature is full of testimony on the problems associated with teacher education. We hear continuously about the irrelevance to teachers of much educational research, of the difficulty of relating theory to practice, of the transitory nature of lessons learned during training (see, for example, Otty 1972; May and Rudduck, 1983). The problems, in summary, appear to stem from the following:

1 Much of the knowledge deployed in this training has not been produced for teachers but for others. The issues and problems posed, the theories elaborated, the form of discourse employed all relate to other epistemologies — sociological, psychological, philosophical, etc.— that seem remote from the practical concerns of teachers.

2 Such knowledge is not under their control. It is produced 'out there' and 'up there' on an apparently superior plane in forms and terms with which they cannot engage. Further, much of this knowledge appears to be critical of teachers. Some sociological arguments, for example, have depicted teachers as unwitting agents of the system or as Machiavellian manipulators. Teachers are small cogs in the mighty wheel. Their own views on the matter do not appear to count (see, for example, Giddens, 1976).

3 In consequence, such knowledge, as *teacher* knowledge, is partial and distorted in a number of ways. Typically, educational researchers deal with discrete aspects, uncontextualized in space or time (Goodson, 1980; Goodson and Walker, 1978). Secondly, such knowledge is produced within a scientific paradigm, whereas many would claim that

teaching is also, and perhaps more essentially, an art (Harris, 1976; Jackson, 1977; Eisner, 1979; Stenhouse, 1984; Rudduck, 1985). Thus, as researchers (rightly) struggle to improve the scientific respectability of their work, so they increasingly distance themselves, in some ways, from the essence of teaching which, it might be argued, is not amenable to scientific methods. Associated with this is the problem of 'perfect form' (Becker, 1966; Faraday and Plummer, 1979) — the presentation of neat, foursquare, accounts where teaching is less precise, messier, more uncertain, more processual. Thirdly, teachers as individuals, the input of a teacher's own personal resources and the degree to which teachers can change situations as well as themselves are largely left out of account. The emphasis has been on structure, rather than self, on constraint rather than volition. In addition to being partial, therefore, it has, for teachers, a negative, pessimistic quality about it. That may of course be accurate, but we do not know that without a more balanced view and assessment. (For other analyses of the weak link between research and practice see Bolster, 1983; Tom, 1985.)

What is involved, therefore, in producing knowledge more central to teachers' concerns? Two major requirements seem fairly clear. First, teachers' knowledge should be *theirs* (Downey and Kelley, 1975; Desforges and McNamara, 1979). In this respect, there are possibilities in constructivist, learner-centred modes of teaching (e.g., Armstrong, 1980; Rowland, 1984). These hold that knowledge is built up by the learner through a process of identification, internalization, reinterpretation, discovery and recognition of the need for new information or skills. Transmission may figure in this, but it is dictated by learner need. 'Reinterpretation' is central here as the learner incorporates knowledge within her own life world and refashions its form and expression to match those particular parameters. As this proceeds, it creates the recognition of need for more knowledge and new forms of expertise. I shall return to this shortly.

Secondly, a new conception of knowledge is required, one that is not simply an extant body of facts and theories, but a living, experiential, processual, flexible, creative, compilation of insights, memories, information, associations, articulations that go into resourcing on-the-spot teacher decision-making and action. It will include the ambiguities, inconsistencies, contradictions of life; what to some outsiders may appear to be trivia, but what to teachers are of the utmost importance; and, as well as empirical and observable facts, the emotions and the subjective (Jackson, 1968; Doyle, 1977; Hitchcock, 1983; Smyth, 1985; Woods, 1985a). It will also include the skill of 'orchestration' — a kind of practical theorizing whereby the teacher blends actions together into a harmonious whole (Woods, 1987).

This at times has been portrayed as common sense, but it is this and more. Schutz (1954) argues:

> By a series of common-sense constructs, (people) have pre-selected and pre-interpreted this world which they experience as the reality of their daily lives. It is these thought objects of theirs which determine their behaviour by motivating it. The thought objects constructed by the social scientist, in order to grasp this social reality, have to be founded upon the thought objects constructed by the common-sense thinking of (people) living their life within their social world.

Discussion on this point has usually been from the standpoint of the social scientists, and how their constructs of the 'second degree' can be made consistent with those of the 'first degree'. This is an essential first step, but the knowledge produced, though more valid, is still that of the social scientist. To turn it into an enhanced teacher knowledge, contributing to its manifold nature, we must carry the process a step further. The problem becomes one of teacher knowledge, in a continuous dialectic, reflecting as far as is appropriate the constructs of the social scientist, which themselves are already firmly based on first degree constructs.

How, then, do we put these two kinds of constructs together, and make this kind of knowledge the property of teachers? One way is through various forms of so-called action research (see, for example, Nixon, 1981; Hustler *et al.*, 1986), which starts from teachers' concerns, and which is often underwritten by constructivist or interpretive models of learning as discussed earlier. This can be combined with 'collaborative research', where a researcher works in close cooperation with a teacher as a facilitator, an enabler, a colleague. As de Waele and Harré (1979) point out, this may not only lead to more valid results, but also is more morally acceptable where the aims include improved practice.

For these kinds of liaisons I have argued elsewhere the advantages of ethnography as a research method (Woods, 1985a, 1986). It offers teachers access to research, control over it, and results that to

them are newsworthy. However, a method that meets the conditions outlined above even more closely, arguably, is that of the life
history. As Goodson (1980) maintains, it both gives historical depth
to ethnography and permits a view of wider socioeconomic and
political circumstances and their effect on personal lives (see also
Dollard, 1935; Ball and Goodson, 1985). More than this, of course,
it is anchored within the teacher's self. Pollard (1985) has argued
that 'self' is the teacher's primary interest-at-hand in the classroom,
manifested in aspects of 'enjoyment', 'workload', 'health and stress',
'autonomy' and 'maintenance of self-image'. Instruction and discipline, he argues, are secondary 'enabling interests' acting in the
service of the primary ones. The self is not only central to immediate concerns, but also to those of past and future, that is, one's career
(Riseborough, 1981; Ball and Goodson, 1985; Sikes *et al*, 1985).
From these studies it is clear that the teacher's self is a major
concern, whether it be in terms of mortification and spoliation
(Riseborough,1981) or of enhancement and reward (Nias, 1981). It
is, in short, the teacher's 'favourite subject' (Quicke, 1985). The self,
it should be noted, in line with the conception of knowledge mentioned earlier is not '. . . a solid, given entity that moves from one
situation to another. It is rather a process, continuously created and
recreated in each social situation that one enters . . .' (Berger, 1963,
p. 106). Perhaps this is why 'self-knowledge' is 'normally so elusive'
and why it is 'perhaps the most important benefit' from teacher
involvement in research (Roberts, 1985, p. 214).

Given this, the life history would appear to be an eminently
suitable method in the compilation of teacher knowledge. It is based
within the subjective reality of the individual in a way that both
respects the uniqueness of individuals and promotes identification of
commonalities among them. It is concerned with the whole person,
within whole contexts.

The subject, therefore, is worthy of study in itself and as a
platform, or observatory, for viewing the rest of the world. The life
history provides equipment for this. But one needs help in the use
of it, and on where to look. This leads to another advantage. In
addition to the prompts to memory and the discipline encouraged in
recollection (for life history method see Denzin, 1970; Faraday and
Plummer, 1979; Bertaux, 1981; Woods, 1985a; Measor, 1984), the
aided life history facilitates teacher articulation. This is important
for two major reasons. First, talking about something aids our
understanding of it. Expression is like the final evaluation stage of
the learning process — not until then can we be sure of the degree

to which we 'have it'. We may only have ill-formulated ideas or hazy memories — talking about them in discussion with a trained, sympathetic listener can add considerably to their substance. Secondly, articulation promotes teacher control of the knowledge produced. As one teacher told me, 'Now the more we talk about it, the more the uncertain things become, you know, fixed.... It is mine, the minute I put it into words, *my* words, I've got it.' Here, then, is the essential moment of appropriation and reinterpretation which helps to establish ownership.

'Talk' has some significance here as compared with 'writing'. The latter is the more conventional and formal mode of expression in education generally and as such is heavily influenced by traditional norms. Certainly expression in writing can help establish ownership, but for many teachers it is a time-consuming experience, too public, too definite, and somewhat alien, (1) since their job is based on action, and (2) because it is firmly embedded within a traditionalist paradigm. This is not to say that the written account is not important. But it is the discussant, the facilitator, who does it on the basis of the recorded discussion. Successive drafts are then worked up between them until both are satisfied that as much accuracy is established and benefit derived as possible. The discussant may introduce other material, concepts, theory from 'out there' possibly to enlighten or otherwise enrich or contextualize the account. The process could also work the other way. Richly detailed and highly valid life histories could do much to enhance our general educational knowledge. Either way the nucleus remains the teacher's own life, and the basis of the organization and expression are as in the teacher's own words (see also Wood, 1985a).

Certain aspects of the value of life histories in the study of education have been discussed elsewhere. Here I wish to focus on another aspect of the educational import of life histories, namely their *reinterpretational* value, that is, their ability to make sense in terms that help bring meaning to extant bodies of knowledge and disciplines that otherwise would be seen by teachers as not only irrelevant but alien, and that help to promote interpretive learning. I shall consider what seems often to be regarded by teachers as the most problematic of these disciplines in this respect — sociology (see, for example, Otty, 1972). The first examples are drawn from one particular life history — that of 'Tom' — other aspects of which have been reported elsewhere (Woods, 1981, 1984, 1985a; Woods and Sikes, 1986). This is useful here as Tom was very sociologically sensitive. He had little professional background in the discipline, having been emergency trained after the war, though he had attended a post-experience part-time diploma course which had contained some sociology. (Already keenly aware of the importance of social factors throughout a lifetime's experiences, he had felt an affiliation for this and it had become incorporated into his modes of thought.) As he said about one of his tutors: 'A lot of what he told me cemented ideas that I'd formed for myself, you know I wasn't really very sure of it. Then I discovered later that there's a ready-made theory that had been used for a long time. But I always find this very pleasant when it happens.'

Labelling Theory

How, then, did sociology manifest itself within the 'teacher domain'? In the following, Tom is showing perfect understanding of labelling theory, the amplification of deviance and teacher typification. These concepts are not 'stuck on' to his comments, as is so often the case in formal education, but they inform them organically. I use the transcript to show Tom's mastery of sociology-in-action, not as material to be used by the social scientist:

> There was some misdemeanour and Posser got sent for and done. Only Tom put in a word for him, all the others were against him, but there was no firm evidence. He denied it strenuously and was very upset. Tom took it upon himself to console the irate boy afterwards. The head's attitude is even if he's not guilty, it doesn't do him any harm, but Tom insists that it does. If he had seen the boy afterwards he might have realised. The thing was, Posser said he wouldn't come after him *every* time. They are driving him to deviance. Of course, some would laugh him to scorn. Assumption number one is that the teacher is always right even though he might make mistakes. The mistakes are reminders, deterrents. The child has a lower status, so it is permissible.

Tom also showed a different approach from most of the rest of the staff to the expulsion of a fifth form boy. The head had recently reported that this boy, Barry Higgs, had been arrested for grievous bodily harm, and that this confirmed him as an inveterate villain and justified their expulsion of him. But it was possible to advance another explanation. Tom thought Barry 'a grand lad', popular amongst his fellows and bright. He had been in the top stream, but was demoted because of behavioural problems. Here, with the general aimlessness of the form, peer group pressure, attitudes of staff, the discipline structure of the school, he became a real deviant. Tom suspected his intelligence had forced him into a leadership position in the class, and also caused him to feel more keenly the abuse, overt and latent, heaped on the form. He had been expelled, branded an outsider, and was now being knocked around by the police. The school had made a new criminal.

Tom exhibited his sociological awareness in considering some of his own colleagues. The following illustrates a characteristic blindness to this kind of insight on the part of others, and suggests his own understanding of pupil culture:

> You take Jim here, grand fellow, I talk to him a lot. But he has his problems, he just doesn't understand. We were walking over to the main block together and we saw a girl doing something and he said 'Look at that! Fancy being allowed to do that!' Whereas I just smiled — I couldn't see anything wrong in it at all! There's a brick wall between Jim and what goes on.

There are numerous similar examples in my notes.

He was also astute on the bureaucratized personality ('Here, we're all caught in a vicious circle. We're restricted in what we can do for them. They get bored and subsequently bolshy, and this leads people to adopt schoolmasterly attitudes towards them, which increase the kids' dislike of the place, and so on'). He was perceptive in typologizing teachers along a scale of bureaucratization in relation to social distance between them and pupils (Waller, 1930). He related people to their social background and development, of which he seemed to know a great deal (especially on Jim, the head, and the deputy), and he was aware of the significance of different contexts.

Self and Society

The interplay between the individual and society is a recurring theme throughout Tom's life history. At his last school an aspect of this was personified in his headteacher and deputy headteacher, whom he saw as slaves to bureaucratic form and external policy. Some of his finest moments came from success in these interactions, which were about securing the best conditions for teaching as he saw it and which invariably involved an intense and often frustrating struggle against people in higher authority. Victories were to be savoured. As well as facilitating expression, therefore, the life history permits a celebration of the self, and enhancement of the primary rewards of teaching.

Tom quoted several examples where he would 'overplay the teacher role', for example, 'to take the sting out of staff meetings ... make the boss look small when he couldn't escape, and yet not do anything wrong, you see. It improved staff relationships, and he deserved to be knocked anyway.' On one occasion he organized staff solidarity against the head in face of some injustice he was perpetrating by suggesting nobody say anything in response to the head's tirade. When he came to Tom, he said

> 'I understand you were here last night and you were ...'
> and I looked at him and smiled, and didn't say anything, and
> I'm not joking, I could see his face getting so red, and I just
> kept smiling at him, and this set the tone then, whoever he
> turned to wouldn't speak. It was lovely! It was superb! It
> was the finest thing I've ever known! Oh, I so enjoyed it.
> And you know the staff felt so much stronger when they
> came out. They realized for once that if you stuck together,
> common policy would beat anyone....

He was also an expert at role-distancing and conveyed this art to his pupils:

> I couldn't just say to the children, he is a fool, he shouldn't
> be a headmaster, but I could say, well, he is the headmaster,
> I owe him an allegiance just as you do, you know, and if
> you only giggle, you know, they get the point.... Isn't that
> what education must be, an alliance, a total alliance? If a
> third element wants to opt out, well that's their problem!

In Tom's case, it might be argued that much of the applied sociological knowledge is already there in advance of the life history. This is true, but in some respects it may have been vauge, ill-formulated and unrealized. He made frequent reference to how talking about his life helped analysis, and included reflectivity (Pollard, 1985):

> 'It may not be very sound you know, I haven't worked it
> out, but basically that's what it boils down to.'
> 'I think it's a bit like that, I think.'
> 'But you see I don't, I'm never analyzed myself. Who does
> normally, you know?'

'I've never thought about it before, but I imagine that to be the case.'

His reaction to doing a life history was: 'I must say I find this most fascinating. . . .' he continuously related his experiences to the past life he had already recounted. His liking for third forms was because their 'searching and rebellion' reminded him of his own rebellious times. His particular form of humour, which allows him to be 'excessively rude' to people, he might have inherited from his father. He had learnt much about pupils from his own schooldays (for example, their need to like a teacher — 'when I look back to my schooldays all bad lessons were with the teachers I didn't like'). His experiences in the army had taught him much about person management and group dynamics . . . and so on (see Woods, 1984, for a full account of these influences). The sociology, if ill-formulated in consciousness, was solidly grounded on a bedrock of experience which had threads running deep into his past.

Culture and Structure

For teachers to engage fully with 'second-order' knowledge, they must have opportunities for reflecting (Pollard, 1985). In some respects this is opposed to what they do in its concentrated immersion. Life histories offer them a vehicle for being reflective and for characterizing the immersion. For example, there are several accounts of the traumas of first teaching experiences (e.g., Blishen, 1966; Otty, 1972). These convey what the immersion feels like, and in their affective expression are cathartic and therapeutic. But they are only the first stage of understanding. There may be a feeling of excited revelation — 'Yes, this is exactly how it is' — and comfort in the knowledge that others experience these things so closely. But as they stand, they lack the inbuilt analysis which allows for the cooler, more studied consideration of cause (though see Hannam *et al.*, 1971; Hanson and Herrington, 1976). Some of these accounts are highly accessible sociologically. D.H. Lawrence's account of his early teaching experiences, projected onto Ursula in *The Rainbow* (see Finch and Scrimshaw, 1980), is a vivid account of the process of transformation into a school teacher, in this case from 'free person' into 'institutionalized role', and a splendid basis for consideration of the complexities of role and one's personal engagement with it. Bethell's (1980) account of why he left teaching for a year is an illustration of the Protestant ethnic in action, a living engagement with a historical psychological imperative and modern work structures. Others describe the experience of 'culture shock' as they come up against the cultures of the staffroom (see, for example, Hammersley, 1980) and of the pupils (Riseborough, 1985). The requirements of the role within these contexts are sometimes much at variance with one's self-image. A teacher reported in Pollard (1985, p. 33), for example, suddenly found that she had to 'become this horrible person who had to be nasty to get control ... it wasn't me in the first place which is why I found it difficult to do.' In contrast to Lawrence, this teacher discovered that as she gained more experience, and her skills and knowledge increased, there was less need to be 'horrible', and her real self came to be enhanced by the job. The point here is that there is more chance of appropriate decisions being made in these circumstances if there are opportunities for reflecting on lives which embrace the whole context and history of the self in its engagement with the external world.

Much of this is about socialization and culture cast in terms of the self, or what C. Wright Mills (1959) might refer to as 'private troubles'. Life histories can also inform our thinking about the personal engagement with social structure, with implications for some of the most prominent public issues of the day. One way to this is through a glimpse of my own life history. Though as a pupil there were many aspects of school that I enjoyed, it was still largely an alien experience to me. At the time I was inclined to blame certain individual teachers for this, for they seemed immovably hostile for reasons that were not altogether clear (for example, I was conscientious about work and reasonably well-behaved in my own view). Only later, and when I had more knowledge of such things, in looking back did I realize that this was the subjective side of social class. This élite grammar school had been forced to open its doors to those who passed the 'scholarship'. Some of the staff were convinced this was the wrong decision, and feared that their erstwhile centre of educational excellence was about to be swamped by ill-bred lower-class children, of whom I was one. The fact that some of them were quite good academically only seemed to increase their resentment, for this increased the threat to the position and privileges of their class. It was only when I had become a teacher myself that I fully appreciated this, as I had to do if I were to 'disalienate' the experience. While teaching promised certain rewards for my 'self', I had to come to terms with these earlier experiences. It was important, too, that I recognized the structural constraints, not only so that I could appreciate the position and attitudes of others, but also because I soon became entangled with them myself.

From here it is possible to see what life histories could do for raising teacher consciousness with respect to other pressing issues such as gender and racial differentiation in schools. There is a danger that a confrontational approach — impressing on them the sexism and racism in their thought and practice — may only achieve opposition and resentment and drive the stanchions of those dispositions further into their belief systems. This is because 'we are what we are' — the products of a lifetime's socialization and adaptation. Coming to terms with teaching is a complex matter, such that adaptations for many are protected by boundaries and counter-armament in the event of threat. Demands for change, therefore, that go to the roots of one's construction of self are very difficult to meet without some examination of how that self has come to be constructed. In relation to gender, for example, reconsideration of childhood experiences within the family, and the influences and pressures operating during adolescence, could provide the first significant loosening in entrenched positions.

Conclusion

I have argued here that teacher education should continue to move towards more teacher-centredness, involving constructivist modes of learning, and a conception of knowledge that embraces the affective, the artistic, the volitional and the processual, and which is grounded upon teacher experience. It would not, however, turn its back on gains made more traditionally on the nature and effects of constraints, for example — but rather seek to establish a new balance on the fulcrum of the self. It is one that recognizes both first and second order constructs, and suggests a third — one that amalgamates the two from the teacher's perspective.

The life history offers one way of doing this. It has the great advantage of being based on the teacher's 'self' — a continuing primary interest, and both object and resource. Nothing could be more relevant to the individual teacher. A life history is therefore a very personal document, yet at the same time, in its attention to the historical, social, political and economic contexts of that life, it offers a means for a fully contextualized view, one that is sensitive to the structures and patterns of events that have a general influence.

The value of the life history is enhanced by the participation of a discussant who lends an interested, informed and sympathetic ear, and who offers help and cues to memory, suggests interpretations, provides like and contrasting experiences, *discusses* and thus helps build up the account through talk, and who provides the written account. There is also advantage in group life histories and generally in building up a number of them to yield 'a new series of personal documents' (Becker, 1966, p. xviii) which would inform our thinking on a range of issues.

Teachers must want to do life histories for them to be of any value. On our 'teacher careers' project (Sikes *et al.*, 1985) some teachers were reluctant at first (understandably — we are not all desperately keen to bare our souls to strangers) and only discovered a value in them after the second or third meeting with the discussant. In general they would be more naturally disposed towards them at key career points — on deciding to take up teaching, after the initial traumas, the 'mid-career crisis', pre-retirement — times of deep self-assessment. They need to be sensitively introduced, as well as sensitively handled. Where this is done, life histories have their part to play in the construction of a meaningful, relevant and living teacher knowledge.

References

ARMSTRONG, M. (1980) *Closely Observed Children*, London, Writers and Readers.

BALL, S.J. and GOODSON, I.F. (Eds) (1985) *Teachers' Lives and Careers*, Lewes, Falmer Press.

BECKER, H. (1966) Introduction to SHAW, C.R. *The Jack-Roller*, Chicago, Ill., University of Chicago Press.

BERGER, P.L. (1963) *An Invitation to Sociology*, Harmondsworth, Penguin.

BERTAUX, D. (Ed.) (1981) *Biography and Society*, Beverly Hills, Calif., Sage.

BETHELL, A. (1980) 'Getting away from it all', *The Times Educational Supplement*, 21 March.

BLISHEN, E. (1966) *Roaring Boys*, London, Panther Books.

BOLSTER, A.S. (1983) 'Toward a more effective model of research on teaching', in *Harvard Educational Review*, 53, 3, pp. 294–308.

DENZIN, N. (1970) *The Research Act in Sociology: A Theoretical Introduction to Sociological Methods*, London, Butterworth.

DESFORGES, C. and MCNAMARA, D. (1979) 'Theory and practice: Methodological procedures for the objectivation of craft knowledge', *British Journal of Teacher Education*, 5, 2, pp. 145–52.

DE WAELE, J-P. and HARRÉ, R. (1979) 'Autobiography as a psychological method', in GINSBURG, G.P. (Ed.), *Emerging Strategies in Social Psychological Research*, London, Wiley.

DOLLARD, J. (1935) *Criteria for the Life History*, New York, Librarians Press.

DOWNEY, W. and KELLEY, A. (1975) *Theory and Practice of Education*, London, Harper and Row.

DOYLE, W. (1977) 'Learning the classroom environment', *Journal of Teacher Education'*, 28, pp. 51–5.

EISNER, E.W. (1979) *The Educational Imagination*, London, Collier Macmillan.

FARADAY, A. and PLUMMER, K. (1979) 'Doing life histories', *Sociological Review*, 27, 4, pp. 773–98.

FINCH, A. and SCRIMSHAW, P. (1980) *Standards, Schooling and Education*, London, Hodder and Stoughton.

GIDDENS, A. (1976) *New Rules of Sociological Method*, New York, Basic Books.

GOODSON, I. (1980) 'Life histories and the study of schooling', *Interchange*, 11, 4, pp. 62–77.

GOODSON, I. and WALKER, R. (1978) 'Telling tales', Paper written for SSRC Seminar on Teacher and Pupil Strategies, St Hilda's Collage, Oxford.

HAMMERSLEY, M. (1980) *A Peculiar World? Teaching and Learning in an Inner City School*, PhD thesis, University of Manchester.

HANNAM, C., SMYTH, P. and STEPHENSON, N. (1971) *Young Teachers and Reluctant Learners*, Harmondsworth, Penguin.

HANSON, D. and HERRINGTON, M. (1976) *From College to Classroom: The Probationary Year*, London, Routledge and Kegan Paul.

HARRIS, A. (1976) 'Intuition and the arts of teaching', Unit 18, Course E203 *Curriculum Design and Development*, Milton Keynes, Open University Press.

HITCHCOCK, G. (1983) 'What might INSET programmes and educational research expect from the sociologist?', *British Journal of Inservice Education*, 10, 1, pp. 9–31.

HUSTLER, D. *et al.* (1986) *Action Research in Classroom and Schools*, London, Allen and Unwin.

JACKSON, P.W. (1968) *Life in Classrooms*, New York, Holt, Rinehart and Winston.

JACKSON, P.W. (1977) 'The way teachers think', in GLIDEWELL, J.C. (Ed.), *The Social Context of Learning and Development*, New York, Gardner Press.

MAY, N. and RUDDUCK, J. (1983) *Sex-Stereotyping and the Early Years of Schooling*, Norwich, Centre for Applied Research in Education.

MEASOR, L. (1984) 'Interviewing in ethnographic research', in BURGESS, R. (Ed.), *Qualitative Methodology and the Study of Education*, Lewes, Falmer Press.

MILLS, C.W. (1959) *The Sociological Imagination*, New York, Oxford University Press.

NIAS, J. (1981) 'Commitment and motivation in primary school teachers', *Educational Review*, 33, pp. 181–90.

NIXON, J. (1981) *A Teacher's Guide to Action Research*, London, Grant McIntyre.

OTTY, N. (1972) *Learner-Teacher*, Harmondsworth, Penguin.

POLLARD, A. (1985) 'Reflective teaching — The sociological contribution', Paper delivered at the Sociology and the Teacher Conference, St Hilda's College, Oxford.

QUICKE, J. (1985) 'Using structured life histories to teach the sociology of education', Paper given at ESRC Conference on Sociology and the Teacher, St Hilda's College, Oxford.

RISEBOROUGH, G.F. (1981) 'Teacher careers and comprehensive schooling: An empirical study', *Sociology*, 15, 3, pp. 352–81.

RISEBOROUGH, G.F. (1985) 'Pupils, teachers' careers and schooling: An empirical study', in BALL, S.J. and GOODSON, I.F. (Eds), *Teachers' Lives and Careers*, Lewes, Falmer Press.

ROBERTS, T. (1985) 'Taking part in research: An inservice activity for teachers', *Durham and Newcastle Research Review*, 10, 54, pp. 213–15.

ROWLAND, S. (1984) *The Enquiring School*, Lewes, Falmer Press.

RUDDUCK, J. (1985) 'The improvement of the art of teaching through research', *Cambridge Journal of Education*, 15, 3, pp. 123–7.

SCHUTZ, A. (1954) 'Concept and theory formation in the social sciences', *Journal of Philosophy*, 51, pp. 257–73.

SIKES, P.J. (1984) 'The life-cycle of the teacher', in GOODSON, I. and BALL, S.J. (Eds), *Teachers Lives and Careers*, Lewes, Falmer Press.

SIKES, P., MEASOR, L. and WOODS, P. (1985) *Teacher Careers: Crises and Continuities*, Lewes, Falmer Press.

SMYTH, W.J. (1985) 'Developing a critical practice of clinical supervision', *Journal of Curriculum Studies*, 17, 1, pp.1–14.

STENHOUSE, L.A. (1984) 'Artistry and teaching: The teacher as the focus of research and development', in HOPKINS, D. and WIDEEN, M. (Eds), *Alternative Perspectives on School Improvement*, Lewes, Falmer Press.

TOM, A.R. (1985) 'Rethinking the relationship between research and practice in teaching', *Teaching and Teacher Education*, 1, 2, pp. 139–53.

WALLER, W. (1930) *The Sociology of Teaching*, New York, Russell and Russell.

WOODS, P. (1981) 'Strategies, commitment and identity: Making and breaking the teacher role', in BARTON, L. and WALKER, S. (Eds), *Schools, Teacher and Teaching*, Lewes, Falmer Press.

WOODS, P. (1984) 'Teacher, self and curriculum', in GOODSON, I.F. and BALL, S.J. (Eds), *Defining the Curriculum: Histories and Ethnographies*, Lewes, Falmer Press.

WOODS, P. (1985a) 'Conversations with teachers', *British Educational Research Journal*, 11, 1, pp. 13–26.

WOODS, P. (1985b) 'Sociology, ethnography and teacher practice', *Teaching and Teacher Education*, 1, 1, January, pp. 51–62.

WOODS, P. (1986) *Inside Schools: Ethnography Educational Research*, London, Routledge and Kegan Paul.

WOODS, P. (1987) 'The management of the primary school teacher's role', in DELAMONT, S. (Ed.), *The Primary School Teacher*, Lewes, Falmer Press.

WOODS, P. and SIKES, P.J. (1986) 'The use of teacher biographies in professional self-development', in TODD, F. (Ed.), *Planning Continuing Practitioner Education*, London, Croom Helm.

11 Learning from Difference: A Collegial Approach to Change

Jennifer Nias

An eighteenth century writer is alleged to have complained, of those making the Grand Tour of Europe, that in their travels many learnt nothing of God, themselves or the world. To judge by the glacial slowness of change within education at all levels, the same could be said of teachers as they move from one class, school or college to another. This chapter seeks to explain this phenomenon by exploring the perceptual basis of teaching and the context in which it takes place. Teaching, it is claimed, consists of making judgments, themselves based upon the learned capacity to receive, analyze, classify and interpret incoming information and to link it to the memory — that is, upon perception. Once established, especially in the dependent years of childhood, perceptual habits are hard to change, particularly when they are shared with others whom we love, respect or admire. Further, alterations in self-perception may be painful, provoking anxiety, uncertainty and a sense of loss. The culture of teaching often protects people from these feelings (by, for example, discouraging open debate about ends) while the hierarchical and bureaucratic nature of schools reduces the likelihood that teachers will be exposed, in a supportive environment, to the challenge of others' views. Lack of time for discussion and scepticism about its value as a crucial tool in the modification of personal and professional perspectives are particular obstacles to change. Notwithstanding, teachers find their own ways of creating groups which present them with alternative ways of perceiving themselves and their environments and support them during the processes of experiment and change. Fostering these groups offers a way towards the continuous re-creation of the professional knowledge from which teaching grows.

No-one can teach without making judgments. Material, means

and manner of presentation, pace, correction and reward have to be matched to the learner and the task, against criteria of cost and feasibility and in relation to other, competing claims on the teacher's resources and attention. With a class the task is more complex still. The classroom environment is crowded, capricious and unpredictable, teachers have other roles and responsibilities beyond fostering pupils' learning; their activities have often to be carried out simultaneously or in very rapid sequence. Under these circumstances, much depends on teachers' ability accurately to judge priorities, initiatives and responses.

Judgments are, however, based upon perception. Teachers are subjected to a constant barrage of incoming information, on all sensory channels. They have to receive, sort and react to it, ignoring some of it, synthesizing some with other, remembered incidents, selecting parts for future recall or present action. The informed guesses which guide many teachers' actions for much of the time depend upon their capacity to process and interpret the information conveyed to them by their perceptions.

Perception is not a passive process, a sensory mirroring of external realith. Physiologists and psychologists searching for ways to express the active, learned nature of perception have coined the term 'schemata'. In her masterly study of the psychology of perception Abercrombie (1969, p. 31), quoting Vernon (1955), describes these 'as persistent, deep-rooted and well-organised classifications of ways of perceiving, thinking and behaving' which are also 'living and feasible'. They are slowly built up as, from birth, we develop and exercise the skills of seeing (or hearing, smelling, tasting, touching).

A single schema generally has a fairly specific referent and, especially in young children, is usually formed by direct sensory experience. Into this schema other similar experience will (in Piagetian terms) be assimilated until the schema has to be modified (through accommodation) by experience of a familiar but non-assimilable kind. For example, many young children have a schema, built through experience, that leads them to expect that they can open a container by lifting off its lid. The behaviour of lidded containers of different sorts, sizes and shapes can be assimilated into this schema until a child encounters screw-tops. Then accommodation has to take place, but the modified schema still enables the child to predict the ways in which containers in general can be opened. Later schemata may be formed or modified by the symbolic representation of sensory experience, often through words, that is, by communication and comparison with the experience of others.

However, not all schemata have precise or single referents. Abercrombie argues that 'many of the schemata which affect our behaviour are of a much more generalised and diffused kind ... [they are] loosely organised in ... vague or ill-defined patterns for which the term "assumption" seems appropriate' (1969, p. 40).

These basic assumptions, perceptual in origin, often determine our attitudes, values and even beliefs since we use them to predict the nature and meaning of incoming information. As Abercrombie (1969, p. 63) so vividly demonstrates, 'We never come to an act of perception with an entirely blank mind, but are always in a state of preparedness or expectancy, because of our past experience.' Indeed, the schemata we employ, by encouraging us to see what we expect to see, may distort the information we receive. Further, the linking and integration of schemata into consistent wholes or loosely organized basic assumptions make it possible to respond to patterns or cues (especially verbal ones). Context, purpose and imagination may also influence whether we attend to part or the whole of something and how we interpret what we perceive. In short, however much we may wish to use our sense organs simply to 'receive' the external world, our nervous system sieves, classifies, organizes and changes the impulses carried by the nerve fibres from the receptors to the brain.

The individual and subjective nature of perception makes it difficult for us to share our basic assumptions with others. Yet 'many of the most potent schemata or assumptions were established before the child could talk and, having been made non-verbally, are very difficult to talk about' (Abercrombie, 1969, p. 73). Individuals may find it hard to discover what their own basic assumptions are or to lay them out to challenge from others. Moreover, accommodation to new experience or ideas seldom takes place if the gap between the known and the new is too great. For change to occur new schemata must normally be brought into suitable relationships with old ones. Thus substantial modifications to a learner's perspectives may need to take place incrementally and over long periods. This is likely to be particularly the case when schemata are interrelated so that change in one involves modification to others.

In addition, our perceptions are linked to those of other people. Because the process of building schemata and assumptions begins at birth, it is deeply affected by the behaviour of those who come into close physical contact with the infant and growing child. Later, non-verbal and verbal communication from these 'significant others' is supplemented by contact with members of a wider social group whose members often have values and behaviour patterns compatible with those adopted by the child's family and/or teachers. Eventually individuals begin to take for granted the attitudes and actions of the 'generalized others' who help to frame their view of their environments. Such 'perspectives' (described by Delamont, 1976, p. 52 as 'an ordered set of beliefs and orientations within which, or by reference to which, situations are defined or construed') are the more powerful as predictive devices because they are shared with and reinforced by others. Since Asch's experiments in 1952, it has been widely accepted that individuals find it easier to sustain a perception or opinion if they have the support in it of at least one other person, that is, if they have a 'reference group' of one or more people. Such groups play an important part in determining and maintaining each individual's generalized attitudes and specific beliefs (Shibutani, 1972; Nias, 1985a). In the process they also inhibit change; by definition there is seldom dissent or creative tension within a reference group.

Moreover, the fact that many schemata are formed, especially at home and at school, in situations where children are physically, emotionally or intellectually dependent upon those who are tending or teaching them, often means that the need to change a basic assumption is tacitly linked in an individual's mind with a challenge to authority. The less ready individuals are, through temperament or training, to make this challenge, the more they will resist perceiving the evidence which would result in accommodation to new ideas. Authority-dependence may be closely linked with a closed mind (Abercrombie, 1969, 1981).

Furthermore, we all have basic assumptions about ourselves as well as about the people and things in our environment. These self-referential schemata, being formed through prolonged, intimate contact with significant others, are particularly difficult to alter. Woods (1981), Nias (1984, 1985b) and Pollard (1985) have all demonstrated that teachers have a sense of personal identity, often expressed in terms of deeply held attitudes and values, which precedes and transcends their choice of an occupational identity (that is, they see themselves as 'me' first and 'teacher' second). In defence of their self-image they not only negotiate relationships with their classes and their colleagues which enable them to 'be themselves' within the classroom, but they also try to arrange their careers (even if it means leaving the profession) so as to maintain a sense of fit between occupation and personal identity.

There is evidence (compellingly presented in Marris, 1974) that all changes in personal identity involve feelings of loss, anxiety and conflict. During any redefinition of self (for example, after bereavement or divorce) people struggle with doubt and pain. Personal change, it appears, is always accompanied by a sense of losing control; the more fundamental the shift, the deeper and more traumatic the uncertainty and the greater the need for reassurance and support. Alterations in occupational identity have a similar effect. Indeed, the closer the identification of the self with work, the more difficult it becomes to modify the individual's occupational attitudes, perspectives and actions without provoking anxiety and causing pain (Marris, 1974, Elliott, 1977).

Teachers are particularly vulnerable in this respect because of the occupational importance which is attached to 'being in control'. Many studies (e.g., Lortie, 1975; Woods, 1979; Connell, 1985) have drawn attention to the fact that teachers think they are judged (by pupils, parents, superiors, peers) in terms of their ability to control children and maintain discipline and that they do not feel themselves to have attained a full professional identity until they are 'in control' (Nias, 1986b). The sense of powerlessness which attends any change in self-at-work is thus aggravated for teachers by the fear that their ability as practitioners is being called in question.

All in all, it is not surprising that adults change their frames of reference with relative infrequency and that their values and assumptions, particularly as these relate to themselves, are characterized by cohesion and stability. Individuals will not modify the minute-by-minute judgments of which their teaching consists as long as they, and other members of their reference groups, perceive the world in unchanged ways. Those who wish to modify their own and other people's professional knowledge must recognize that the un-learning of established ways of perceiving and the learning and practice of new ones is a lengthy, hard and potentially painful process in which the challenge and support of others play a crucial role.

This is not to argue that a change in perspective can never take place suddenly; St Paul's experience on the road to Damascus has its educational counterparts (see, e.g., Razzell, 1968). Nor is it to claim that interaction with adults is the only experience which brings about accommodation to others' perspectives. Descriptions of classroom innovation stress the importance both of pupils and of the resources available for teaching them (see, e.g., Holmes, 1952; Marshall, 1965; Lewis, 1971), and the current experience of secondary teachers in the UK, implementing new curriculum initiatives such as

TVEI and CPVE, bears this out. Moreover, a pair of critical friends can provide one another with the right blend of challenge and support to bring about mutual accommodation to new perspectives (Nias, 1985a).

Discussion within a group of their peers is also a powerful means of exposing people to different viewpoints, of encouraging them to lay out their basic assumptions for comparison with others and of supporting them through personal change (see, e.g., Abercrombie, 1974; Abercrombie and Terry, 1979; Lintott, 1986). However, it follows from the claims made earlier in this chapter that, to be fully effective as a change agent, such a group needs to have certain characteristics. It must be big enough to provide a diversity of views but small enough to allow everyone to be heard. Members must be mutually supportive, but ready to encourage challenge and tolerate disagreement, even conflict. They must be willing to accept responsibility for their own ideas, imaginings and actions and to work through any changes in these that they may wish to make. Their relationship must be as egalitarian as possible, though the group is likely to have a leader who is willing to use his/her authority to protect and encourage the free expression of views. The group will be long enough in existence and meet sufficiently often for challenge and change to take place.

Unfortunately, neither teaching as an occupation nor schools as institutions favour the development of such groups. Abercrombie (1981) points out that the human race spends nine months in the womb and a further ninety years trying to achieve independence while maintaining attachment. Our long childhood and the fact that we have to learn most of our survival knowledge from adults or older siblings encourage an unconscious dependency upon those who are bigger, stronger or older than we are. This is perpetuated by the way in which much formal education takes place. At all stages of our schooling we are likely to acquire the assumption that information comes from above, downwards. Unless they challenge this attitude, people who become teachers will repeat the pattern; all that has changed is their position in the transmission process.

The tacit belief of many teachers that their responsibility is to dispense knowledge which pupils need to learn may underlie their tendency, revealed by many classroom studies in the past decade, to do most of the talking in classrooms, to control pupils' social interaction as well as their learning by this means and to equate speaking with teaching. There have been few studies of adult interaction outside the classroom, but Ashton (1975) emphasized that primary teachers found it difficult to discuss their aims with their colleagues; they made statements rather than listening and responding to one another. On in-service courses with experienced teachers, I have found the same. Evidently there is much in teachers' occupational lives to encourage them to talk, little to encourage the habit of listening.

Teachers are often reluctant to engage in a genuine exchange of views on educational issues, especially within their own schools, a characteristic which may derive in part from the nature of the training that they receive. Historically, English teacher training institutions have been asked to undertake simultaneously and with inadequate resources a number of mutually incompatible tasks (Nias, 1972). At the same time, teacher education has lacked a tradition of debating philosophical differences or educational priorities, when to do this would lead to intellectual conflict (a situation which may have been exacerbated by the small size of many colleges and the resulting discomfort of dissension among the staff). The unity, naturalism and pragmatism of Froebel and Dewey have been more influential than the dialecticism of Hegel and Marx in shaping the training of most primary and many secondary teachers. As a result, some basic assumptions (about, for example, the nature of childhood innocence, the need for 'good relationships') are so deeply embedded in many primary teachers that they do not see the need for discussion of them.

Furthermore, English teachers are generally trained to work with children in classrooms, not with adults in schools. They are given little understanding of schools as institutions or preparation for negotiation or conflict resolution among their colleagues. When differences occur they are often resolved, at least on the surface, by reference to authority. As a result, few structures exist within schools to deal with the disagreements which inevitably arise from time to time, given the different frames of reference used by individual teachers. Moreover, in primary schools in particular, the pervasive existence of 'good relationships' as an unchallenged educational aim often results in the proscription of negative emotions (e.g., anger, jealousy) among adults as well as children. In short, potential conflict in school staffrooms tends to be treated as a pathological symptom rather than as a naturally occurring phenomenon, the resolution of which can lead to personal and collective growth (see, for example, Hartley, 1985; Pollard, 1985; Yeomans, 1985; Nias *et al.*, 1987).

The structure of schools as institutions does little to discourage or counterbalance these occupational characteristics. It is a commonplace that teachers are short of time. Without further resources it is very difficult to see how they could meet within school hours, regularly, consistently and without interruption. The crowded nature of the school day offers every obstacle to the airing of different professional and personal perspectives and every incentive to repetition of the well-tried and familiar.

So too does the segmented organization of schools, especially large secondary ones. Buildings, timetables, departmental structures make it hard for teachers to talk to anyone who is not part of their administrative group. Beyond and sometimes within this group pervasive hierarchies inhibit discussion. Yet when peers talk to one another, the views of those from different organizational levels are seldom represented. Staff selection procedures often militate against recruiting for diversity of aims and opinions, and when variety does exist conflicting reference groups protect their members from having to face the challenge of fresh perspectives (see, for example, Connell, 1985; Southworth, 1986). Finally, lacking practice in discussion with those who do not share their basic assumptions, teachers find it hard to take full advantage of such opportunities when they are available (e.g., on in-service courses). Instead, they tend to focus in their initial encounters upon the trivial or technical (Lintott, 1986; Schools Council, 1981).

On the face of it, these occupational and organizational characteristics seem sufficiently deep-rooted and pervasive to ensure that teachers are seldom exposed to fundamental challenge from their colleagues. Nevertheless, some teachers do appear to have found their own ways of using each other's perspectives to foster and support personal growth and change. The accounts below are taken from semi-structured interviews with forty-five mid-career primary teachers (Nias, 1986a, 1986b). They did not arise from direct questions about the extent of personal change or the processes by which it had taken place, but rather from loosely framed inquiries about the experience of being a staff member. All the interviewees were well-known to me and most had been interviewed eight to ten years previously, in their first decade of teaching (see, e.g., Nias, 1981, 1984, 1985a). Full details of the methods used are given in Nias (1986a, 1986b).

The first account is paraphrased from an interview with a woman with fifteen years' service in primary and special schools:

It started with the head, though she didn't seem to do

much — indeed in some respects she seemed quite lazy, but that was good because it made us take the initiative and get on with it. Then she just let it happen. What she did, though, was always to support us — she made us feel secure. She made us feel good about ourselves; it was the first time I'd ever met anyone who said teaching was important and teachers were great.

There were six of us, seven with the head, and although she was head of the whole school she seemed one of us. We all worked down the same end [of the school building] to start with but not afterwards. I can't remember how we came together as a group, but I'm sure it's important that none of use was hung up on status or role. One of the people we learnt most from was a welfare assistant ... we were all willing to learn from each other, ready to take on other people's roles and to try and see things from their point of view.

It was very important that we didn't feel the need to compete. Somewhere along the way we lost the need to defend ourselves to each other, our egos stopped being important. You weren't afraid any more of making a fool of yourself and you could admit when things were going badly. I felt absolutely secure in that group. I suppose we all did which is one main reason why it was so important. You could be completely open.

I can't really say how it worked — it was 'organic'; if that doesn't sound silly. It just happened. It was important that we all shared certain values — mostly that we all took the job seriously and wanted to do it well, but also that we had the same basic idea about, for example, how the children should be treated. But we didn't agree about everything. You influence each other. I changed my views on corporal punishment, but stuck my ground on competition and brought the others with me — which was hard because we were all brought up to be competitive and our children are competitive too.

I suppose that's where the openness comes in. If you're a group, and one or two members change their minds or have a new idea then you all change a little, otherwise you don't stay a group. That's why it is good if new people come in ... [a new teacher] joined us one year, and she was very different to the rest of us in her views on teachers always being right. We had to accept her ideas a bit but you could see her changing her ways within months of arriving. If you don't change a little, you ossify. But we did need to keep changing — if that had stopped happening, and nobody had changed we could easily have all stopped growing. It didn't happen, but you could see that it could have done.

We didn't meet as a whole group very often. There wasn't time, though sometimes after school we'd all sit down for half an hour or so, and occasionally we went out for lunch all together and had longer for talking. Somehow the ideas seemed to move between us by osmosis. But we did talk a lot in overlapping twos and threes, yes, a lot, about all sorts of things, as they came up. That was terribly influential. It was the constant talking, and the openness that helped me to change.

It made us feel very together, because we knew each other so well, and gave each other so much support. We didn't see much of each other outside school but if there had been more time we could have been friends and done things together as well.... It was a tremendous feeling, I missed them terribly when I moved on. I still think about it. We really changed that whole school in the time I was there, and the parents changed too because we spent a lot of time talking to them as well. We couldn't any of us have done it on our own.... It was probably the most important and formative experience I've ever had.

The second is taken from an interview with a man, recently appointed as a headteacher after ten years in the classroom:

Working with Sarah and Alan was my first experience of team work.... It changed an awful lot of my outlook.... I honestly don't know [how it happened]. Partly to do with the building — it was an open-plan unit of four classes and we had three of them. The other person — the fourth person who changed a couple of times — never entirely fitted into the group.... We were always talking, putting the world to rights.... It did me a lot of good. It persuaded me — it got me listening to other people and it got to a stage when I was secure with them, in particular to take their criticisms. I can remember vividly being told by Sarah in a friendly way, long before we were reasonably good friends, 'Look, you're not going to make any progress while you're continually putting backs up left, right and centre, couldn't we try it this way?' and my reply was 'No', but she repeated the exercise and it did me a lot of good.... Alan was like that too. We all fitted in together, though it wasn't always easy. Like me, he was pretty neurotic to start with. We very quickly realised that we had things to learn from him as well. I think that's what made the difference. In certain areas he was clearly the leader and it provided him with a degree of security that we were willing to listen to him too....

The head didn't have anything to do with [the development of this group], in fact we must have been rather a pain from his point of view. It was Sarah really, she started us off.

We didn't meet formally, there was no need to — it was the usual times, mostly after school, lunch times, in the morning, sometimes whenever we felt the need to, but working together, there's always something that's happened or some child or an idea that one of you wants to talk about.

The third description was given by a woman teacher with eight years' classroom experience:

[In my first school, the head] had a definite philosophy about the way he wanted his school to run.... If he didn't agree with you, he'd tell you, often in a public and rude manner, but you could take that because ... he didn't bear any grudges, and let you carry on expressing yourself the way you felt was best, and you could talk to him, too. I think the energy [in the school] came from having a body of professional people who were interested and did things together.... There was a lot of talk .... I miss it.... We didn't always agree, but we spent a lot of time doing things for school together and we learnt from each other.... Perhaps we'd make it a social occasion too — we were always going out together. [By contrast, in this job] we're finding the need more and more for young teachers to get together, to give each other ideas, to spark off from one another. In fact we're trying themselves ... [and] to develop [part of a school] where we can meet and be together.

In my first school, you could talk about philosophy and argue about it and if your view was different from somebody else's you could have an argument. In this school you can't, you can't really have any views at all because you're not sure whether anyone will agree with you and if they don't agree with you they hold it against you. So if it's part of you, something you've believed in all your life and you're holding it in all the time then you have problems, don't you, if you can't express yourself? Then Beth came along and she isn't like that at all, so we huddle in the little corners and talk about things we feel passionately about. I go home to her house in the evening if there's a problem we really want to thrash out. She's brought me out a lot ... made me realise the ways I can change and helped me do it.... I wish there was a group of us, like there was in my first school ... [if I could change on thing here] it would be to make the staff be far more open and honest about teaching and while they're actually at school, to work as a team. We're just not benefitting from everybody's experience and ideas and they're too isolated, everybody is and nobody's happy because there isn't unity, was aren't a group.... I think we'd benefit an awful lot if it opened up and we could talk to each other. I think the rest would follow then.

It would obviously be unsound, methodologically and substantively, to derive from these three accounts extensive claims about the ways in which teachers make or change their professional knowledge. In speaking as they did, none was responding to questions about the extent or nature of change in themselves or others, and this topic was not a prime focus of the research. The accounts leave many questions unanswered: Who decided that these particular teachers should share a staffroom or a teaching space? If it was the head, did he/she intend that individuals should change one another's perspectives? Who are the 'fourth teachers' in the second account and why did they not become members of the group? Did all three groups impose a joint perspective upon newcomers rather than freeing them to discover and modify their own? Was Beth — in the third account — helping the speaker to change or confirming her in her existing viewpoint?

Notwithstanding such gaps in the available evidence, and the attendant difficulty in drawing valid conclusions from it, these teachers all made several similar points. First, the experience of being a group member was a powerful and enjoyable one, both personally and professionally. Second, groups developed because proximity and a common task brought individuals together and gave them a reason to talk. Third, in each group there was tacit agreement among members on basic educational values, an agreement which enabled them to work together despite their differences. Fourth, once the habit of talking had been formed, members found it so valuable that they made time for it whenever they could. Fifth, their discussions shared certain characteristics: because members of the group felt secure with one another they talked very openly; topics for discussion arose spontaneously and naturally among members and were not imposed upon them; no firm boundaries were drawn between personal and professional concerns; differences of opinion were sanctioned, even welcomed; individuals were willing to learn from one another. Sixth, relationships in the whole staff group or the relevant sub-group were non-competitive and relatively egalitarian. Each group had a leader in the sense that someone took the initiative in starting the discussions, but he/she then became a member of the group, allowing and encouraging leadership to move among the others as seemed appropriate to them all. Seventh, as a result of all these characteristics, the group acquired a life and identity of its own, but eighth, this served not to enforce conformity upon its members but to enrich their thinking and behaviour, individually and collectively. Through their twos, threes or small groups members found 'a new kind of stability based on the recognition and acceptance of ambiguity, uncertainty and open choice' (Abercrombie, 1969, p. 171).

It seems that groups of this kind, characterized, within commitment to a common task, by equal power relations, willingness to expose, through talking, differences in perspective and practice and mutual support for modifications in both, offer a way of understanding and encouraging pedagogical change. The fact that such groups develop despite the cultural and structural obstacles placed in their way by the nature of teaching and of schools should not, however, be a cause for complacency. Rather, it highlights the need to remove these obstacles and encourage teachers to create their own challenging yet supportive environments, stimulating enough to provoke growth and sufficiently secure to nurture it. The kind of developments most obviously needed are: acceptance by headteachers and administrators that discussion of teachers' own concerns is a worthwhile professional activity and provision of more time within the school day for talking; encouragement of contexts (e.g., open-plan units, team teaching, shared curriculum responsibilities) in which shared coping brings small groups of people together with common starting points for discussion; recruitment for diversity and organizational provision (e.g., through interdepartmental working parties) for its expression; acceptance at all levels of the educational system of the value of disagreement, set within a secure environment; provision in all kinds of teacher education for open discussion and the sharing of perspectives; emphasis within management training upon the need to reduce hierarchical practices and encourage collegial discussion, and to develop leaders who will listen and support without losing their power to protect individuals from the group or to help them uncover their own basic assumptions.

Such changes within the organization of schools and the practice of teacher education would also lead into theoretical fields such as social psychology and psychotherapy which are at present relatively little used by educationalists. One example is S.M. Foulkes, an English group psychotherapist whose intellectual roots are in the critical theory of the Frankfurt School and whose writings (though scattered and diffuse) are extremely relevant to many of the ideas explored in this chapter (e.g., the learnt nature of attitudes and assumptions; the relationship between the individual and the group; the importance of communication between group members) (see Pines, 1983; Abercrombie, 1983; and, for the work of Foulkes himself, Foulkes, 1948, 1964; Foulkes and Anthony, 1965). Another is M.L.J. Abercrombie, a zoologist whose seminal work (1969) on *The Anatomy of Judgement* first made plain the importance of perception in teaching and learning. She herself drew heavily on Foulkes' work in her practice and writing as a teacher of medical, architectural and education students (see Abercrombie, 1969; Abercrombie and Terry, 1978, 1979). Marris (1974) is a social psychologist whose work on bereavement has enhanced the understanding of many theorists and practitioners concerned with personal and occupational change. Other notions used in this chapter, such as reference group and personal identity, lead into related academic fields. It could be argued that educational theorists stand in as much need as classroom practitioners of fresh perspectives on their work. In Nias (1987) I have attempted to apply this message to my own thinking.

In this chapter I have presented evidence to suggest that practical and theoretical developments which encourage teachers to discuss their differences in supportive and egalitarian groups could be a powerful tool in the modification and propagation of new kinds of professional knowledge. Yet I do not see such developments as being swift or easy to achieve. In the absence of structural change, it is up to individual heads, teachers, administrators and teacher educators to do what they can to create and foster contexts in which practitioners, in the company and with the support and help of their peers, can explore, understand and, if they so desire, change their perceptions and the judgments which spring from them.

References

ABERCROMBIE, M.L.J. (1969) *The Anatomy of Judgement: An Investigation into the Processes of Perception and Reasoning*, Harmondsworth, Penguin.

ABERCROMBIE, M.L.J. (1974) 'Improving the education of architects', in COLLIER, K. (Ed.), *Innovation in Higher Education*, London, NFER.

ABERCROMBIE, M.L.J. (1981) 'Changing basic assumptions about teaching and learning', in BOUD, D. (Ed.), *Developing Student Autonomy in Learning*, Worthing, Nichols.

ABERCROMBIE, M.L.J. (1983) 'The application of some principles of group analytic psychotherapy to high education', in PINES, M. (Ed.), *The Evolution of Group Analysis*, London, Routledge and Kegan Paul.

ABERCROMBIE, M.L.J. and TERRY, P.M. (1978) *Talking to Learn*, Guildford, Society for Research into Higher Education.

ABERCROMBIE, M.L.J. and TERRY, P.M. (1979) *Aims and Techniques of Group Teaching*, 4th ed., Guildford, Society for Research into Higher Education.

ASCH, S.E. (1952) *Social Psychology*, Englewood Cliffs, N.J., Prentice Hall.

ASHTON, P. (1975) *Aims of Primary Education: A Study of Teachers' Opinions*, London, Macmillan for Schools Council.

CONNELL, R. (1985) *Teachers' Work*, London, Allen and Unwin.

DELAMONT, S. (1976) *Interaction in the Classroom*, London, Methuen.

ELLIOTT, J. (1977) 'Developing hypotheses about classrooms from teachers' practical constructs: An account of the work of the Ford Teaching Project', *Interchange*, 7, 2, pp. 2–22.

FOULKES, S.H. (1948) *Introduction to Group Analytic Psychotherapy: Studies in the Social Integration of Individuals and Groups*, London, Heinemann.

FOULKES, S.H. (1964) *Therapeutic Group Analysis*, London, Allen and Unwin.

FOULKES, S.H. and ANTHONY, E.J. (1965) *Group Psychotherapy: The Psychoanalytic Approach*, Harmondsworth, Penguin.

HARTLEY, D. (1985) *Understanding the Primary School*, London, Croom Helm.

HOLMES, R.G.A. (1952) *The Idiot Teacher*, London, Faber.

LEWIS, F. (1971) *And Softly Teach*, London, Black.

LINTOTT, B. (1986) 'Group work in a course for teachers', mimeo, Cambridge, Cambridge Institute of Education.

LORTIE, D. (1975) *School Teacher*, Chicago, Ill., University of Chicago Press.

MARRIS, P. (1974) *Loss and Change*, London, Routledge and Kegan Paul.

MARSHALL, S. (1965) *Experiment in Education*, Cambridge, Cambridge University Press.

NIAS, J. (1972) 'Value-persistence and utility in colleges of education', *Education for Teaching*, 89, 3, pp. 29–34.

NIAS, J. (1981) 'Commitment and motivation in primary school teachers', *Educational Review*, 33, pp. 181–90.

NIAS, J. (1984) 'Definition and maintenance of self in primary education', *British Journal of Sociology in Education*, 5, pp. 267–80.

NIAS, J. (1985a) 'Talking, listening and identity: Reference groups in primary education', in BALL, S. and GOODSON, I. (Eds), *Teachers' Lives and Careers*, Lewes, Falmer Press.

NIAS, J. (1985b) 'A more distant drummer: Teacher development as the development of self', in BARTON, L. and WALKER, S. (Eds), *Social Change and Education*, London, Croom Helm.

NIAS, J. (1986a) 'Schools as well as children: Why mid-career teachers need their colleagues', mimeo, Cambridge, Cambridge Institute of Education.

NIAS, H. (1986b) 'What is it to "feel like a teacher"? The subjective reality of primary teaching', mimeo, Cambridge, Cambridge Institute of Education, Paper given at British Educational Research Association Conference, Bristol, 1986.

NIAS, J. (1987) *Seeing Anew: Teachers' Theories of Action*, Geelong, Deakin University Press.

NIAS, J., SOUTHWORTH, G. and YEOMANS, R. (1987) *Primary School Staff Relationships*, research in progress, Cambridge Institute of Education.

PINES, M. (1983) 'The contribution of S.H. FOULKES to group therapy', in PINES, M. (Ed.), *The Evolution of Group Analysis*, London, Routledge and Kegan Paul.

POLLARD, A. (1985) *The Social World of the Primary School*, London, Holt, Rinehart and Winston.

RAZZELL, A. (1968) *Juniors: A Postscript to Plowden*, Harmondsworth, Penguin.

SCHOOLS COUNCIL (1981) *Making the Most of the Short In-Service Course*, by Jean Rudduck, Working Paper 71, London, Methuen.

SHIBUTANI, T. (1972) 'Reference groups as perspectives', in MANIS, J. and MELTZER, B. (Eds), *Symbolic Interaction: A Reader in Social Psychology*, 2nd ed., Boston, Mass., Allyn and Bacon.

SOUTHWORTH, G. (1986) 'By appointment or staff selection? A case study of the appointment of a teacher to a primary school', mimeo, Cambridge, Cambridge Institute of Education, Paper presented to British Educational Research Association Conference, Bristol.

WOODS, P. (1979) *The Divided School*, London, Routledge and Kegan Paul.

WOODS, P. (1981) 'Strategies, commitment and identity: Making and breaking the teacher role', in BARTON, L. and WALKER, S. (Eds), *School, Teachers and Teaching*, Lewes, Falmer Press.

YEOMANS, R. (1985) 'Are primary teachers primarily people?' *Education 3–11*, 13, 2, pp. 6–11.

PART III

Pedagogical Action

12 Transforming Teaching through Intellectualizing the Work of Teachers*

John Smyth

This chapter takes as its starting point the need to rethink fundamentally the ways in which teaching and the work of teachers are regarded, and hence the kind of knowledge that informs and shapes the pedagogical practices of teachers. The particular stance taken here is that the work of teachers is a form of mental or 'intellectual' labour, quite distinct from technical or manual forms of work. The historical importance of this distinction lies in the dominant images of teachers as 'technicians' (Scheffler, 1968; Hartnett and Naish, 1980; White, 1979), 'civil servants' (Bullough, Gitlin and Goldstein, 1984; White, 1979) and 'executives' (Berliner, 1980). Teachers have long been vulnerable, and their work susceptible to domestication.

To reconceptualize the nature of teachers' work as a form of intellectual labour amounts to permitting and encouraging teachers to question critically their understandings of society, schooling and pedagogy. It involves acknowledging the claim made by Kohl (1983) about the need for teachers actively to assume the responsibility for theory making (and theory testing), or accept the fact that these will be made for teachers by academic researchers and others only too willing to assume that task. For Kohl (1983), this is inevitable if teachers unwittingly, or otherwise, bargain away their educational power by giving up their responsibility as intellectuals. Indeed he says, 'When teachers fail to develop and use educational theories . . . they open the door to stifling curriculum proposals devised by stodgy academics with no real sense of what goes on in the classroom' (p. 28).

---

* This is a revised and abridged version of a paper presented to the annual meeting of the Australian Association for Research in Education, University of Melbourne, November 1986.

What is important here is not the emphasis on the intellectual per se, but rather the political, social and moral imperatives of uncontested power, authority and domination which such a perspective opens up for critique and reasoned moral action. In proposing a focus on 'the intellectual' I am not suggesting that teachers become aloof, abstract, or detached from the real world of teaching — this is a misconstrual of what it means to be an intellectual. Gramsci (1971) argues that what is important about intellectual work, and hence the activities of intellectuals, is not their cognitive function, often seen as existing independently of issues of class, culture and power, but rather their political and social prowess in developing the potential to engage with and transform dominant theoretical traditions. Kohl (1983) claims an intellectual to be a person who '. . . knows about his or her field, has a wide breadth of knowledge about other aspects of the world, who uses experience to develop theory, and questions theory on the basis of further experience' (p. 30). But, even more important than that, Kohl (1983) argues that an intellectual is above all '. . . someone who has the courage to question authority and who refuses to act counter to his/her own experience and judgement' (p. 30). Greene (1985) claims that many teachers fail to do so:

> . . . because the processes that go on in their institutions strike them as so automatic, there seems to be no alternative but to comply. Their schools seem to resemble natural processes: what happens in them appears to have the sanction of natural law and can no more be questioned or resisted than the law of gravity. (p. 11)

It was Gramsci (1971) who argued the more general case for reclaiming the theoretical tradition of the intellectual, and Aronowitz and Giroux (1985) an Giroux (1985a, 1985b, 1985c) who have given more recent expression and impetus to those ideas in the context of education and schooling. Their work is closely associated with Gramsci's (1971) challenge to the allegedly value-free neutral nature of intellectual activity; it is this that represents his major theoretical advance. His disavowal of the intellectual as being apolitical is well put by Giroux (1985b):

> Inherent in such a view is the notion that the intellectual is obligated to engage in a value free discourse, one that necessitates that he or she refuses to take sides on different issues, or refuses to link knowledge with fundamental principles of emancipation. Such a view reinforces the idea that

intellectuals are free floating and detached in the sense that they perform a type of labor that is objective and apolitical. (p. 86)

The essence of Giroux and McLaren's (1986) argument is that a reconstitution of teachers' work will result in teachers being construed as:

> ... bearers of critical knowledge, rules and values through which they consciously articulate and problematize their relationship to each other, to students, to subject matter, and to the wider community. This view of authority exposes and challenges the dominant view of teachers as primarily technicians or public servants whose role is to implement rather than to conceptualize pedagogical practice. Moreover, the category of emancipatory authority dignifies teacher work by viewing it as an intellectual practice with respect to both its formal characteristics and the nature of the content discussed. Teacher work becomes a form of intellectual labor opposed to the pedagogical divisions between conception and practice, and production and implementation, that are currently celebrated in a number of educational reforms. The concept of teacher as intellectual carries with it the political and ethical imperative to judge, critique, and reject those approaches to authority that reinforce a technical and social division of labor that silences and disempowers both teachers and students. (pp. 225–6)

What is significant about this reconceptualization of teachers' work is that it provides a basis from which to argue against the encroachment of those bent on treating teaching as a particular species of instrumentalism. This should not be interpreted as a narrow claim to change the teaching role — on the contrary, what is being argued for is a change in perspective by those outside schools, away from a particular limited view of pedagogy. While it is true that pedagogy refers to a general systematic procedure for advancing learning, there is also a sense in which to act pedagogically means to act in ways that 'empower' learners. Pedagogues ask questions, while articulating their theories about teaching and learning — they verbalize why they do what they do in their teaching, interrogating their knowing so as to uncover why it is they accept current practices, and questioning the veracity of the social conditions that support and sustain them. In Simon (1985) and Giroux's (1985a) terms, this amounts to a 'critical pedagogy' in which knowing is an ideological process that requires continual clarification and elaboration of the relationship between knowledge and the social order. According to Simon (1985), the various ways of knowing are organized around particular 'taken-for-granted' assumptions and practices that permit certain questions to be posed, while actively suppressing others.

What is needed is a way of reclaiming knowledge about teaching that acknowledges and questions its socially construed nature and the way it relates to the social order. To take some examples:

> why do I insist on external rewards and punishments to make kids learn?
> why do I define the 'good' kids as the 'quiet' kids?
> why is it that I insist on equating 'workbook work' with 'reading'?
> why do I regard 'on-task time' as synonymous with 'learning'?
> why is it that I have come to regard 'getting through the material' as the prime goal of my teaching?

Questioning habitual pedagogical practices in this way necessitates asking other pointed questions that seek to unravel the social, cultural and political forces that have shaped our teaching, and that prevent us from dislodging those deeply entrenched practices. Such questions include:

> where do my ideas about teaching/learning come from historically?
> how did I come to appropriate these ideas?
> what social and cultural conditions cause me to continue to endorse the ideas I hold to be true about teaching/learning?
> whose interests do my ideas actually serve?
> what power relationships between myself and students are expressed in my teaching practices?
> do my practices accommodate to the dominant ideology?
> how do I encourage resistance by those who are oppressed?
> in view of this, are there grounds for radically changing the way I teach?

To regard teaching in this way is to adopt a viewpoint that involves critique and transformation. Simon (1985) argues that such a 'transformative critique' has three interrelated moments:

First, transformative critique views knowledge as socially produced, legitimated, and distributed and seeks to make explicit the ways in which such production, legitimation, and distribution take place. Second, knowledge is apprehended as expressing and embodying particular interests and values, implicating issues of power and ethics in all expressions of knowledge. Third, seeking to negate the 'objective' nature of knowledge and forcing the educator to confront the relation between knowledge, power, and control, critique additionally requires the articulation and consideration of transformative action — that is, action that would alter the distribution of power and increase the range and scope of possibilities for individually and collectively defined projects. (p. 1119)

Giroux and McLaren (1986) argue that what is involved here is a process in which teaching and learning '... is linked to the more political goal of educating students to take risks and to struggle with on-going relations of power in order to alter the oppressive conditions in which life is lived' (p. 226). All of this recognizes that schools are socially constructed realities in which there are continuous struggles among contending groups to have their particular lived reality of schooling recognized.

Adopting a critical stance towards teaching and learning, therefore, involves more than being negative and carping (Carr and Kemmis, 1983). It requires, as Apple (1975) claims:

... a painful process of radically examining our current positions and asking pointed questions about the relationship that exists between these positions and the social structure from which they arise. It also necessitates a serious in-depth search for alternatives to these almost unconscious lenses we employ and an ability to cope with an ambiguous situation for which answers can now be only dimly seen and which will not be easy to come by. (p. 127)

A critical pedagogy of schooling goes considerably beyond a reflective approach to teaching. For Giroux (1983), the defect of the reflective approach is that it is severely constrained and limited by what it ignores. Being critical, or engaging in critique, involves analysis, enquiry and critique into the transformative possibilities implicit in the social context of classrooms, and schooling itself. The intent of critical pedagogy is that of 'liberation' (or emancipation), in the sense that people:

> ... are increasingly free to choose from a range of alternative perspectives on themselves and their social worlds. This freedom of choice requires the ability to see one's own views of what is good or right, possible or impossible, true or false, as problematic, socially constructed, and subject to social and political influence. (Berlak, 1985, p. 2)

But here Giroux (1981) offers a caveat: the goals of emancipation are not '... like shopping lists that one draws up before going to the supermarket; they are goals to be struggled for and defined in specific contexts, under specific historical conditions' (p. 220). A truly critical pedagogy involves an examination of existing social relationships at three levels: that of history, of current practice (including its hierarchical bases), and of the potential to transform arrangements in the future. Simon (1984) claims that to act critically means figuring out:

> ... why things are the way they are, how they got that way, and what set of conditions are supporting the processes that maintain them. Further ... we must be able to evaluate the potential for action that [is] embedded in actual relationships. To think these tasks through requires concepts that can carry a critique of existing practice. (p. 380)

Where the critical perspective becomes especially poignant is in situations (such as the present) where there ae intensified moves towards increased centralism in education, with their reductionist and predetermined curriculum guidelines, frameworks and packages, and concomitant prescription of pedagogical procedures (Buswell, 1980). This trend, which is part of a much broader attempt to deskill workers generally (Braverman, 1975), is at least partly obscured by the allegedly benign technical nature of work and its objectivist claims to be concerned only with managerialist matters of efficiency and effectiveness in schooling. As we all know, such approaches are far from value-free; they have a well-developed corporatist agenda designed among other things to get teachers to 'lift their game'.

Because of economic crises facing governments, and the tightening fiscal squeeze, it has not been difficult for policy-makers to generate politically compelling arguments about the need to ensure value for the taxpayer's beleaguered educational dollar. The emphasis has been upon the economic rationalization of educational systems, with the requirement that teachers attend to the business management canons of 'standardization', 'efficiency', and 'effectiveness'. This push has been aided and abetted by the educational technocrats who, through their reports, have provided a form of ideological control. The plea for economic accountability in educaion has meant an intensification of moves towards the scientific management of schools and school systems.

The problem with the technocratic view of education and teaching is that the emphasis on 'excellence', 'quality', 'efficiency', and 'effectiveness' brings severely into question the ability of teachers to provide the kind of intellectual and moral leadership necessary to enable children to be educated. What are rehearsed are liturgical solutions regarding what is considered by some to be important in schooling. What is not opened up for debate and contestation are the fundamental deficiencies in the ways schools are conceived and organized. What we have, therefore, is what Giroux (1979) terms 'a dispending of the culture of positivism' which serves only to bolster and reproduce the orthodox view of what schools and teaching are about. Furthermore, such conceptualizations detach students and teachers from their language, customs, rituals, experiences and histories; what is posited in their place are managerial forms of discourse about the nature of schooling that are alien to the cultural lives of people in schools. Because of the power of language, what occurs in schools is a kind of pedagogic dislocation as teachers and students become confused about the legitimacy and potency of their own lived practical experiences in the light of hegemonic 'management pedagogies' (Giroux, 1985c). The kind of imperatives that emerge as important in schooling are: the reduction and standardization of knowledge; the measurement of attainment against arbitrarily determined objectives and standards; and the allocation of teaching resources so as to maximize output. Part of the pseudo-respectability attaching to the technocratic view is what Ryan (1986) sees as '. . . its scientistic language, reflecting an instrumentalist orientation to carefully-defined and measurable goals, [and which] gives the perennial politics of control a gloss of sophisticated modernity' (p. 30). The discourse of management pedagogy actually seeks to supplant the idiosyncratic and value-laden experiences of classrooms, teachers and students. But herein lies the curious paradox — there is also a simultaneous and continuous struggle against the goals and objectives set by others outside classrooms. This becomes clearer when we accept a 'dialectical' view of power that amounts to a working against frozen social relationships that constrain and deny transformative possibilities. As Giddens (1979) put it:

> Power relations ... are always two-way, even if the power of one actor or party in a social relation is minimal compared to another. Power relations are relations of autonomy and dependence, but even the most autonomous agent is in some degree dependent, and the most dependent actor or party in a relationship retains some autonomy.... (p. 93)

If teachers are to challenge and ultimately supplant this dominant technocratic view of schooling, it is necessary that they be articulate about the nature of their work, and where they are located historically and pedagogically in it, while also being conscious of its social and political purposes. It means that teachers must go beyond the roles of technicians, managers or efficient clerks imposed upon them by others, and must be unwilling to continue to accept the way things are in schools. Even where these externally contrived agenda appear to be rational, sensible and humane, the inability of management pedagogies adequately to understand, let alone grapple with the complexities in classrooms, creates a situation of opposition for teachers. What must not be overlooked (cf. Smyth. 1986) is that unequal power relations in schools (between individuals and groups) are *established and constructed* through the lived experiences of people in schools. As such, they can be 'disestablished' and 'deconstructed' in the way people choose to live, work and ultimately penetrate the object of their struggles. What is needed is a faith in the power of teachers to reflect upon, resist, and change the oppressive circumstances in which they find themselves (Giroux, 1981, p. 216).

As Giroux (1985a) argues, what is at stake is not simply disempowerment of teachers, who are losing control of the basic conditions of their work, but rather that the increasing technicist burdens being imposed on teachers to implement the dictates of educational experts are altering the fundamental division of labour and thereby changing teachers' own perceptions of their role as reflective practitioners. Countering this tendency means that teachers must engage in the creation of a culture of teaching in which the agenda is one of rendering problematic the cultural forms and content of classroom instruction itself. McLaren (1986) put it in these terms:

Once we understand the classroom as an embattled symbolic arena where classroom and street discourses collide and where teachers and classroom peer group struggle over how reality is to be signified, and in what manner and style the cultural terrain is to be engaged, then we, as teachers can begin to situate classroom reform in both the fight for material equality and the forging of a new symbolic sphere. (McLaren, 1986, pp. 253–4)

To regard teachers' work as a form of intellectual labour is to endorse Freire's (1972) 'problem posing' view of education, in which actors '. . . develop their power to perceive critically the way they exist in the world with which and in which they find themselves; they come to see the world not as a static reality, but as a reality in process, in transformation' (p. 56).

What this amounts to is a form of 'resistance' — a way of teachers and students mediating the contradictory lived experiences of schooling so as to address the problems of the hidden curriculum (Apple, 1971). For Giroux (1983), this involves more than mere oppositional behaviour which, while it is active, does not address the underlying issues of domination. He argues that resistance involves '. . . uncovering the degree to which . . . [action] speaks to a form of refusal that highlights . . . the need to struggle against the social nexus of domination and submission' (p. 109). Giroux's (1983) notion of power (which he sees as being inextricably connected to knowledge) is closely tied to his view of resistance. Rather than power being uni-directional, he sees it as permitting and encouraging 'progressive alternatives' even within the most hierarchical and oppressive of relationships. By way of example, he says: 'Within most authoritative modes of classroom discipline and control there are fleeting images of freedom that speak to very different relationships' (p. 79). It is in this context that Giroux (1985b) sees teachers as 'resisting intellectuals' capable of inserting education into the political sphere '. . . by arguing that schooling represents a struggle over power relations' (p. 87). He sees students as having to be involved too in the struggle to overcome injustices, and to humanize themselves in the process. Doing this requires giving students not only '. . . an active voice in their own learning experiences' (p. 87), but also ways of engaging in critique so as to see the relationship between problems of everyday life and the pedagogical practices enacted in classrooms.

This means rejecting the instrumentalist transmission view of education in which external experts determine content which is then relayed to passive students; it requires in its place a radically different alternative (Shor, 1980). It means accepting that knowledge does not exist independently of the meaning and significance which students attach to it by virtue of their previous experiences, their class, and their culture. Unlike behaviourist forms of knowledge, this approach to knowledge does not attempt to 'place beyond criticism what is always potentially contentious' (Ryan, 1982, p. 25). Rather, it is concerned with teachers and students working in ways that challenge '... culturally-induced distortions' and allow '... previously-submerged insights' (Ryan, 1982, p. 25) to surface and provide the basis for a variety of pedagogical strategies. Clearly, such reflective and inquiring approaches are at variance with centrally prescribed curriculum guidelines, and viewpoints that are concerned with cost-effective systems of educational delivery.

As long as technocrats are allowed to coopt and domesticate educational thinking and discourse within an outcomes-oriented managerialist ideology, then educational debate will be restricted to a concern about a sterile measuring of results against objectives. The bigger questions about the nature of the 'educational good' will continue to go unanswered. As Van Manen (1977) put it, a preoccupation with technical concerns actively prevents a consideration of the inequitable nature of the society we live in and of the role schools play in maintaining that inequality. The consequence is that teachers are increasingly forced into a situation of 'epistemological consumerism' in which the kind of choices that exist are from the growing array of curriculum, evaluation and pedagogy hawked around by others. For Van Manen (1977), the danger in this instrumentalist 'expert-user' dichotomy lies in its superficial understanding of both the interpretive and critical processes of teaching and learning.

If, as Apple (1983) argues, Western societies are becoming increasingly caught up in fiscal crises, then mass produced materials become a de facto mechanism for effectively exercising centralized control over schools and trivializing the nature of teachers' work. There is a deskilling process at work whereby teachers are robbed of their creativity and initiative (Apple and Teitelbaum, 1986) and in their place: '... a call for the separation of conception from execution; the standardization of school knowledge in the interest of managing and controlling it; and the devaluaton of critical, intellectual work on the part of teachers and students for the primacy of practical considerations' (Giroux, 1985c, p. 377). In this scheme, teachers are seen as passive recipients who act as 'executors' of 'the laws and principles of effective teaching' (Zeichner, 1983, p. 4). It is precisely this ideology that impregnates the recently released US Department of Education (1986) document *What Works: Research about Teaching and Learning*. While trying to espouse an honest broker role, the document posits normative structures about teaching and learning that standardize pedagogical practice. While making a pretence to objectivity and claims to tentativeness by virtue of including only those research findings '... about which research evidence and expert opinions were consistent, persuasive, and fairly stable over time ...' (p. 1), the document has a broader political agenda — to establish and maintain a conservative and uncritical view of teaching and learning. Recommendations in the form of recipes for action are put for the alleged benefit of teachers, parents and educational communities on topics such as: the virtues of increased homework; the desirability of enhanced time-on-task; the value of hard work; the importance of high teacher expectations; the desirability of direct instruction; memorizing; frequent testing; rigour in subject matter; preparation for the world of work; and the like.

Far from actually emancipating or liberating teachers, corporatist measures like this serve further to entrench feelings of subservience and dependence among teachers. There is no sense in which action of this kind invests teachers with the capacity to explore, understand, and transform their own thinking about the means and the ends of teaching (Smyth, 1984, 1985). Instead, there is a kind of educational consumerism in which the relations are those between 'supplier' and 'consumer' — with educational research acting to amass scientific evidence in support of the need for more 'educational packages' and for their more accurate 'delivery to the consumer' (Illich, cited in Fried, 1980, p. 5).

By reconstruing the nature of teachers' work, as argued in this chapter, so as to emphasize its intellectual nature, it becomes possible to locate changes in teaching within the broader transformations occurring in the workforce generally. We are able to see, for example, how the devaluation of teachers' work (Darling-Hammond, 1985) is part of a more general process of the degradation of labour (Braverman, 1975). It becomes clearer too that the category of the intellectual is helpful in providing '... a theoretical basis for examining teacher work as a form of intellectual labor, as opposed to defining it purely in instrumental or technical terms' (Giroux, 1985c, p. 378). As Greene (1985) argues, once teachers come in touch with their own understandings, confrontations, and lived reality, then they are able to project situations in which their students, in turn, are empowered to make sense of their lived situations. Indeed, once it has become possible to be clearer about the intellectual nature of teachers' labour — and of the critical, creative, and insightful nature of what is required (Smyth, 1987) to develop in children the skills necessary to play active roles as citizens in a democracy (and not to be mere technicians or civil servants) — then '. . . the concept of intellectual [becomes] the basis for interrogating the specific ideological and economic conditions under which intellectuals as a group need to work in order to function as critical, creative human beings' (Giroux, 1985a, p. 28).

References

APPLE, M. (1971) 'The hidden curriculum and the nature of conflict', *Interchange*, 2, 4, pp. 27–40.

APPLE, M. (1975) 'Scientific interests and the nature of educational institutions', in W. PINAR (Ed.), *Curriculum Theorizing: The Reconceptualists*, Berkeley, Calif., McCutcheon.

APPLE, M. (1983) 'Work, gender and teaching', *Teachers College Record*, 84, 3, pp. 611–28.

APPLE, M. and TEITELBAUM, K. (1986) 'Are teachers losing control of their skills and curiculum?' *Journal of Curriculum Studies*. 18, 2, pp. 177–84.

ARONOWITZ, S. and GIROUX. H. (1985) *Education under Seige: The Conservative, Liberal and Radical Debate over Schooling*, London, Routledge and KEGAN PAUL.

BERLAK, A. (1985) 'Back to the basics: Liberating pedagogy and the liberal arts', Paper presented to the annual meeting of the American Educational Research Association, Chicago.

BERLINER, D. (1980) 'The teacher-as-executive: Administering a learning environment', Paper presented to the South Pacific Association of Teacher Education conference, Perth, May.

BRAVERMAN, H. (1975) *Labor and Monopoly Capital*, New York, Monthly Review Press.

BULLOUGH, R. GITLIN, A. and GOLDSTEIN, S. (1984) 'Ideology, teacher role, and resistance', *Teachers College Record*, 86, 2, pp. 339–58.

BUSWELL, C. (1980) 'Pedagogic change and social change', *British Journal of Sociology of Education*, 1, 3, pp. 293–306.

CARR, W. and KEMMIS, S. (1983) *Becoming Critical: Knowing through Action Research*, Geelong, Deakin University Press.

DARLING-HAMMOND, L. (1985) 'Valuing teachers: The making of a profession', *Teachers College Record*, 87, 21, pp. 205–18.

FREIRE, P. (1972) *Pedagogy of the Oppressed*, Harmondsworth, Penguin.

FRIED, R. (1980) *Empowerment vs Delivery of Services*, Concord, N.H., New Hampshire State Department of Education.

GIDDENS, A. (1979) *Central Problems in Social Theory*, Berkeley, Calif., University of California Press.

GIROUX, H. (1979) 'Schooling and the culture of positivism: Notes on the death of history', *Educational Theory*, 29, 4, pp. 263–84.

GIROUX, H. (1981) 'Pedagogy, pessimism, and the politics of conformity: A reply to Linda McNeil', *Curriculum Inquiry*, 11, 3, pp. 211–22.

GIROUX, H. (1983) *Theory and Resistance in Education: A Pedagogy for the Opposition*, Amherst, Mass., Bergin and Garvey.

Giroux, H. (1985a) 'Intellectual labor and pedagogical work: Re-thinking the role of teacher as intellectual', *Phenomenology and Pedagogy*, 3, 1, pp. 20–32.

GIROUX, H. (1985b) 'Critical pedagogy and the resisting intellectual', *Phenomenology and Pedagogy*, 3, 2, pp. 84–97.

GIROUX, H. (1985c) 'Teachers as transformative intellectuals', *Social Education*, May, pp. 376–9.

GIROUX, H. and McLAREN, P.(1986) 'Teacher education and the politics of engagement: The case for democratic schooling', *Harvard Educational Review*, 56, 3, pp. 213–38.

GRAMSCI, A. (1971) *Selections from the Prison Notebooks*, Ed. and trans, Q. HOARE and G. SMITH, New York, International Publishers.

GREENE, M. (1985) 'Teacher as project: Choice, perspective, and the public space', Paper presented to the Summer Institute of Teaching, Teachers College, Columbia University.

HARTNETT, A. and NAISH, M. (1980) 'Technicians or social bandits? Some moral and political issues in the education of teachers', in Woods, P. (Ed.), *Teacher Strategies: Explorations in the Sociology of the School*, London, Croom Helm.

KOHL, H. (1983) 'Examining closely what we do', *Learning*, 12, 1, pp. 28–30.

McLAREN, P. (1986) *Schooling as Ritual Performance*, Boston, Mass., Routledge and Kegan Paul.

RYAN, B. (1982) 'Accountability in Australian education,' *Discourse*, 2, 2, pp. 21–40.

RYAN, B. (1986) 'Revising the agenda for a democratic curriculum', *The Australian Journal of Education*, 30, 1, pp. 66–84.

SCHEFFLER, I. (1986) 'University scholarship and the education of teachers', *Teachers College Record*, 70, 1, pp. 1–12.

SHOR, I. (1980) *Critical Teaching and Everyday Life*, Boston, Mass., South End Press.

SIMON, R. (1984) 'Signposts for a critical pedagogy: A review of Henry Giroux's "Theory and Resistance in Education"', *Educational Theory*, 34, 4, pp. 379–88.

SIMON, R. (1985) 'Critical pedagogy, in HUSEN, T. and POSTLETHWAITE, N. (Eds), *International Encyclopedia of Education: Research and Studies*, London, Pergamon.

SMYTH, J. (1984) 'Towards a "critical consciousness" in the instructional supervision of experienced teachers', *Curriculum Inquiry*, 14, 4, pp. 425–36.

SMYTH, J. (1985) 'Developing a critical practice of clinical supervision', *Journal of Curriculum Studies*, 17, 1, pp. 1–15.

SMYTH, J. (1986) 'Changing what we do in our teaching: Let's stop talking about it', *Australian Journal of Teaching Practice*, 6, 2, pp. 16–31.

SMYTH, J. (1987) *A Rationale for Teachers' Critical Pedagogy: A Handbook*, Geelong, Deakin University Press.

US Department of Education (1986) *What Works: Research about Teaching and Learning*, Washington.

VAN MANEN, M. (1977) 'Linking ways of knowing with ways of being practical', *Curriculum Inquiry*, 6, 3, pp. 205–28.

WHITE, J. (1979) 'The primary teacher as servant of the state', *Education* [UK], 3, 13, pp. 18–23.

ZEICHNER, K. (1983) 'Alternative paradigms in teacher education', *Journal of Teacher Education*, 34, 3, pp. 3–9.

13   Teachers Working with Teachers to Transform Schools

Ann and Harold Berlak

The first question we pose to teachers in a workshop or course is: 'What are the most difficult problems you face as teachers?' The answers we've heard in recent years are remarkably similar: too much paper work, not enough time to teach; lack of discipline; working mothers don't devote enough time to their children; not enough respect for teachers. Our goals are always the same: to help teachers fulfil their role in the democratic process — encouraging critical thought by students and helping them to become 'empowered'. Some may find these objectives offensive because they think pursuing them will only serve to aggravate our social and educational ills; for others these objectives are so often proclaimed as to have become vacuous.

Nevertheless, in a society that professes democracy, critical thought and empowerment are primary objectives of all schooling from pre-school through university. As poverty increases daily around the globe, as work becomes increasingly alienating, and the dangers to the planet multiply, achieving these goals becomes vital for survival. The purpose of teacher education is to help teachers to help their students address these realities. In this chapter we describe our efforts and a specific approach for working collaboratively with teachers to achieve these ends.

Critical thought is a process of freeing oneself from dependence upon take-for-granted ways of viewing and acting in the world, and seriously entertaining and evaluating alternative possibilities. These may be alternative possibilities for understanding and organizing classrooms, for bringing up children, for analyzing literature, or for dealing with the problems of unemployment or terrorism. To evaluate alternative courses of action we must see connections — connections among everyday events, patterns of behaviour, and cultural, social, political, and economic forces. In a phrase, it is to see the relationship of 'micro' to 'macro'.

Empowerment implies contributing to the shaping of society, rather than being subjected to the power of others. It goes beyond critical thought and includes a readiness to act with others to bring about the social conditions that one has chosen through a process of collaborative, critical inquiry. Action requires courage, but it also requires the possession of knowledge and skills necessary to change the situation — a classroom, school, or any other arena of human activity.

If we as teachers hope to encourage critical thought in others, we must engage in it ourselves. Throughout our teaching careers we must participate in an ongoing, collaborative process of re-evaluation of, and liberation from, our taken-for-granted views.

The role of teacher educator, and of teacher education more generally in a democracy, is to help set in motion this process of critical thought and empowerment, or to nurture and help sustain its development. In practice this means that we as teacher educators must ourselves engage in, and stimulate in teachers, a re-evaluation of teaching practices, and of our explicit and implicit views of teaching, students, the nature of knowledge and learning, and the social and political system. It also requires a corresponding process of entertaining alternative and oppositional viewpoints, including some that will be considered subversive. Finally, but of great importance, it includes developing practical ways to express these new understandings in everyday practice through changes in curriculum and pedagogy.

This is, of course, far easier said than done. What makes the critical examination of alternatives difficult is that the process incurs resistance because it involves a re-evaluation of much of what people believe, including what they have learned in their prior schooling and from exposure to the media over their lifetimes and at present, and from most other social interactions as well.

The sources of resistance are personal and structural — that is, the resistance is in us as well as in the particular situations we are in. For example, questioning one's taken-for-granted views about teaching will involve most teachers in the re-evaluation of the notion that teachers are the 'natural' ones to set standards, or that competition is an effective motivator of students. Notions of standards and competition are tightly interwoven with a net of other beliefs that make up the worldview we use to orient us in our daily lives. Questioning such assumptions, therefore, has implications for all the others, and re-examination of any one may threaten to unravel the entire fabric of beliefs and ideas that guide our actions in and outside the classroom.

The structural constraints on independent thought are equally strong — to re-evaluate the role of competition as a motivator, or the locus of control over standards, is to confront, for example, the organization of athletics, the line and command structure within schools, and the hierarchical organization of the workplace outside schools as well.

A Framework and Approach to Collaborative, Critical Inquiry

The challenge is to encourage independent thought and empowerment while overcoming resistance. There is, of course, no one best way to proceed. Over several years we have used a 'dilemma analysis framework' we developed, described in our book *Dilemmas of Schooling: Teaching and Social Change,*[1] to guide critical inquiry. We identified sixteen dilemmas, divided into three sets (see Figure 1). The first set deals with how teachers exercise control; the second focuses on teachers' implicit and explicit views of knowledge and learning; the third focuses on their underlying conceptions of fairness, justice and equality. Looking at teaching through the lenses of the sixteen dilemmas enables teachers to describe and re-evaluate their taken-for-granted practices. Each dilemma poses questions and represents alternative possibilities for teaching.

The dilemma framework rests on an assumption that it is possible for individuals to reflect upon their past and present experience, to come to see the familiar in new ways, and, as a consequence of changed understandings, to change habitual patterns of teaching. By engaging in such inquiries with others, we can come to see that we are not condemned to teach in ways that mindlessly recreate the status quo.

Teachers' patterns of teaching convey meanings to their students. One way of thinking about the role we as teachers play in social continuity and change is to consider the meanings various *patterns* of resolution to the dilemmas convey to succeeding generations — meanings about social control, the nature of knowledge and learning, justice and equality. The questions of how persons — and the society — come to take for granted particular conceptions of what is just, or come to believe some forms of knowledge are of

Ann and Harold Berlak

Figure 1. Dilemmas of Schooling

Control set:

1. 'Whole' child v. child as student — (realms)
2. Teacher v. child control — (time)
3. Teacher v. child control — (operations)
4. Teacher v. child control — (standards)

Curriculum set:

5. Personal knowledge v. public knowledge
6. Knowledge as content v. knowledge as process
7. Knowledge as given v. knowledge as problematical
8. Learning is holistic v. learning is molecular
9. Intrinsic v. extrinsic motivation
10. Each child unique v. children have shared characteristics
11. Learning is individual v. learning is social
12. Child as person v. child as client

Societal set:

13. Childhood continuous v. childhood unique (childhood)
14. Equal allocation of resources v. differential allocation (allocation)
15. Equal justice under law v. *ad hoc* application of rules (deviance)
16. Common culture v. sub-group consciousness

Source: Berlak and Berlak (1981).

special and outstanding worth, can be posed in terms of what patterns of resolution to particular dilemmas convey these meanings. How we as teachers have encouraged, or might encourage, particular traits or viewpoints — autonomy, flexibility, civic courage, for example — can be posed in terms of what patterns of resolution are more or less likely to convey such traits.

The dilemma analysis framework can be used for critical inquiries by groups of teachers or parents and teachers in varied settings. We clarify its use by presenting a rather general outline of how we have used it with teachers who have had little prior exposure to alternative perspectives on teaching or on society more generally.[2]

Using the Dilemmas to Reframe Problems Teachers Pose

The purpose of inquiry is to work collaboratively with teachers to help one another re-view or reformulate teaching problems, and search for alternative ways to overcome them. Each cycle in the inquiry process begins with a problem facing the schools as framed by the teachers. In one recent workshop I[3] began by examining one of the most frequently cited: 'Students' lack of respect for authority.' As the group began to examine this concern it became clear that underlying it was the taken-for-granted assumption that for most a very salient attribute of a good teacher is being a good disciplinarian — having good 'control'.

Such assumptions can be problematized and the entry problems reformulated by framing them in terms of each of the dilemmas. In the early stages of the inquiry the group leader selects the particular dilemmas to use for reformulation of the entry problem several have posed. In the case cited, the problem of not enough respect for authority, I began by deconstructing with their help what they meant or implied by 'respect'. Did they mean they wanted our students to be docile/polite/obedient? At some point I suggested that we could formulate the issue in terms of the dilemma 'Knowledge as given v. knowledge as problematic.' We considered what knowledge, values, or perspectives we as teachers want students to accept without question, as givens; and what we want them to take as problematic. Do we want our students to obey the instructions of all teachers? If not, when do we want them to obey? Under what circumstances? Do we want them to 'know' that Beethoven was great? That Hitler was evil? That instructions from authorities should be followed? Or questioned? To believe that US corporations should divest their South African holdings? That the economy works in terms of supply and demand? That our government is controlled by the people through popular elections?

As we discussed such issues I asked them to consider the possible effects on their students and on the society more generally of the alternative possibilities embedded in these questions. How are our students affected by learning that scientific facts are beyond question, rather than constantly being revised? What kind of society are we shaping when we teach that the primary purpose of US foreign policy is to extend democracy?

Each of the dilemmas can be used as a lens to illuminate alternative possibilities for responding to any entry problem. For example, the problem of respect for authority can also be considered in terms of the 'Childhood continuous v. childhood unique' dilemma. This dilemma poses the question to what extent childhood should be treated as a unique period of life during which young people should be subject to different rules than adults. Does 'respect' mean, perhaps, that children should be expected to obey until they reach a certain age? If so, what age? To what extent should teachers of primary children treat them as mini-adults and encourage them to be sceptical of authority? If so, what aspects of authority should they be encouraged to question? If not all children should be encouraged to question authority at a particular age, then which children? Only the 'brighter' ones? The top track?

As before, the group examines alternative possibilities for resolving the dilemmas by considering the consequences of differing patterns. How will teaching children to obey until, say, the age of 11 affect their willingness to think critically as high school students or as adults? Will a particular pattern of resolution have a different effect on poor than on more affluent children? And so on.

Each cycle concludes with a return to the problem as originally posed, and a consideration of alternative possibilities for addressing it suggested by the prior analyses. We ask how shifts in patterns of resolution to one or more of the dilemmas might address the original problem. In this case would high school students' respect for teachers and for the schooling process increase if teachers placed greater emphasis on childhood continuous — giving students more, not less, responsibility for their education — or if schools conveyed the fascination and delight of pursuing knowledge, by emphasizing more frequently its problematic nature?

Let us consider briefly another problem the teachers in that workshop posed: not enough time to teach. Discussion soon revealed that most of the teachers saw the use of standardized test scores to evaluate their students and themselves as one of the major sources of pressure on their time. We began the cycle with the question why the tests interfere with teaching rather than support it. I suggested we proceed by looking at the problem in terms of the dilemma 'Knowledge as process v. knowledge as content', by asking what are their actual as opposed to their preferred patterns of response to this dilemma. Day by day what is the balance or emphasis between teaching students processes of thinking and analyzing, compared with focusing on students' retention of content or information? Then, upon reflection, what balance do we prefer — what emphasis is best for the kind of society we hope to be creating? What meanings about learning and knowledge will students develop if, year after year, they are tested almost entirely on their knowledge of content rather than thinking processes?

By reformulating the problem in these terms the teachers focused on and clarified the implications of what most already knew from experience to be true — their increasing preoccupation with 'covering' particular realms of knowledge. We then examined alternative possibilities for responding to the entry problem. The response most frequently suggested and easily adopted was to set aside time to teach for the tests and sneak in curricula they valued more whenever possible.

But the teachers recognized that this was really a partial and unsatisfying alternative. We all recognized the need to dig deeper, to look for more satisfactory solutions. As in the case of the teaching cycle discussed above, where teachers wanted to try a more heavily problematic emphasis in their classrooms, we knew the changes we endorsed would not be easy to adopt. To understand why this is so, we moved next to a process we call autobiographical analysis.

Autobiographical Analysis

As we have indicated, problematizing taken-for-granted views and teaching patterns requires unraveling an interwoven net of ideological assumptions. This network of assumptions 'naturalizes' current practices, creating the illusion that the practices are inevitable and/or desirable or correct. Autobiographical analysis is essential for stimulating a re-view of these naturalized assumptions, for clarifying viable alternatives, and for making significant changes in teaching. An autobiographical analysis entails coming to understand how our personal and cultural (including school) experiences have converged to convey the taken-for-grantedness of particular patterns of resolution. By inquiring into the origins of particular patterns or preferences a teacher may come to see, for example, how the almost exclusive emphasis on public knowledge, knowledge as content, and teacher control of standards in her own school experiences, made it nearly inevitable that she would replicate this pattern in her own teaching. Only as we come to view our own actions and preferences as products of historical as well as biographical forces, rather than as natural or inevitable, can we escape the ideological assumptions that underlie teaching practices, and engage in reflective teaching.

Sharing autobiographical analyses also encourages teachers to re-evaluate their own preferred and habitual teaching patterns, because it reveals how different experiences of group members have shaped different postures towards each of the dilemmas. This sharing of experience — learning as social, to use the dilemma language — is crucial not only for the role it plays in helping teachers understand the socially constructed nature of their own practices, but also for gaining the pedagogical knowledge teachers need to enable them to express their intentions in their classroom practice.

Analyses of Schooling Are Not Sufficient

Unfortunately, it is all too easy for autobiographical analyses — in our terms, examination of the origins of particular patterns of resolution — and re-views of the consequences of our classroom practices to be vacuous and to mock the process of independent thought. This will occur if such inquiries are conducted within the taken-for-granted macro frameworks or worldviews of the dominant culture.

Most of us have been exposed almost exclusively in our prior education to economic, political, and social analyses that reinforce and support rather than question the common wisdom, and most are almost entirely unfamiliar with oppositional views. Whether 'well-educated' or not, we are usually unaware of how much of what we take as true about society is really problematic.

Teacher education programs typically reinforce mainstream views. One of the most significant ways they do this is by conveying what Jonathan Kozol calls the 'no connections' view of the social process.[4] They do so by failing to illuminate the relationship of macro to micro, of history to biography, of psychology to sociology, of school to society and to social continuity and change. The way teacher education programs are generally organized reinforces the 'no connections' orientation, segmented as most are into foundations, curriculum, and pedagogical components.

We can neither understand the origins of our own behaviour and successfully engage in autobiographical analyses, nor evaluate alternative patterns of resolution in terms of their effects upon our students, unless we seriously entertain alternative and oppositional historical, political, economic, and social perspectives in society, and see the connections among individual action, schooling, and these perspectives. For example, for teachers to analyze the origins of their tendencies to become bogged down in teaching grammar rather than teaching students to write, they must look beyond the classroom and school, ask why, in spite of the fact that standardized tests cannot assess writing, school systems invest so heavily in standardized tests, and in textbooks and workbooks that focus on mastery of grammatical rules. Inquiries that stop short of considering a range of economic and political perspectives on such questions, including those that draw attention to the role power and privilege play in the definition of valued knowledge, to the requirements of the work world and how these requirements shape schools, to ideology and the imprinting of consciousness, will be superficial and of limited value.

If teachers do not know that environmental and foreign policies are heavily influenced by corporate interests, or that their government routinely engages in efforts to manipulate public opinion, how can they adequately consider whether they should emphasize teaching patterns that lead their students to accept or question authority? If teachers are to question the excessive classroom time devoted to standardized tests and whether the educational and financial costs are justified, they must consider how the current forms of 'objective' tests not only affect students but also serve economically and politically powerful interests — the testing industry, state or district testing and evaluation offices — and how a test-driven pedagogy and curriculum may exacerbate tracking and economic inequalities in the wider economic, social, and political arenas. When, as in this particualr workshop, no students express alternative macro perspectives, the group leader must provide them by offering hypotheses about origins and consequences of teaching practices, and by selecting appropriate readings and films.

Conclusion

We have sketched the initial stages of a continuing process of inquiry. The process is composed of a series of cycles, each beginning with a problem posed by members of the inquiry group, and proceeding with an analysis of the problem for the purpose of finding practical answers. Though by itself the dilemma language is not sufficient, we have shown how it can help orient critical inquiries.

But analysis is not the end of critical inquiry. Its purpose is to encourage teachers to act with others to bring about a more just and humane world. Each cycle is intended to move us closer to transforming schools and society. As the course or workshop draws to a close, teachers are at different points along this road. In workshops such as the one described above, where no-one had had much prior exposure to alternative or oppositional viewpoints, most teachers reach the point where they begin to make plans to shift some patterns of resolution. All were able to select and use as lenses those dilemmas that promised to clarify alternative possibilities for addressing their problems, possibilities previously unexplored because they are connected to ideological assumptions the teachers had never questioned.

In any course or workshop some teachers will move beyond this point. The dilemmas will have become a part of their language, and they will be able to define dilemmas of their own; they will be able to analyze the origins and consequences of their teaching in terms of alternative and oppositional macro perspectives. Having reassessed many of the basic assumptions about school and society that they had previously accepted without question, these teachers will have become transformative intellectuals.[5] They will be ready to join with others to change the institutional and political structures beyond their classrooms that limit them, and to work with the many others, teachers, administrators, teacher educators, and parents, who are already engaged in the ongoing process of critical inquiry in schools, in teacher centres, teacher support groups, and networks to regain control of their own classrooms and to create schools that encourage critical thought and empowerment.

Notes

1 BERLAK, ANN and BERLAK, HAROLD (1981) *Dilemmas of Schooling: Teaching and Social Change*, London, Methuen.
2 The position discussed here is discussed at greater length in chapters 5, 8 and 9 of *Dilemmas of Schooling (ibid.)* This account is based on a theoretical conception that draws upon George Herbert Mead, Georg Lukacs, Paolo Freire, Raymond Williams, and others.
3 The 'I' in this example refers to Ann Berlak.
4 JONATHAN KOZOL (1975) *The Night Is Dark and I Am Far from Home*, New York, Sabury.
5 See STANLEY ARONOWITZ and HENRY GIROUX (1985) *Education under Siege*, South Hadley, Mass., Bergin-Garvey.

14 Teachers, Journals and Collaborative Research

David H. Tripp

This chapter is about the possibility and value of a more symbiotic relationship between practising classroom teachers and teacher educators through a form of collaborative research with substantive outcomes for both educational theory and practice; that is, achieving the development of teachers' professional practice through research, while at the same time enabling researchers to study the classroom processes of schooling. Specifically, the approach outlined has been developed for an in-service course on classroom action research, the required pay-off of which lies, as always, in the possibilities for and effectiveness of action by the teachers in their own classrooms. Fundamentally that is a matter of how teachers and researchers can together engage with classroom practices at a more theoretical level to answer questions of 'what' and 'why' rather than merely of 'how'.

That emphasis on the theoretical is not mere academic indulgence: as I have shown elsewhere, teachers tend to approach their teaching with what may be termed a 'practical problematic' (Tripp, 1984), seeing as problematic only what is to be done; but what one does and how one does it depend upon understanding exactly what is happening and why it happens thus. So in the main section of this chapter I shall endeavour to show how it is possible to use teachers' journal entries to enable teachers and researchers to be active collaborative agents in the struggle to connect the all too often dichotomized realms of theory and practice.

This approach was developed from two major premises: first, to research the hidden curriculum and teachers' practical knowledge, one must find a way of working which monitors teachers in the process of examining, articulating and critiquing the values implicit in their practice, using what is learned from them as data for more formal, public research; second, it is increasingly necessary to offer to teachers some of the responsibility for and benefits of educational research (Tripp, 1986b). Such premises require research strategies which are collaborative in nature and symmetrical in control, outcomes and benefits. Of course, collaboration between educational researchers and teachers has been frequently tried and is much discussed, but very little real collaboration has occurred: rather there have been various degrees of participation by teachers in the work of outside researchers. However well-intentioned, researchers appear to have stopped short of the vital step of sharing control of research with teachers. Elbaz (1983), for instance, effectively excluded her teacher from the choice of the research question, thus casting her as the research object of an outside 'professional' researcher.

In contrast, I believe a collaborative model is one where teachers make their own choices and are active, self-reflective researchers into their own practice and situation. For the outside researcher, working collaboratively means that the teacher's experiences in those roles are the research data. Only then can the learning be symmetrical in that the teacher learns as much as the researcher. However, under those conditions the overall substantive outcomes are markedly different: the teacher's gains are principally in the form of improved practices and understanding of their teaching, whilst the researcher gains data for theorizing about schooling and teachers' practical knowledge. It is in terms of those outcomes and the processes by which they are achieved that the nature of the research must be determined. Collaborative research in the classroom thus takes place between two consenting but somewhat schizophrenic professionals who share a common bond: a teacher-researcher and a researcher-teacher educator. I shall attempt to illustrate one way these people can together relate the theory and the practice of teaching.

Teacher Journals and Theory

Teacher professional journals, in the simplest definition, are similar to a diary in that the teacher mainly writes accounts of what happened; but they are distinguished from a diary by being more focused, reflective and analytic because teacher-researchers try to explain and account for educational phenomena (see Tripp, 1986). Like a diary, journals are primarily for the journalist's own use, which is important in this case, for it is through their choice of what items to record in their journals that the practitioners set the research agenda.

Setting a research agenda in this way is not without difficulties. For instance, one important criticism that is often made to me about working from the journal entries written by teachers is that it inevitably leads to both a very ad hoc in-service course and research programme, and hence to the lack of any coherent understanding by any participant. This criticism is most frequently levelled at the rather random way in which one must approach substantive theories, generally located as they are in other disciplines. It has been suggested for instance that I can do no more than 'raid the cognate disciplines', and in so doing both decontextualize the theories and deny students a parsimonious approach to understanding. The cognate nature of the disciplines is currently much in dispute, however, and they are now regarded less as coherent forms of knowledge (Hirst, 1974) or realms of meaning (Phenix, 1964), than socially constructed, institutionally legitimated conventions serving the vested interests of particular groups (Barnes, 1977). Second, it is precisely because most so-called educational theories are located in specific subject disciplines that they are inapplicable to classroom contexts (Egan, 1983) and many teachers are rightly suspicious of them. Third, beginning with the concerns of teachers as expressed by their journal items is not necessarily incoherent nor does it inevitably lead to superficiality. It is a matter of establishing a dialectic between teachers' and tutor's inputs. Specifically, the tutor not only suggests and negotiates which of all the items generated to pursue, but the very act of concentration upon a particular item or theory tends to elicit other directly related items which can be built into a sequence both enabling and making worthwhile an often detailed incursion into theory.

I present the following account of a tutorial session as an example of the way one can use the unplanned contributions of journal items as a way into explanations and applications of grand theory. This sequence began with a casual, almost apologetic, reference to a journal item:

> Carole had not spoken much during the early part of the session, so I asked her whether she would like to say anything about her week. 'Not really,' she said, 'I just object to the way students take such obvious delight in messing up the lessons that I have planned. It really gets to me sometimes.

I've just written about that.' My immediate response was to suggest that it may well be that her students didn't actually realise that she did plan and prepare lessons ... 'Perhaps,' I said, 'they think that lessons just happen because you are a trained teacher whose job and expertise it is to make such things happen.' Carole replied to the effect that they must know that she planned and prepared lessons, because she told them at the start of each lesson exactly what they were to do that session, and she couldn't do that if she hadn't planned well in advance. We then launched into a discussion about whether the students would read her lesson introduction in such a way. The group split on whether it was so obvious that they couldn't miss it, or whether lessons were so similar in construction not only for each teacher, but also across teachers in the school, that they were taken for granted as habitual routines which needed little or no planning. Carole agreed to ask her students about it, and the following week she reported that the students were amazed that she put time and effort into planning each lesson. (DHT 17.XI.86)

Although it was clearly a matter of both substance and interest, as is so often the case with questions raised by teachers about their practice, so far as I was and am aware, there is no obvious or specific theorization of this matter in the classroom research literature. As we began discussing this subsequent evidence, I introduced a way of regarding the curriculum that was available in the literature, namely that there were at least three curricula in operation at any one time: the formally planned syllabus learning; the informal and unplanned spontaneous learning that is often introduced by students' questions about the formal curriculum; and the hidden curriculum that has been the subject of so much sociological work over the past decade. My speculation was that students would fail to distinguish among or would conflate the three, and so would tend to see all learning as occurring under the most obvious informal category.

We then went on to consider the kind of evidence which might inform such a hypothesis, and found that no teacher in the group ever allowed students to see their lesson plans and programmes; that it was seldom possible to mark off the previously planned from the spontaneous when teaching interactively (further, that in fact teachers would wish actively to disguise one from the other for all sorts of professional reasons); and that other structures (such as the expectation that a relief teacher would be able to continue with an absent teacher's work) would reinforce the impression that one of the skills of an experienced teacher was the ability to teach anything to anyone at anytime. In such ways the discussion of journal items becomes anchored in, but also moves between, an account of theories in the literature and anecdotal evidence from the teachers' practical experience.

To broaden the context and opportunity to contribute to this topic, I suggested that an assumption which we make about situations in which we all participate is that the act of participation necessarily means that all the participants have a common definition and understanding of the situation, which means in effect that we take it for granted that others see the situation in the same way that we do. One result of such an assumption is that we then tend to project our unexamined assumptions onto others who, because they have a very different viewpoint, may not in fact share them.

Judy then contributed an anecdote about a viewpoint which was giving her some bother:

> As she had earlier promised them, Judy took her year 5 class out of school to draw the birds at the harbour. On the day, she stressed to them that the outing was conditional upon their following certain rules, such as staying together, not running on ahead, walking properly and not fooling about. In the event, before they had gone very far, a cry and a wail from the back turned out to be Fiona falling over, grazing her knee and claiming that she had been tripped by Alan. Judy stopped to apply tissues, only to find that the rest of the class had carried on down the street. She sent a runner down to call them back, and, when they had returned to her, told them that as they could not behave they were returning to school. A few days later, another teacher was doing some language extension work with Rosemary's class, and she asked them to recount a recent incident that they felt strongly about. She was tape recording the lesson, so, because they talked about how angry they were with Judy about the non-visit to the harbour, the other teacher passed the tape on to Judy. Judy found that the students were very resentful about the whole matter, saying:
>
> 1 She had hay fever and so was only looking for any excuse to cancel the whole thing;

2 She made a quite unnecessary fuss over Fiona, when normally she would have simply given her a tissue and told her to get on;

3 She had told them to walk on in front of her so she could see them all, and as she hadn't told them to stop, they'd simply carried on as told;

4 They'd not run on, but had come back as soon as she asked them to.

It was, Judy rather ruefully said, all quite devastatingly true, but valuable in that they had surprised her by demonstrating how perceptive they were, and how cogently they could express their comments. She had also found the substance of this feedback useful if somewhat salutory, and she suggested that it might be a good idea to find out on a more regular basis what her students thought of her actions. (DHT 20.IX.86)

The analysis of journal items is not, and should not always be, a matter of original theorizing, though as I suggested with the previous journal entry, because the so-called theories of education generally have little applicability to classrooms, one does often have to do just that. With reference to the idea of collaboration, if one is working with practising teachers, then the emphasis should be upon the value of theory to their understanding of their journal items, and not, as academics can all too easily tend to view it, the value of teachers' journal items as supporting data for a particular theory in the form of instances and exemplifications. It is not a matter of introducing theory with a prepared disquisition upon a known theory, moving on to an invitation to the teachers to contribute items to which the theory might usefully apply (although that was, I incidentally confess, the way I was operating a few years ago). Rather, it is a matter of the academic dealing with the concerns of the teachers as they are raised in their journals, using the insights of whatever theory might be usefully applied.

The approach can make life difficult for an academic, but it does not mean that one has to be able instantly to produce intellectually adequate accounts of any relevant theory straight off the top of the head, so to speak. It is usually sufficient to point out that there is a theory that would suggest a certain analysis, and then, if it is felt to be important, to follow up the incident with an account of the theory and a detailed analysis of the incident in the next session.

Or, depending upon the group, ask them to do that for themselves during the week.

In this case I took the former course, and at the time merely stated that it would be useful to deal with the fact that Rosemary's students were not telling her about her teaching through the theory of communicative competence. This I merely introduced by suggesting that some theorists would view her problem as a question of whether there was something about the structure of her communicative relationships with her students which resulted in her not normally having access to the evaluations of her teaching that they appeared to be constantly making in any case. As I then put it, the idea of communicative competence suggested that people often did not speak, not because they were linguistically incapable of doing so, but because they were, by one thing or another, prevented from speaking, and in some cases, literally not allowed to.

Note that in order to pursue that theory, I chose not to pursue the other obvious matter raised by the incident, namely the processes by which Judy was making judgments about the intention and significance of her students' actions. Specifically demonstrated by this case was the way in which her expectation of trouble led her to misclassify the intent behind their actions, thereby treating them unfairly in their eyes. My decision to ignore that matter in order to introduce the idea of communicative competence presents another point. As a tutor, one finds such choices are as inevitable as they are common, nevertheless, they too must be submitted to critique. In this case I justified my decision on the grounds that, first, Judy was already consciously critical of the lack of feedback from her students and was wondering what and/or if (and the 'what' and the 'if' are always mutually constraining) to do about it. Second, because it was still fairly early in the course, something that was already well theorized in the literature and for which a whole range of practical outcomes were already available seemed to be more appropriate than the critique of an aspect of her teaching.

In the following session I reintroduced the matter of communicative competence with a carefully prepared account of some of the more relevant features. I explained that it was quite clear that whereas the students were in certain respects competent to provide the kind of feedback which Judy found valuable, they did not do so directly or intentionally, and indeed, it was only under very exceptional and chance circumstances that they had been able to do so at all. Pointing out something like this to a teacher can be done more easily if there is a theoretical framework and a language in which to do it. With that in mind I had previously introduced this group to the Berlaks' book on the dilemmas of teaching. In that currently underestimated but very important contribution to the theory of teaching, Berlak and Berlak (1981) show how teaching can be seen to consist of a series of dilemmas. How a person acts in a particular situation is principally determined by how they perceive the choices they have. So, what dilemmas a teacher will perceive and how they will resolve them will be greatly influenced by who they are, their personal and professional histories, their values, motivations and aspirations.

Partly because we had already been using the Berlaks' dilemma language (so it was an analytic device with which the group felt comfortable), and also because it offered a direct but neutral way into the analysis of an incident (as it presented a problem definition of the situation rather than an evaluative one), I continued by pointing out that, as was typical of a dilemma situation, Judy was both attracted and repelled by the incident. The dilemma she faced was whether to enable her students to make and then to provide her with their evaluations of her teaching (thereby opening herself up to what might be a process of critique which might generate unknown side-effects and perhaps a life of its own); or whether to prevent her students from making and expressing their evaluations of her teaching (thereby shutting herself off from what might on occasions be a source of very useful information).

However, to return to the main point about the use of theory in journal analysis, we resumed our discussion with a pooling of experience and judgments about the issue. We then moved on to the theory of competence in communication, seeing it as a very rich one because it has been developed in different ways in the work of three major theorists. Considering the incident from these perspectives, we found first that in Chomsky's (1965) principally cognitive and grammatical sense of competence it is obvious that the students were competent to generate the linguistic forms necessary to convey clearly and forcefully their views to Judy. That much is demon-strated by the fact that they did so to another teacher. However, the fact that they did not do so to Judy directly, but only through the mediation of that other teacher, could only be explained by a theory which had the capacity to treat such facts as social and political phenomena. Because that capacity is a feature of both Hymes' and Habermas' notions of communicative competence, their theories could be used to inform this incident.

Although the theories of Hymes and Habermas are related and overlap, they have different emphases: Hymes would point to the other than linguistic though still essentially individual social competencies which form the set of preconditions necessary for the students to communicate their perceptions directly and intentionally to their teacher; Habermas would point to the political nature of the institutional constraints upon the relationships between the two parties.

It was Hymes' demand that even 'on its own terms, transformational theory must include more than the grammatical' (1971, p. 57), that led him to formulate fourfold requirements for communicative competence:

> (a) systematic potential — whether and to what extent something is not yet realised, and, in a sense, not yet known; ...
> (b) appropriateness — whether and to what extent something is in some context suitable, effective, or the like; (c) occurrence — whether and to what extent something is done; (d) feasibility — whether and to what extent something is possible, given the means of implementation available. (Hymes, 1971, p. 157)

In the first two of these four terms the students were communicatively competent, and in the other at least partially. Clearly they had the 'systematic potential' to generate the communication in a linguistic sense, and they also had a sound and detailed understanding of the governing rules which structured the situation; that much is shown by the way in which the substance of their message was an evaluation of it. So they had something to say and the language in which to say it. Second, they managed the matter of appropriateness well too, for they responded according to the social context offered by the rules of the task set by the second teacher. They were in fact so competent in that respect that one could say they appropriated the task to their own ends. It is harder to judge the extent to which they were also competent with regard to 'occurrence' and 'feasibility', because although they did effectively communicate with their teacher, it was not altogether of their doing: it was more a matter of chance and an intermediary. But as communicative competence is a question of degree rather than a dichotomy, it seems that in Hymes' as well as Chomsky's terms, these students were competent.

The fact that they did not, and by all accounts could not, communicate their ideas directly to their teacher would seem therefore to turn on the political, that is, on the matter of power in the teacher-pupil relationship. It was to that aspect of communicative competence that Habermas (1968) turned his attention. Briefly, he contrasted 'systematically distorted communication' with an 'ideal speech situation'. In the latter, he suggested that limits to or closure of dialogue would not be due to constraints such as the power of one party, lack of access by or to participants, or shortage of time. In an ideal speech situation the opportunity to select and perform would be symmetrical among participants, as would the opportunity to assume particular roles, so that through rational processes, mutual understanding and thereby agreement would obtain. However, most speech situations are distorted in a systematic way, by history, interests, status, rituals or accident, to favour one party or the other.

Although Habermas thought in terms of the importance of the anticipation of an ideal speech situation, rather than the possibility of it being frequently if ever realized, in all of these regards classroom communication is one of the most severely distorted. The teacher tends to decide who is able to talk when, to whom, for how long and about what. Because a teacher could choose to negotiate such procedures, or to allow the students to control them entirely for themselves, it is the teacher who also decides these matters. That Judy found herself without access to her students' evaluations of her teaching behaviour must be seen as almost entirely within the realm of her choice, and therefore within the realm of her action. In that respect, Habermas indicates very clearly the criteria for ideal speech situations; his theory offers a starting point and guide to the changes that would have to occur in a classroom if students were to participate more democratically.

One has to be careful about the language one uses in matters and moments such as this, because our tendency is to translate what are essentially personally made professional decisions, and conditional upon circumstance, into generalized normative ones. It is all too easy for the group to say to Judy that she should now do this or that to enable her students to provide feedback to her. If that is allowed to happen, then the whole effect of the journal entry, the willingly taken risks and professional self-exposure, has merely been a means of increasing the level of outside control of a teacher's judgment by others, concomitantly decreasing the professional autonomy of the teacher concerned, and hence the collaborative nature of the enterprise.

The Berlaks' dilemma language helps, because if one has established that what one does about any one dilemma in a particular situation is the product of other decisions about a whole chain of other dilemmas pertaining to and resolved in a whole series of other situations and events, then the choice of whether Judy would now go on to action research ways of gaining more access to her students' existing evaluations, whether she should not only do that but also teach them how to make such evaluations and provide them with the opportunity for increased activity in that respect, must remain just that, an open choice, and one which Judy alone would be competent to make. So it is at that point that the teacher again takes control of the practical implications of the research by deciding whether to change a practice or not.

But the tutor-researcher does not necessarily cease to be involved in the action. In this case, for instance, were the teacher to decide to action research how she could utilize the evaluations her students were making of her teaching normally, naturally and in any case, the researcher would not only be a 'critical friend' (Ingvarson, 1986) to her planning, but would also continue to support her in monitoring the change of practice. The tutor, by documenting as a publishable study the precise structures she created in order to do that, the rules governing their operation, and the outcomes of the changes, would then have a local and bounded but traditional research outcome to their work. If the tutor-researcher were working in a similar situation to mine, he or she would support and make a case study of an action research project immediately, and then, over a far longer period, attempt to cumulate and generalize across person, time and space, the findings of a number of such bounded instances.

In this case, Judy decided not to pursue the matter immediately: she had, in her words, 'Only mentioned it because it seemed so interesting.' Although if she had decided to continue with it the researcher would have had an excellent opportunity to put some of Habermas' notions to empirical test, the lack of further development in this instance does not mean that the researcher has gained little from the collaboration. On the contrary, insofar as I was involved in this case at all, the benefit to my professional practice was considerable in furthering and deepening my understanding of a particular theory and way of working.

With regard to my research, it did perhaps represent a very small increment of data and understanding by itself; nevertheless, it was one which has contributed to my 'pure' research in several ways. First, having had it drawn to my attention, I have made a note to observe and investigate the communicative structures in the next classroom case study I perform. Second, I have been working for some time on the features of classrooms that need to be included in a case study to provide what is termed in anthropology an account 'comparable' with other case studies (Tripp, 1985), and communicative competence requires consideration in that regard. Third, the raw data always remain for further analysis and cumulation: I also have a new case record. Although it is at present a solitary instance of communicative competence in classrooms, over the years I expect to collect others so that I might contribute to the empirical development of the theory. Fourth, the incident is an extension of our still very limited knowledge of the hidden curriculum: we need more published accounts of incidents which reveal its presence and nature. This example supports two principles which I am currently investigating: first, that because teaching is a cultural activity there must always be a hidden curriculum of one kind or another; second, that because the hidden curriculum is an enacted cultural structure there will always be a number of different features hiding, confusing and contradicting as well as supporting and reinforcing any particular values position. This incident is very important in revealing an ideological contradiction, which gives rise to the tension creating dilemmas of teaching. Last but by no means least, I, like most educational researchers, also teach a great deal. Because this instance originated within my own teaching it possesses a verity and immediacy which makes it excellent workshop material to be used with other students.

Conclusion

It is not easy to conclude a chapter in which I have simply tried to illustrate a way of working and the outcomes that may be achieved. If there is an argument or narrative for which a conclusion would be appropriate, however, then it has to do with developing future possibilities for the collaborative research process outlined. I would emphasize two major strengths of the approach: first, for teachers it facilitates active involvement in the generation of a more systematic and shared (and thus scientific and objective) understanding of their own practice, the effects of which not only indicate improvements to it, but also tend to enhance the professional standing of teaching and teachers. Second, for researchers it ought to lead to a better theoretical understanding of the culture, site and person-specific nature of classrooms in particular and schooling in general.

Acknowledgments

My thanks to my partners in this work: Rosemary Brown, Maureen Chandler, Peter Fowlie, Paul Ganderton, Maralyn Hand, Peg Malcolm, Jeanette McCahon, Linda Moran, Maureen Thompson.

References

BARNES, B. (1977) *Interests and the Growth of Knowledge*, London, Routledge and Kegan Paul.

BERLAK, A. and BERLAK, H. (1981) *Dilemmas of Schooling*, London, Methuen.

CHOMSKY, N. (1965) *Aspects of the Theory of Syntax*, Cambridge, Mass., Massachusetts Institute of Technology Press.

EGAN, K. (1983) *Education and Psychology*, London, Methuen.

ELBAZ, F. (1983) *Teacher Thinking*, London, Croom Helm.

HABERMAS, J. (1968) *Knowledge and Human Interests*, London, Heinemann.

HIRST, P.H. (1974) *Knowledge and the Curriculum*, London, Routledge and Kegan Paul.

HYMES, D. (1971) 'Sociolinguistics and the ethnography of speaking', in AIDENER, E. (Ed.), *Social Anthropology and Language*, London, Tavistock, pp. 157–63.

INGVARSON, L. (1986) 'With critical friends, who needs enemies? in FENSHAM, P. *et al.*, *Alienation from Schooling*, London, Routledge and Kegan Paul, pp. 344–50.

PHENIX, P. H. (1964) *Realms of Meaning*, New York, McGraw-Hill.

TRIPP, D. H. (1984) 'From autopilot to critical consciousness: Problematizing successful teaching', Paper presented at the Bergamo conference, Dayton, Ohio.

TRIPP, D. H. (1985) 'Case study generalisation: An agenda for action', *British Educational Research Journal*, 11, 1, pp. 33–43.

TRIPP, D. H. (1986a) 'The teachers' professional journal: An illustrated rationale for teacher/researcher partnership in curriculum research', Paper presented at the annual conference of the American Educational Research Association, San Francisco.

TRIPP, D. H. (1986b) 'Excellence in teaching: The ideology of educational research', Paper presented at a symposium, Problematizing Excellence in Teaching, at the annual conference of the South Pacific Association for Teacher Education, Perth, Western Australia.

15 Teachers' Emerging Texts: The Empowering Potential of Writing In-Service

Janet L. Miller

> The teacher can no longer simply accept what is transmitted by 'experts' and feel he is properly equipped to interpret the world. He cannot even rely on the authority of accumulated knowledge or the conventional wisdom on which so many people depend. He must make decisions of principle, which may make necessary a definition of new principles, more relevant norms and rules. Therefore, he must become accustomed to unconventional presentations of situations around him, to ways of talking with which textbooks cannot deal. Only if he breaks with fixed, customary modes of seeing can he remove the blinders of complacency. Only then can he take responsibility for his pursuits of norms and meanings. (Maxine Greene, *Teacher As Stranger*)[1]

Pre-Text: An Introduction

Teachers are story-tellers; daily, in the lounge, in the lunchroom, in faculty meetings after school, they spin out interwoven and episodic tales of Jim's clowning, Sara's resistance, or the creeping laziness of the entire third period class. Every teacher has a version of the drama, terror and history of life in the classroom, and for a brief time that collective life seems a bit more manageable through the re-creation and sharing of these ongoing and often embellished sagas.

As I watched the thirty-two high school teachers assemble for our first meeting of the Writing across the Curriculum in-service course, what struck me was that teachers' story-telling often becomes anthologized, separated and automatically indexed into genres of subject matter and grade level. These people lingered by the coffee pot, clutching brief cases and shuffling bulging canvas bags, carriers of students' papers and students' stories. As they filled their cups again, hoping to store energy for the day ahead, they slowly filtered by one another and grouped themselves into comforting clumps of subject matter specialists, still telling stories of the social studies roleplayer or the budding scientist who exploded eighth period.

As instructor in this ten-week liaison, I was faced with a living montage of the structure of the disciplines: teachers identified with the subjects they teach and filled with the stories of others. To break through these structures of objectified knowledge, to collapse the myth that the disciplines as well as the teachers themselves were immutable entities became the point of our work together. It was the refocusing of the story-telling that provided the frame for teachers' emerging texts, for the telling of their own stories within their evolving conceptions of themselves as active creators in both the curriculum and writing processes.

I approached the teaching of this in-service course with apprehension grounded in my own resistance and struggles to find a voice within my writing. By extension, my research in writing thus far had focused upon explorations of teachers' self-concept as writers and had emphasized the personal and reflective nature of such inquiry as one means of understanding the potential of writing as discovery for both teachers and their students.[2] These case studies had allowed me to explore teachers' conceptions of themselves as writers; further, they had provided a context in which to examine the extent to which such self-concept, moulded by teachers' own schooling experiences and biographical situations, influenced the attitudes and approaches with which they then presented writing experiences to their students.

As I began work with these high school teachers, I wished to extend my initial case study research by involving the teachers in their own active pursuits of meaning. Further, I hoped to enhance such pursuit by involving them not only in their own self-reflective research but also in classroom research. Educational research can become a liberating and empowering activity by involving teachers in the research process itself.[3] Such involvement might lead not only to further understandings about the writing process, for example, but also, and more importantly, to teachers' sense of efficacy.

James Britton sees the day-to-day work of teachers as embodying the concept of research as discovery, and calls the interactive nature of teaching a 'quiet form of research'. Britton argues that teachers are researchers; every classroom interaction becomes a form of inquiry that leads teachers to some further discovery, reflection or inference.[4] Positing teachers as researchers allows them to participate in the dialectic of theory and practice that may contribute to their empowerment.

Thus, as I faced these teachers, I was convinced of the potentially liberating nature of our interactions. I saw the in-service context as providing a variety of ways in which together we could interpret and enact the concept of process. Further, by establishing the nature of the in-service course as collaborative, I hoped that together we could move the traditional conceptions of in-service from a passive to an active conception of involved and concerned peers. The writing process and its attendant applications to subject areas beyond the English classroom comprised the 'content' of the course. At the same time that content could become metaphor not only for the processes of reflection, discovery and action in which teachers could engage, personally and collectively, but also for the larger conceptions of curriculum and its creation that our work would address.

Mayher, Lester and Pradl describe the kernel of this potentially enlarging metaphor:

> The composing process is essentially a meaning-making process. As the writer begins percolating and drafting, there's often only a vague sense of intention or purpose. The full thrust of ideas has not yet emerged and part of the cycling back and forth among the percolating, drafting and revising involves the writer in shaping purposes and refining intentions.... The meaning that thus emerges from one's text, and has been the focus of rereading it, is a result of this forward-backwards motion of the composing process. This interaction — returning to reread the text from a different angle of vision — plays a key role in helping the writer push forward to create meaning.[5]

Sondra Perl has characterized this forward-backwards interaction:

> Retrospective structuring ... refers to all of the backward movements in the process. They're things that do not follow any linear logic. People go back to the words on the page in order to go forward.... And they also go back to a 'felt sense,' a feeling they have about the topic that's not yet in

words. It's a kind of vague, fuzzy intention they have. . . .
The other term, the other direction, is what I call 'projective
structuring.' This is also a mental posture, a way writers
need to take their audience into account. I see this as an
outward looking, forward looking, projecting out to call up
a sense of one's audience.[6]

These constructs identified within the composing process are analogous to parts of the method of *currere* proposed by Pinar as one
means of situating one's self at the centre of the study of educational
experience. In Pinar's positing, curriculum is defined as one's educational experience not only of the text per se but also of all interactions and interpretations that surround one's learning activity. Our
study of writing as a way of learning and discovery in the various
disciplines may become embedded within a larger study of ourselves
as we are engaged in that study of writing. Pinar describes this
method of examining the nature of one's educational experience:

One responds to educational situations, whether they be
artifacts like poems or actors like teachers or peers or com-
binations of these in certain understandable ways. We can
decipher the educational meaning of the present by studying
this response. The method is . . . (a) regressive, because it
involves descriptions and analysis of one's intellectual
biography or, if you prefer, educational past; (b) progressive, because it involves a description of one's imagined
future; (c) analytic, because it calls for a psychoanalysis of
one's phenomenologically described educational present,
past, and future; and (d) synthetic, because it totalizes the
fragments of educational experience (that is to say the response and context of the subject) and places this integrated
understanding of individual experience into the larger political and cultural web, explaining the dialectical relation
between the two.[7]

The regressive and progressive processes of *currere*, in particular, encompass the retrospective and projective structuring of the
composing process, and provide an enlarging framework within
which to view writing and the teaching of writing as parts of a
discovery process that illuminates individual meaning-making. The
writing process is a microcosm of those processes which allow the
writer, the learner, the teacher to return again and again to the text
of his or her educational experience, to reread that text from new

angles of vision, and to 'push forward to create meaning.'

These, then, were my conceptions and expectations for our work together in this writing in-service course. At the same time I was aware of the difficulties and the resistance that might cloud my vision of our experiences together. I, too, always had rotated through the room to my fellow English colleagues, exchanging stories of our latest Regents impasse, and hoping to get a set of papers graded before the meeting started. Further, I knew that the ongoing critiques of education and educators continued to perpetuate not only the fragile morales of teachers but also the constant pressures on them to perform via their students' achievements. I hoped to balance such perceptions and deeply-felt pressures by drawing upon the analyses that continue to emerge, particularly from those working in curriculum studies,[8] and which focus upon the structural and functional characteristics of schools that perpetuate larger issues of control, hierarchical order, and submersion of individual autonomy.

However, as I began my introductory remarks and then inquired about the expectations and needs of these quietly waiting and clearly apprehensive teachers, the balance which I so clearly had articulated in my internal monologue wavered in the rush of teacher requests for linear prescriptions, neatly packaged for immediate diffusion. My carefully constructed conceptual dialectics of theory and practice, self and others, writing and discovery, teacher and researcher, unraveled as I realized that I had replicated the very tactics that I thought I was attempting to redress. I had created the conceptual frameworks of our work together, and thus had violated the very processes to which I was committed. I had perpetuated the hypocrisy by deciding the nature and direction of our work together, rather than allowing our interactions to evolve as part of the larger 'pushing forward to create meaning.' While I resisted the prescriptive and packaged nature of these teachers' initial requests, I also realized that I could not expect these teachers to begin to tell their own stories until I had erased the predetermined plot-line and characterization in my own.

We only could begin then with the priorities that these teachers clearly had enacted in the structuring of themselves into subject matter specialists. Further, the title of the in-service course itself reified the conception of separate disciplines whose content and modes of inquiry could be learned through the process of writing. My script had included analysis of such conceptions of curriculum so as to move beyond epistemological bases to the broader vistas offered by curriculum conceptions that acknowledged the relevance of social, human and personal themes;[9] however, we could move to such examinations only if we together roughed out a draft that might include such conceptual revisions. Our work together, like the composing process itself, became a series of explorations and discoveries of our individual and collective emerging texts.

Teachers' Emerging Texts

Teachers' memories of their first writing experiences as students comprised our first step in these regressive and retrospective processes. I shared memories, briefly sketched in a journal entry, of my eighth grade English teacher who formed grammar teams and had us run relay races to diagram sentences at the blackboard. He coached us from the side of the room screaming, 'Adverb, adverb,' or admonishing us to remember the rightful place of the direct object. As I described the perpetual knot in my stomach that this 'fun' approach to the teaching of grammatical structures had created, the teachers began to smile, reconstructing their own variations on this theme. The translation of these memories into initial journal entries became a natural extension which eased the tension of this newly formed collective.

Some were willing to share recollections of their student writing experiences. The following is an excerpt from an English teacher's journal:

> Earliest of all my recollections is that of Mother Lucia talking at me from behind wire-rimmed glasses, through whitewashed picket fence teeth. When the writing was good, she said, 'Very nice, Bernard.' When the writing was not so good, Hell enlarged its mouth to receive me. By the time I was twelve, I had learned to play it safe.

A social studies teacher expressed the fears that characterized many of these teachers' memories of writing:

> Most likely, I could have written a book entitled *The Fear of Writing*. I had such bad experiences in my elementary years. I was always afraid to write. I had a fear of being corrected grammatically. In fact, this was all I thought writing was — grammar. No-one ever asked me to write down my feelings.

These recollections capture the consensus experience of writing as a series of mechanical and linear drills, culminating in a grammatically correct and finished product. Many teachers simply could not recall learning to write in the same way that they vividly could remember the reading groups and their 'blue-bird' participation in them.

As we shared these early recollections, many teachers began to express not only their lack of confidence in their own writing but also their apprehensions regarding this in-service experience. While curious about the concept of writing as discovery, many concurrently were attending with the idea that this course would be good for them, much in the way that cough medicine, vegetables and practising the piano would make us stronger and better people.

Teachers' negative experiences with writing and the accompanying resistance of many to the in-service course per se thus created the focus of our initial explorations. We opened each successive meeting with journal writing; while I encouraged the sharing of entries and read from my own journal periodically, I did not require the exposing of any journal reflections. I wished only at this point to encourage these teachers to write. Many later revealed that this private journal writing constituted the first time and place in which they had been able to write in any type of reflective manner. Often these reflective entries did not focus upon issues of schooling or pedagogy but rather upon personal incidents and feelings with which they were grappling. The retrospective and larger regressive processes emerged within these contexts, as I continued to encourage reflection upon their early memories of school writing.

A science teacher noted the cumulative effects of these micro and macro processes:

> The time in the beginning of each class when we are given the opportunity to express ourselves on paper shows me writing needs to be incorporated into my routine. The more often pen is set to paper, the easier it becomes. The scare of the emptiness of paper and mind is lessened.

To enhance their reflections upon the development of their concepts of writing and themselves as writers, I requested that the teachers collect samples of their writing from as early in their schooling experiences as possible. Some brought in scrapbooks compiled by proud parents; we poured over neatly penned notations next to 'The Black Cat Poem', Halloween, 1953, or 'Alex's Speech, Third Grade, 1950, as Washington Crossing the Delaware'. Children again, they recalled the fear of reciting in front of the class or the embarrassment as whiskers fell one by one from the Halloween cat mask. Teachers' own texts were emerging and were becoming part of the larger story that collectively we were penning. One teacher expressed his delight in the present story creation: 'Praise God! No examples of my past writing exist. All destroyed, they cannot indict me. I can start afresh. A born-again writer, my sins have been thrown into the sea of forgetfulness.'

As the weekly sessions evolved, we utilized our writing reflections as basis for approaches to writing within specific classroom contexts. We constantly attended to the paradox of student resistance to writing as the mirror of our own fears and reluctance to incorporate writing into learning and teaching experiences. Thus every technique or approach that we explored and our responses to it became context for our own class writing. We wrote in pairs, standing and staring at brown paper taped to the walls, brainstorming clusters of ideas and topics which appeared as splotches of red and green and blue magic-markers, connected by circles and arrows. We practised talk/write, and peer group editing and zero drafts. Throughout, we all noted, in discussion as well as in journal entries, the difficulties we experienced in these activities. Those difficult spots were differently located for each of us, obviously, depending upon prior experiences and conceptions; but instead of ignoring or moving quickly through these rough areas, we concentrated on them as further revelation of individual points in the retrospective and prospective structuring of writing as well as the regressive and progressive analysis of that educational experience. In such a forward and backwards processing we were able to transcend the categorization of activities as appropriate for social studies as opposed to mathematics, for example, and we emerged not with lists of subject-specific writing exercises but rather with the initial sketches and drafts of possible integration and interaction among the personal, social and contextual nature of teaching and learning.

The Text of In-Service

Louise Wetherbee Phelps argues for an integrative theory of composition that acknowledges '... the cooperative enterprise whereby writers and readers construct meanings together, through the dialectical tension between their interactive and interdependent processes.'[10] While she develops a model of the interactions between texts and readers as basis for an integrative concept of coherence, she draws attention to the shared experiential frames that permit us to comprehend socially shared ideas of possible or typical objects, facts or situations. She takes the reader's perspective in her examination of coherence, and while she acknowledges the incompleteness of the theory without the writer's view, she does illuminate an important metaphoric shift toward a more subjective and deeply contextualized view of written language:

> It is not simply a question of taking into account the rhetorical motives and functions of writing as social action, but of recognizing that written thought — thought which emerges through writing into situational contexts — is radically social and intersubjective through its very constitution as a discourse. The metaphor of writing as creating an autonomous meaning-object focuses attention on the subjectivity of the writer and handles the social nature of language largely as a property of the finished object to affect an audience. The new metaphor leads us to ask how texts effect the joint construction of meaning as a basis for complex negotiations between discoursers over attitude, belief, and action in the world.[11]

Whether the text is the formalized knowledge of the disciplines or the teacher's notes to herself as she approaches the seventh period chemistry lab, these texts become cuing systems that can '... evoke performances from its readers that are both bound and free, receptive and interpretive.'[12] If teachers have experienced writing as a means of reflection and analysis of their own situational contexts as teachers, then that larger form of text becomes the point of possible interaction and interpretation among the teacher, the student, and the subject matter content. In this way, content is not reified as objective entity and curriculum becomes a part of the processes of teaching and learning. Neither writing nor curriculum is conceived as linear and sequential product, but rather reflects the dynamic interactions and 'joint constructions of meaning' that truly can empower both teacher and student.

So too, by conceiving of text not only as content but also as metaphor for teachers' and students' experiencing of that content, the analogy is extended to include what Phelps calls 'virtual discourse time' which carries the reader '... forward on a moving point of focused attention, alternately looking backward to the text's "past" and ahead to its "future".'[13] Further:

> The design of a text — its fully realized and relatively fixed coherence as a meaning-object — stabilizes for the reader only in retrospect (and even then it is always subject to reinterpretation).... Design is characteristically timeless, independent both of the virtual time in which the thought process and action of a discourse evolve and the real time lived by the reader and writer. Design for the reader is the product of an effort to step back from the immediacy of ongoing integrations to put the textual meaning at a distance and contemplate it.[14]

To encourage teachers to become readers and writers of their own texts is to acknowledge the concurrent necessity of a 'timeless' aspect for the creation of that text, a space in which they may step back and contemplate the coherence of its past as well as its future. This requires the acknowledgment of the retrospective and prospective nature of teaching as well as of writing; further, this requires the synthesis of regressive and progressive analysis of teachers' texts so as to enable teachers to engage with other teachers and with students in the joint constructions of meanings and in negotiations 'over attitude, belief and action in the world.'

Ten weeks of engagement with these thirty-two teachers did contribute, in a sense, to that necessary suspension of time. The in-service course itself, organized into two sessions during the school day because of the split schedule of the overcrowded high school, allowed the teachers to step away from their daily pressures and routines, to explore and reflect upon possibilities for themselves and their students, and then to step back into the press of students in hallways and classrooms, now reading the texts that they constantly created together from a new angle of vision. Our working together, over a sustained period of time, enabled each of us to reclaim our actions in the world through the redefinition of not only the constructs of writing and curriculum but also our roles in these constructions of meaning.

Further, the in-service context provided a time and place in which teachers could reflect upon the lives that they brought to the acts of writing and teaching; it allowed for the spontaneous telling of their own stories, for what James Britton calls 'shaping at the point of utterance.'[15] It is at this point of spontaneous meaning-making, emerging and moving forward from that suspended point of reflection and contemplation, that teachers, in focusing upon and sharing their emerging texts, enact for their students the potential of learning itself as process and discovery.

A teacher of special education students writes of changes:

> On the first day that I attended the writing class, I was nervous about writing, and especially of sharing my feelings and writings with my classmates. However, even though I may not be a better writer than before, I don't get nervous about it any more. I'm still not as good as I'd like to be, but my thoughts seem to flow more freely.

An English teacher for fifteen years noted: 'To see teachers become excited over their writing and to see them talking with each other about it all and rushing back to use it with their students and even their families — made this an enlightening experience.'

As the teachers began to share their writing experiences with their students and provide opportunities for students to write in class, not just as a way to reiterate course content but rather as a 'central humanistic way of knowing',[16] they also began to move beyond the confines of separated and reified notions of curriculum and of their roles in perpetuating such reification. They began to acknowledge what James Moffett has termed the 'very dangerous' possibilities of transforming culture inherent in the writing process:

> As a way of carrying one's thought beyond received ideas, writing ... may change youngsters. Composing, after all, means putting together. Composing is making sense. An authentic author is not a plagiarist or a paraphraser but someone who puts things together for himself or herself.... But if adult society as a whole fears losing the minds of the young, teachers in particular fear losing their own minds if they try to teach the way they know they should. They fear the loss of classroom control and of status if they allow youngsters to choose the content and form of what they read and write. Making students active and teachers reactive seems like a gratuitous relinquishing of power. But empowering others is the teacher's job.[17]

By experiencing the retrospective and prospective structuring of their own writing experiences, and by engaging in the regressive and progressive analysis of those experiences, teachers could begin to encourage their students to engage in those same processes. At that point of relinquishing content and form in favour of process, teachers empowered not only their students but also themselves. A mathematics teacher describes the change in her ninth grade class:

> These kids were consolidated from overenrollments in other classes (my St. Elsewhere group) in mid-October and were filled with hostility 'til January. In the last few weeks, I've introduced the journal writing and suggested that we try to use this as a way to talk with one another about this class. Now they insist on their ten minutes daily of journal writing and I think that we've come together as a class.

A special education teacher describes his first attempt at employing journal writing with a student:

> This student was arrested for breaking and entering an elementary school, vandalizing, robbing, defacing school property. To make his escape, he stole a horse from a nearby farm and three hours later tied it to someone else's fence on the other side of town. All this while already on parole. So now I have him writing about this in his journal. Even his days in court and his court result showed up in his journal entries. He's coming to class and he waits for me after class to read his journal entries. That's more than he's ever done before. I can only go with it.

Our work together thus far has become a collection of individual stories, connected by intertwining motifs. We are meeting again for a second year, each of us somewhat changed by our shared experiences. I approach this second chapter of our emerging texts no longer as the outside reader but as another story-teller, adding one more perspective to the collective chronicle. The teachers, having begun to tell their own stories as well as those of their students, now can gather together not as segmented representatives of the disciplines but rather as individuals who together create those suspended moments in which we may acknowledge the larger texts of our lives and their bearing upon our educational roles.

As our own texts began to emerge, we all agreed that we could only 'go with it', moving to new points of view from which to reread those texts in order to engage in 'joint constructions of meaning' with ourselves and our students. The story continues.

Notes

1 MAXINE GREENE (1973) *Teacher As Stranger*, Belmont, Calif., Wadsworth Publishing Company, p. 8.

2 See, for example, JANET L. MILLER (1983) 'A search for congruence: The influence of past and present in preparing future teachers of writing', *English Education*, 15, February, pp. 5–16; JANET L. MILLER (1982) 'Reflections and reciprocal remembrances: A case study of self concept and the composing process', *Arizona English Bulletin*, 25, November, pp. 194–204.

3 See, for example, JEAN I. ERDMAN (1984) 'Teaching writing as a potentially liberating activity', *Lifelong Learning*, 8, November, pp. 4–7; PATTI LATHER (1985) 'Empowering research methodologies', Paper presented to the American Educational Research Association, Chicago.

4 JAMES BRITTON (1983) 'A quiet form of research', *English Journal*, April, p. 90.

5 JOHN S. MAYHER, NANCY LESTER and GORDON M. PRADL (1983) *Learning to Write, Writing to Learn*, Upper Montclair, N.J., Boynton/Cook Publishers, p. 36.

6 *Ibid.*, p. 37.

7 WILLIAM F. PINAR (1975) 'Search for a method', in W.F. PINAR (Ed.), *Curriculum Theorizing: The Reconceptualists*, Berkeley, Calif., McCutcheon, p. 424.

8 See, for example, JEAN ANYON (1979) 'Ideology and US history textbooks', *Harvard Educational Review*, 49, 3, pp. 361–86; MICHAEL W. APPLE and LOIS WEIS (Eds.) (1983) *Ideology and Practice in Schooling*, Philadelphia, Penn., Temple University press; HENRY GIROUX (1981) *Ideology, Culture and the Process of Scholling*, Philadelphia, Penn., Temple University Press; HENRY GIROUX, A. PENNA and W.F. PINAR (Eds) (1981) *Curriculum and Instruction: Alternatives in Education*, Berkeley, Calif., McCutcheon.

9 JAMES B. MACDONALD (1975) 'Curriculum theory', in W.F. PINAR (Ed.), *Curriculum Theorizing: The Reconceptualists*, Berkeley, Calif., McCutcheon, p. 9.

10 LOUISE WETHERBEE PHELPS (1985) 'Dialectics of coherence: Toward an integrative theory', *College English*, 47, January, p. 14.

11 *Ibid.*

12 *Ibid.*, p. 18.

13 *Ibid.*, p. 22.

14 *Ibid.*, p. 23.

15 MAYHER *et al.*, *op. cit.*, p. 40.

16 JAMES MOFFETT (1985) 'Hidden impediments to improving English teaching', *Phi Delta Kappan*, 67, September, p. 54.

17 *Ibid.*, pp. 53–4.

16 Professional Learning through Collaborative In-Service Activity

Christopher Day

This chapter represents an attempt to contribute to knowledge about the design and long-term impact of school-focused in-service work on the professional practices of teachers. It describes a model of professional learning and intervention which had its origin in classroom-based in-service work with individual teachers (Day, 1981). The work had resulted in changes at various levels, but the main gain for those involved at the time is illustrated in the comment:

> ... the setting of a higher standard. I can't think of any other way in which you'd be so compelled to examine yourself and force yourself as high as you possibly can.... You try it and if it works, then you've reached a level to which you must always afterwards aspire, and compare whatever else you do with that.... (Day, 1985, p. 144)

Some five years later one of those involved wrote:

> I can attest to the validity of this model of reflection and theory building. There has been a shift in pedagogy which had come about through the critical evaluation of current practice in the light of both personal and public theory.... Close reflection upon practice became an irradicable [sic] habit. I discerned a ripple effect which caused me to employ the evaluative method learnt in one area upon others.... (Day, 1985, p. 146)

In this work five main principles had operated:

1   effective learning occurs in response to the confrontation of issues by the learner (this reveals discrepancies within and between thought and action);

2   decisions about teaching should stem from reflection on
    the effects of previous and current actions (this results in
    a reassessment of thinking by the teacher about his
    thinking and behaviour);
3   effective confrontation of issues requires the maximizing
    of valid information (this results in a desire by the
    teacher to change);
4   effective long-term professional learning requires internal
    commitment to the process of learning and freedom of
    choice for the learner;
5   teachers need support in achieving changes — partly
    because old routines dominate and new routines need
    support to develop.

These principles form the conceptual basis for the in-service work
reported in this chapter; and the assumptions are that (a) much
knowledge about practice is implicit, so teachers have a limited
understanding of their theories-in-use, (b) insofar as assumptions
about the influence of internal and external factors and the nature of
classroom (and school) practice remain unquestioned and unprob-
lematic, these are likely to limit a teacher's capacity to evaluate his
work and thus achieve greater effectiveness, (c) terms such as 'reflection' and 'informed choice' are taken to imply the need for explicit
examination of thinking and practice, (d) teachers are capable of
being self-critical but are constrained by psychological and perceptual factors and those of socialization, time and energy.

Course Context and Description

The course was designed by a group of ten people which consisted
of one Inspector/Adviser and two headteachers from each of four
counties in the East Midlands region of England. Planning meetings
were chaired by the writer who was designated Course Director
(though in effect he acted as team leader). The need for courses for
headteachers had been identified through a regional consultative
structure in which the teaching profession, higher education and the
local education authority advisory services were represented; and
the focus for the courses was the management of professional and
curriculum development. Each course aimed to help the headteachers to assess and, where appropriate, enhance the quality of
their work by providing learning environments which would pro-

vide opportunities for reflection upon and confrontation of past and current experience, in work in which self and peer appraisal was a central part. A central focus for the course was school-based work which was negotiated with the course planning/tutorial team and monitored by course members themselves and their peers through regular small-group meetings to which they were mutually account-able. The planners did not operate on a deficit or deficiency model of teaching, but viewed learning as an integral part of teaching and the teachers as being the 'locus' of issue identification and problem-solving.

The intentions of the course were divided into four areas:

1   To cater for a mature group of professionals, by allowing space for the participants to contribute from their own wide experience and knowledge;
2   To facilitate the use and exchange of experiences, through group work; it was hoped that idea-exchange would be legitimized;
3   To undertake worthwhile school-based activities, by carrying out negotiated practical activities in their own schools which would be of professional relevance;
4   To allow flexibility, by providing activities during the course which would be relevant to rural as well as inner city schools.

Members of the Inspectorate and advisory services from the four counties selected the headteachers from the list of applicants on the basis of an agreed set of criteria concerning experience in post, size of school, male-female balance, and likely commitment to pro-fessional development. The majority of the schools had pupils in the 5–11 age range and were situated in suburban or small town environments. Three-quarters of them had between 101 and 300 children.

Each course lasted over an eighteen-month period and had five phases:

Phase 1 Pre-course task   June–July
Phase 2 First regional residential component September
Phase 3 Supported local school-based work September–
                                                                     March
Phase 4 Second residential component   April
Phase 5 Follow-up conference   January

The headteachers on the planning group acted as small-group leaders during the residential components, and as individual counsellors, facilitators and monitors of local group meetings (ten teachers in each group) in their area which were held during Phase 3 of the course. Additional tutors were used as appropriate for specialist lecture and workshop sessions, and at the beginning of the course each member was given a resource book which contained a selection of relevant readings from the literature.

The evidence presented is the result of triangulation of the perceptions of the author, those of the evaluators who gathered data through interviews, questionnaires and non-participant observation, and the reflective comments of a random sample of 50 per cent of the participants on each course which were elicited by questionnaire nine months after each course ended. In essence it is perceptions of change which are being presented and related to central issues which must be faced by all those with a major stake in teacher learning: (1) the relationship between course learning and teachers' thinking and practice and (2) the ways in which teachers' thinking and practice may be influenced by in-service work which is based upon particular models of professional learning and change.

The expectations of the teachers who applied to attend the course were made clear not only in the publicity but also through a further letter which formed the basis for an informal contract. Among other things this stated that school-based work was required as part of the 'on-the-job' learning during the course and this would be documented and used in Phase 4 of the course as a basis for compiling a post-course booklet concerning problems and strategies of professional and curriculum development. This booklet would be considered during Phase 5 of the course. Both the structures of the course and the predominance of small cross-county group seminar work with applied investigations in schools by the participants indicated a clear assumption on the part of the planners that the course would form a part of the ongoing professional development of teachers. As such it would draw from the practical knowledge that teachers had, and the professional contexts in which they worked; and it sought to enhance these.

Planning for Reflection, Confrontation and Change: Action Research

Action research has been defined as the 'study of a social situation with a view to improving the quality of action within it', and as providing 'the necessary link between self-evaluation and professional development' (Elliott, 1983). Its concern is to 'promote improvement in practice and improvement in understanding simultaneously' (McCormick and James, 1983). While this movement originated in America, it has grown in England in the last twenty-five years largely through the efforts of Lawrence Stenhouse (1975, 1979), John Elliott (1976, 1978a, 1978b, 1980) and in Australia through those of Grundy and Kemmis (1981) and Kemmis *et al.* (1982).

Elliott (1983) sees similarities between this and the Aristotelian idea of deliberative inquiry:

> First, it is concerned with developing strategies for realizing educational values which cannot be clearly defined in advance, and independently of, the chosen means. Secondly, it is a process in which practitioners accept responsibility for reflection, and do not simply depend on the analyses of external investigators. The outside researcher's role is to stimulate reflection by practitioners, and the former's 'accounts' or 'hypotheses' are only validated in dialogue with the latter. Thirdly, and as a consequence of the above points, action-research always proceeds from the perspective of the practitioners' ends-in-view. And finally, it is a necessary condition of the professional development of teachers.

The course planners took the view that research was integral to learning about practice and so built this in as the central feature of the course design. The assumption was that although most teachers are capable of reflecting on their thinking and practice, few have the time or energy to do this systematically or deliberatively. Most engage in what Elliott (1983), writing in the context of self-evaluation and professional development, calls 'unreflective self-evaluation based on tacit practical knowledge'. (In the same work he defines practical knowledge as that which 'is derived from their own and others past experience.') Elliott goes on to argue that for teachers to be truly autonomous, responsible, and answerable they must have opportunities to engage in 'deliberative inquiry' on past, current and future practice (see also Schwab, 1969; Reid, 1978). Thus there was a recognition that the quality of the teacher's reflective framework is a decisive factor in his development and that opportunities for the growth of clarity and awareness of one's own thinking and behaviour must therefore be built in to the course structures. This process of making explicit hitherto implicit and thus unchallenged thinking and practices would lead under certain conditions to self-confrontation. Decisions concerning change would then be taken by individuals. The teachers themselves acted as researchers (Stenhouse, 1975) within an action research model which involved conscious *reflection* and '*consciousness raising*' through school-based inquiry and dialectic provided by course tutors, peers and invited lecturers/workshop leaders.

Indeed, the planners viewed teachers as 'connoisseurs' or potential connoisseurs who were able not only to distinguish between what is significant about one set of learning and teaching practices and another, to recognize and appreciate different facets of their teaching and colleagues' or pupils' learning, but also, as critics, to 'disclose the qualities of events or objects that connoisseurship perceives' (Eisner, 1979). Individual acts of connoisseurship would be strengthened by peer support which was built into the course structure and processes. Furthermore, it was hypothesized that teachers would give serious consideration to findings which they themselves had made, and that in this way their understandings and perceptions of their work would be enhanced.

While not dismissing attempts to 'bolt on' to teachers' thinking externally generated knowledge, the action research model of learning asserts that connections among thinking, learning and action are both acquired and made explicit through a mixture of prescribed, negotiated and self-generated work which is perceived as relevant and appropriate by each individual teacher. Teachers are enabled to confront their beliefs in the light of new personal and practical knowledge; reflection and confrontation are seen as a necessary prelude to transformation.

Constraints upon Professional Development: The Need of Intervention

Although it is assumed that professional development is a normal rather than exceptional process, much on-the-job learning will inevitably be at an implicit level and almost certainly remain private, with its validity untested. Thus, while most teachers are capable of reflecting upon their performances in the light of reflection and, where appropriate, recognizing the need for change and changing them, the extent to which change will be implemented will be limited by the psychological and social environment or context in which the teachers work and by their perceptions. For example, the classroom and school in which they work contain much more 'information' than they can handle, and their decisions about practice are concerned with finding ways in which they can survive, cope and teach effectively in a world which is stable. Thus practices are in a sense rules of action which allow them both to maintain a stable view of, for example, the classroom or the school and to give priority to certain kinds of information while ignoring other kinds. They are theories of control. A new headteacher very quickly develops assumptions about practices which allow him or her to cope with the complexities of being a headteacher. However, since it is rare for these to be made explicit or tested, the possibilities for evaluating those assumptions — which underpin his or her role — are minimal. To survive in a school it will be necessary for him/her to accept into his or her system of behaviour the often unstated norms and expectations of the community and his or her colleagues in school. In the staffroom setting, for example, talk about teaching is governed by assumptions about the nature of talk about teaching. Thus what happens in the classroom or school and what is said to happen in the classroom or school may be quite different, and it may not be surprising if the 'doctrine' of headteacher as educationist is contradicted by 'commitments' which arise in the situation of headteacher as practitioner (Keddie, 1971).

There are both perceptual and contextual constraints which may militate against teachers exercising their capacities to be self-critical and to identify problems. Indeed, all but the newest headteachers, like teachers, are likely to have found their own personal solutions to problems shortly after entering the school. These enable them to strike a balance between opposing forces of teacher personality factors, ideological factors, presentation and nature of material, external requirements, and the characteristics of pupils (Lacey, 1977). It is only when the head or teacher perceives that this personal solution is itself inadequate that he or she will be moved to search for means by which he or she can change.

Even this search, however, is likely to be hindered. Once teachers have developed a personal solution to any problems of teaching which they perceive — and this is usually achieved without any systematic assistance from others — it is unlikely that this solution will again be significantly questioned. Argyris and Schön (1976) characterize this pattern of teacher development as 'single loop' learning, in which theory-making and theory-testing is private. In a world of restricted professionality, professionals protect themselves and colleagues by speaking in abstractions without reference to directly observed events. This has the effect of both controlling others and preventing others from influencing oneself by withholding access to valid information about oneself. They suggest that moving to 'double loop' learning, in which our theories and practices are made public, will provide a means of increasing effectiveness. However, this in itself creates problems:

> ... to reverse the process and make the theory explicit for purposes of self-evaluation is to draw attention once more to myriads of additional variables, and to raise the possibility of paralysis from information overload and failing to cope ... to continue for any length of time to treat all one's actions as problematic is a sure recipe for mental breakdown.... (Eraut, 1977)

It follows that 'providers' of in-service work have a major responsibility to ensure not only that teachers have regular opportunities for self-evaluation but also that moral and intellectual support is provided during this process.

The assumptions of the course planners were, therefore, that:

1 there should be opportunities for private and public reflection and confrontation of thinking and practice;
2 support would be provided for this through a curriculum which would be part prescribed (by the planners, the majority of whom were themselves headteachers), part self-generated (through school-based work), and part negotiated (by means of small peer challenge and support groups which met throughout the year and acted as reference points);

By these means they hoped to ensure:

3 internal commitment to the process of learning (not just the products); and
4 freedom of choice for the learner (in terms of decisions about change).

That the residential phases and their contents were built around the school-based work reflected the planners' desire to minimize or avoid problems of need identification, transfer of knowledge and ownership often associated with the more traditional patterns of in-service, while at the same time avoiding the problem of parochialism which is associated with purely school-based work. The course may therefore be described as 'school-focused'.

The emphasis upon school-based work is important, since it underlined the planners' subscription to the 'practicality ethic' of teachers. They believed that course members would value the work if they perceived it as having direct and tangible practical benefits for themselves and their schools.

It will be clear, then, that the course was designed specifically to enable teachers to reflect systematically on their thinking and practices; and to provide active support for them both in their learning processes and in the planning, implementation and evaluation of changes in thinking and practice which arose through the school-based action research which, with the learning networks, formed the central core of the course. The processes by which this was achieved are represented in Figure 1. These processes clearly link deliberative reflection and inquiry, self-confrontation, and the sharing of insights gained from this as essential ingredients in professional learning. The next part of this chapter illustrates the responses of the course members to this.

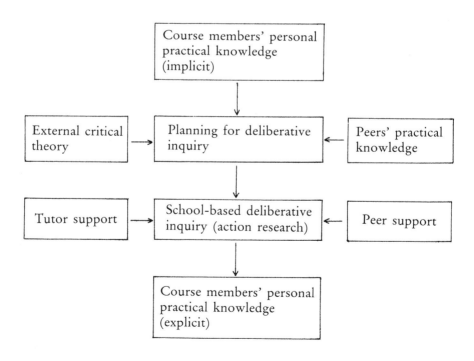

Figure 1. An In-Service Professional Learning Process

The Teacher's Views

The majority of the sixty headteachers who attended stated that the most important factor for attendance was the course title. The questionnaire replies revealed that their expectations of the course related directly to its implicit purposes of providing opportunities for self-reflection and confrontation, sharing work, ideas and knowledge with colleagues, and, through this, the development of improved practice. Responses to each of these purposes are represented in the comments below.

Self-Reflection

I have been a headteacher for five years — but I needed a course which would help me to review my school, appraise my own role and that of the staff and help me in planning the future development of the school.

there are obviously no answers, so I am hoping that I will be made to look critically at myself, my methods and my situation. . . .

Sharing Problems

As a new headteacher, I hope that this course will give me an opportunity to discuss with other headteachers some of the problems that occur during the course of one's work . . . . I believe most heads (newly appointed) are ill-prepared for the job, including myself and the desire to perform my role satisfactorily should be helped by a course such as this.

By the end of the first residential part of the course three key responses emerged from the heads. First, the sharing of problems had clearly occurred:

It was interesting to hear the points of view from teachers in other areas. . . . I found the group work to be of particular value because of the interaction generated . . . we quickly got to know each other and a lot of worthwhile work followed on.

Second, they had all perceived that the pre-course task — 'the identification of an issue or problem' — which had also been discussed in groups during this phase, had helped them view their work from a new standpoint. This confirmed that the opportunities for self-reflection had been taken up. However, support was already needed by some. 'I feel I have achieved a lot from this course. However, I have left feeling even more wretched knowing that there are many things wrong with my school and I cannot put them right fast enough.'

By the second and final residential component the teachers had experienced many months of school-based work (individually negotiated during Phase 2) which they had documented. The range was considerable, and included the development of staff appraisal, the establishment of job descriptions, classroom observation and curriculum development. Evidence of changes of thinking about the course and, more importantly, of a perceived development of critical awareness through assisted self-confrontation was revealed through the questionnaires and interviews. The 'critical input' in Phase 4 itself was described as 'thought-provoking', 'useful' and 'challenging':

> I came prepared to criticize this as being nothing to do with my needs — I thought that more 'simulation work' was what was called for. The content . . . made me think very deeply and put me under pressure (I had to make responses), therefore it was more relevant to my present needs . . . .

In terms of self-reflection, expectations had also been realized for many of the heads. One commented: '. . . it has made me think and take stock. It has made me realize what I have yet to do. I am aware this is probably only a beginning and it is up to myself now to build upon this course. . . .' Another identified his move from the implicit to explicit:

> . . . finding a range of solutions to problems and looking at the complex task of headship, not least of which is the many relationships which have to be forged and fostered. In my work I now feel a great deal clearer about 'where I am going and why'. Philosophies which had been held but not defined are now understood and therefore I can pass them over to others more easily.

Another comment typifies the response to the 'practicality ethic' (Doyle and Ponder, 1976):

As a new head, it had helped me considerably in the organization and planning of my work in areas of curriculum development, staff development and role definition. When taking up the complex challenge of a new post, time is needed to reflect and assimilate before moving forward. . . .

The value of 'sharing' also continued to be raised in comments by heads, focusing on the group meetings held during Phase 3 of the course (the school-based work):

They were valuable not least because we became friendly and relaxed with the members of our group. This led to frank discussions which in turn gave a positive feeling to the next residential phase.

They were useful, in my opinion, as it gave us all a chance to meet up again and talk about the course once more and to relate to each other our progress in school — if any — and our difficulties.

We discussed each other's real thinking.

Reflections on Professional Development and Change with Reference to In-Service Work

It is important to remember that teachers' learning does not begin and end with in-service courses, nor indeed with any process of intervention by outsiders, whether they be colleagues, in-service educators or researchers. All we can ever hope for is a partial picture which will assist in understandings. As one course member stated:

The changes in my thinking and practice had started before the course, but were mostly intuitive, not clearly defined — something I felt ought to be done. . . . I needed help and support. The course was invaluable. It gave me this. It made me analyze the situation more clearly, evaluate it and gave me the stimulus to carry on. . . .

This both supports previous findings that teachers' thinking in its natural state is usually at an intuitive level (Stenhouse, 1975; Clark and Yinger, 1977) and indicates the kinds of support needed if they are to engage in deliberative inquiry (Elliott, 1983) which may lead to decisions about change. Although it is evident from the testimonies received that teachers, like children, are at different stages of development and levels of maturity, and that they have different specific needs and different ways of conceptualizing these, it has been possible to identify a common thread which runs through. It would appear that developmental needs may be assisted by work which enables teachers to engage in reflection, self-confrontation and a consideration of new knowledge which confronts past and current thinking and practice. The focus for this should be both the work context and a venue removed from the work context in which the teacher may reflect, be introduced to new and relevant critical theory which is self-generated, generated with peers through open dialogue and generated by outside 'consultants'. There must, however, be a direct relationship between the two in the work undertaken; the model for promoting the professional development of teachers in Figure 2 illustrates this relationship.

Conclusion

The underlying assumptions in work of this kind are that professional development cannot be forced — it is the teacher who develops (active), not the teacher who is developed (passive); the need for change must be internalized if effective change is to occur; the client must have ownership of his own learning experience; and the in-service educator's role is consultative and collaborative.

Professional practice is found in attitudes, beliefs and ideologies which are expressed in words and actions. These words and actions occur in several contexts — the classroom, the staffroom, the in-service course — and may not always be compatible (Keddie, 1971; Argyris and Schön, 1976). Practice is therefore dynamic rather than static, and those who wish to learn about it must find ways of gaining access both to its context and to its expression. Both the context and expression may be different at different times for different people (Kelly, 1955). The argument here is that enhanced opportunities for professional development and change can be presented through school-focused in-service work which is designed to focus on teachers' intrinsic need to increase their professional effectiveness, to do their job to the best of their ability. In this context, where new understandings and practices do occur, they are unlikely to founder on the rocks of transference (to a different context), ownership (by a particular individual or group), or adoption (by unwilling parents). Through such models as the one described

Christopher Day

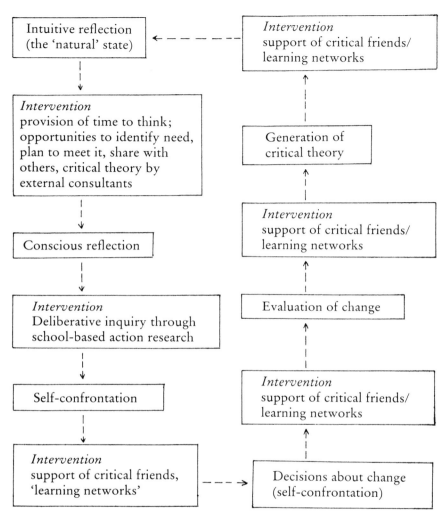

Figure 2. An In-Service Model for Promoting the Professional Development of Teachers

here not only are teachers' thinking and practice likely to develop over the long term, but also both teachers and those who seek to learn about and contribute to the enhancement of their natural professional development will move beyond their own perceptions to broader understandings.

References

Argyris, C. and Schön, D. A. (1976) *Theory in Practice: Increasing Professional Effectiveness*, San Francisco, Calif., Jossey-Bass.

CLARK, C. M. and YINGER, R. J. (1977) 'Research on teacher thinking', *Curriculum Inquiry*, 7, 4, pp. 279–305.

DAY, C. (1981) *Classroom Based In-Service Teacher Education: The Development and Evaluation of a Client-Centred Model*, Education Area Paper No. 9, University of Sussex.

DAY, C. (1985) 'Professional learning and researcher intervention: An action research perspective', *British Educational Research Journal*, 11, 2, pp. 133–51.

DOYLE, W. and PONDER, G. A. (1976) 'The practicality ethic in decision-making', *Interchange*, 8, pp. 1–12.

EISNER, E. W. (1979) *The Educational Imagination*, London, Collier-Macmillan.

EISNER, E. W. (1984) 'Can educational research inform educational practice?' *Phi Delta Kappan*, 65, 7, pp. 447–53.

ELLIOTT, J. (1976) 'Preparing teachers for classroom accountability', *Education for Teaching*, Journal of the National Association of Teachers in Further and Higher Education, 100, Summer, pp. 49–71.

ELLIOTT, J. (1978a) 'What is action research in schools?' *Journal of Curriculum Studies*, 10, 4, pp. 355–7.

ELLIOTT, J. (1978b) 'Classroom research: Science or commonsense', in McALEESE, R. and HAMILTON, D. (Eds), *Understanding Classroom Life*, Windsor, NFER.

ELLIOTT, J. (1980) 'Implications of classroom research for professional development', in HOYLE, E. and MEGARRY, J. (Eds), *Professional Development of Teachers: World Year Book of Education*, London, Kogan Page.

ELLIOTT, J. (1983) 'Action research: A framework for self-evaluation in school, Schools Council Programme 2, *Teacher-Pupil Interaction and the Quality of Learning Project*, Working Paper No. 1, Cambridge, Cambridge Institute of Education.

ERAUT, M. E. (1977) 'Accountability at school level: Some options and their implications', in BECKER, T. and MACLURE, S. (Eds), *The Politics of Curriculum Change*, London, Hutchinson.

GRUNDY, S. and KEMMIS, S. (1981) *Educational Action Research in Australia: The State of the Art*, Mimeo, Geelong, Deakin University.

KEDDIE, N. (1971) 'Classroom knowledge', in YOUNG, M. F. D. (Ed.), *Knowledge and Control*, London, Collier-Macmillan.

KELLY, G. A. (1955) *The Psychology of Personal Constructs*, New York, Norton.

KEMMIS, S. et al. (1982) *The Action Research Planner*, Open Campus Program, Geelong, Deakin University Press.

LACEY, C. (1977) *The Socialisation of Teachers*, London, Methuen.

McCORMICK, R. and JAMES, M. (1983) *Curriculum Evaluation in Schools*, London, Croom Helm.

Reid, W. A. (1978) *Thinking about the Curriculum*, London, Routledge and KEGAN PAUL.

SCHWAB, J. J. (1969) 'The practical: A language for curriculum', *School Review*, 1, Autumn, pp. 1–24.

STENHOUSE, L. (1975) *An Introduction to Curriculum Research and Development*, London, Heinemann.

STENHOUSE, L. (1979) *What Is Action-Research?* Mimeo, University of East Anglia, Centre for Applied Research in Education.

Notes on Contributors

ANN BERLAK is a Professor at Webster College, St Louis, Missouri. With her husband, Harold, she is co-author of *Dilemmas of Schooling* (Methuen).

HAROLD BERLAK is Professor of Education at Washington University, St Louis, Missouri. He is editor of *The Public Education Networker*, a communiqué committed to democratic ideals in public schools.

LANDON BEYER is Associate Professor and Chair of Department of Education at Cornell College, Mt Vernon, Iowa. He has published widely in journals and is interested in critical theory in pre-service teacher education.

ROBERT BULLOUGH is Professor in Education Studies at the University of Utah, Salt Lake City. He is a co-author of *Human Interests in the Curriculum: Teaching and Learning in a Technological Society* (Teachers College Press).

CHRISTOPHER DAY is Head of the In-Service Education Unit at the University of Nottingham. He is a frequent presenter at international conferences and has particular interests in teachers' thinking and how to utilize that through in-service.

FREEMA ELBAZ teaches in the School of Education at the University of Haifa, Israel. Her major published work is *Teacher Thinking: A Study of Practical Knowledge* (Croom Helm).

SARA FREEDMAN is a member of the Boston Women's Teachers' Group and has a particular interest in presenting a feminist perspective on teaching. She is also an editor of *The Radical Teacher*.

ANDREW GITLIN is Associate Professor in Education Studies at the University of Utah, Salt Lake City. He is a regular contributor to education journals and is currently working jointly with Smyth on a book entitled *Beyond Teacher Evaluation*.

GLENN HUDAK is Assistant Professor in Education at the Center for Teaching and Learning, University of North Dakota. Current interests include the contributions students can make to knowledge about teaching.

JANET MILLER is Associate Professor in the School of Education and Human Services, St John's University, New York. She is also the managing editor of *The Journal of Curriculum Theorizing*.

JENNIFER NIAS is a tutor at the Cambridge Institute of Education. She has published the results of her research extensively in education journals.

ANDREW PICKARD is Senior Lecturer in Educational Studies at Manchester Polytechnic. Along with his colleague JOHN PEARCE, who is a co-contributor to this volume, he has been working towards an epistemology that addresses the practical aspects of teaching.

JOHN SMYTH is Chair of the Centre for Education Studies and an Associate Professor in the School of Education, Deakin University, Australia. He is editor of *The Australian Administrator* and has just published *Learning about Teaching through Clinical Supervision* (Croom Helm).

ALAN TOM is Chairman and Professor in the Department of Education, Washington University, St Louis, Missouri. He is also author of *Teaching as a Moral Craft* (Longman).

DAVID TRIPP is Senior Lecturer in Education, Murdoch University, Western Australia. He is also co-author of a recently released book entitled *Children and Television: A Semiatic Approach* (Polity Press and Stanford University Press).

JAMES WALKER is Senior Lecturer in Social and Policy Studies, Faculty of Education, University of Sydney, Australia. He is the author of two recent books: *Louts and Legends: Male Youth Culture in an Inner City School* (George Allen and Unwin) and *Learning Cultures: Teachers and Students in an Inner City School* (George Allen and Unwin).

PETER WOODS is a Reader in Education at the Open University. He is a frequent writer on aspects of teachers' life histories and is author of *The Divided School* (Routledge and Kegan Paul), *Sociology and the School* (Routledge and Kegan Paul) and *Teacher Careers: Crises and Continuities* (Falmer Press).

Index

Abercrombie, M.L.J., 138–40, 142, 150
academic discourse
  and commonsense orientation, 60–1
  and cultural orientation, 61–3
  formation of, 59–68
  nature of, 60–5
  and student knowledge, 55–69
  and technical orientation, 63–5
action research, 35, 36–44, 123, 179–91, 210–20
  bases of, 35
  and change, 212
  definition of, 210–11
  epistemology of, 36–44
  methodology of, 35
Anatomy of Judgement, The, 150

Aristotle
  and deliberative inquiry, 211
  and 'phronesis' and 'techne', 29

Art Is Education (AIE) program, 118n5

Berlak, A. and Berlak, H., 169–78, 186, 188–9
Britton, J., 194–5, 202

careers lessons, 103–4
Carnegie Forum on Education and the Economy, 23–6, 27–8
centralization

and education, 107–18, 160, 164
Chomsky, N.
  and competence, 186, 187
class placement, 77–8
classroom research
  see action research
classrooms
  communication in, 57–68, 183–8, 189–90
  context of, 190
  disruption in, 62
  rarefaction in, 65–7
  resistances in, 55–6, 60–8; *see also* teachers, and resistance
  and student communication, 62–3
  and student cultures, *see* student cultures
  student knowledge in, 55–69
  as teachers' sanctuaries, 91–2
collaborative research, 123, 179–91
  see also action research
common schools [USA]
  compartmental organization in, 108–9
  curriculum in, 107–8, 110–11, 117
  hierarchy in, 109
  rationalized programs in, 108, 111, 112, 115, 116–17
  structure in, 107–19
  teacher evaluation in, 109–10
  teacher relations in, 114–5
  teacher roles in, 110–18